LIVING ALTERITIES

SUNY Series, Philosophy and Race
Robert Bernasconi and T. Denean Sharpley-Whiting, Editors

LIVING ALTERITIES

Phenomenology, Embodiment, and Race

EDITED BY EMILY S. LEE

Cover art courtesy of Lisa Goodin.

Published by State University of New York Press, Albany

© 2014 State University of New York

For information, contact State University of New York Press, Albany, NY
www.sunypress.edu

Production by Ryan Morris
Marketing by Michael Campochiaro

Library of Congress Cataloging-in-Publication Data

Living alterities : phenomenology, embodiment, and race / edited by Emily S. Lee.
    pages cm. — (SUNY series, Philosophy and race)
  Includes bibliographical references and index.
  ISBN 978-1-4384-5016-2 (paperback : alk. paper)
  ISBN 978-1-4384-5015-5 (hardcover : alk. paper) 1. Phenomenology. 2. Human body
(Philosophy) 3. Race—Philosophy. 4. Merleau-Ponty, Maurice, 1908-1961. I. Lee, Emily S.,
1971– editor of compilation.
  B829.5.L563 2014
  142'.7—dc23
                              2013012907

              10   9   8   7   6   5   4   3   2   1

CONTENTS

            Boundary at La Frontera
            EDWARD S. CASEY   189

Chapter 9: Pride and Prejudice: Ambiguous Racial, Religious,
            and Ethnic Identities of Jewish Bodies
            GAIL WEISS   213

Chapter 10: Body Movement and Responsibility for a Situation
            EMILY S. LEE   233

Chapter 11: The Future of Whiteness
            LINDA MARTÍN ALCOFF   255

            Contributors   283

            Index   287

ACKNOWLEDGMENTS

Let me begin by thanking all the contributors to this anthology. It is a pleasure to bring together in this volume so many philosophers whose work I have long admired. It is especially wonderful to discover not only that they write such important philosophy, but that their generosity matches their professionalism.

I want to also thank California State University at Fullerton. Some of the contributions from this book were originally presented at the 40th Annual Philosophy Symposium on "Phenomenology, Embodiment, and Race" in 2010. This volume could only come together because the philosophy department—both its faculty and its students—carry on such great traditions that are well supported by the university.

I'd like to thank Lisa Jong-Soon Goodlin for permission to use her piece, Untitled, (ducks) from the series, "Lost and Found," as the cover art. I have been a long admirer of Goodlin's art; see more of her work at lisagoodlin. com.

Last, but not least, I want to thank my circle of family and friends. I hope you know who you are. Without you, I cannot imagine how to live my day-to-day life.

INTRODUCTION

Emily S. Lee

Race and the Relevance of Embodiment

Philosophy of race has explored many reasons for the history of race and racism within the context of a desire for empire building and within individual prejudices. Empire building and colonialism have been relegated more or less as untenable practices and ambitions. Most present-day societies legally prohibit intentional individual racism. So, to explain the persistence and tenacity of racism, philosophy of race has more recently focused on racism as embedded in the social/institutional structures of society and the subconscious and even unconscious levels of consciousness. Both these levels do not directly address the materiality of race. And yet both the social structural and the individual subconscious levels of analysis rely on perceiving the embodiment of race. A focus on race, on the material, the physical features of race may shed more light on racism's perseverance.

Adamantly insisting on the pivotal role of embodiment, Patricia Williams writes, "[t]he simple matter of the color of one's skin so profoundly affects the way one is treated, so radically shapes what one is allowed to think and feel about this society, that the decision to generalize from such a division is valid."[1] Because of the confluence of the materiality of the body with meanings and significations, embodiment is central to race.[2] The meanings of body features change historically (as well as which and how body features symbolize), but significations persistently saturate body features.

Chandra Talpade Mohanty writes, "[p]articular racial myths and stereotypes change, but the underlying presence of a racial meaning system seems to be an anchoring point of American culture."[3] The color of one's skin imparts meaning about the person's intelligence or kinds of intelligence; the at times presumed (and projected) size and shape of various parts of the body communicate meaning about the person's sexual prowess and hence, proximity to animality; the amounts of hair in different areas of the body transmit information about the person's propensity toward violence. The egregious impact of these prevalent meanings of body features, with its accordance to the various degrees of the status of humanity, was attested to historically in our past of slavery, segregation, and immigration laws. Yet still not obvious is the lived reality of carrying forth every day in a body with its associated subjectivity. Every day, in the banal, minute interactions with members of society, one's body sets the parameters for what constitutes the reasonable response from others. One's body informs the rationale for the person who refuses to enter the same elevator.[4] One's body conveys one's professional position when dressed in a pair of jeans and a T-shirt.[5] One's body displays one's likelihood for punctuality.[6] These intimate moments give rise to distinct experiences that accumulate into a particular life.

Embodiment in General

As central as embodiment appears to be in the question of race, philosophy of race has so far only limitedly explored the role of embodiment. At least part of the initial focus on the conscious intent and on the unconscious projections of racism to the neglect of the role of embodiment might reflect philosophy's own dualistic theoretical history of dividing ideas and matter; thinking things and nonthinking things; consciousness and the body. This split reflects the philosophical tradition from Plato and Descartes, which not only insists on the possibility of such separation, but also prioritizes ideas, thought, and the inner workings of the subject. Because of this metaphysical distinction, and its prioritization of consciousness, the understandings of race and the analysis of racism may have underemphasized the role of embodiment because the body has been relegated to the status of unthinking matter.

Of course, a tradition in philosophy argues for metaphysical monism and denies any substantive distinctions between thinking beings and non-thinking beings. The most persuasive argument against dualism and de facto for monism is that if the world is metaphysically reducible to two kinds of beings, how do the two beings—completely different in kind—have contact or awareness of each other?

Without insisting on either position here, much recent work argues that human beings' particular form of embodiment conditions cognitive processes. Human bodies' upright postures, human bodily distinctions of front and back, as well as the limitations of human body movements impact human cognitive connections. For example, Hubert Dreyfus has been arguing for a while now against mainstream cognitive theory's position that the mind functions through representations; the position that the mind relies on representations reflects dualist conceptions. Only with the complete separation of the mind and the body does the mind require a representation of what appears or occurs in the physical world.[7] In place of these theories of mind's reliance on representations, Dreyfus argues that the form of the input conditioned by the materiality of the body directly influences thought. Referring to neural networks designed to simulate cognitive processes, he writes, "the body-dependence of shared generalizations puts disembodied neural networks at a serious disadvantage when it comes to learning to cope in the human world. Nothing is more alien to our form of life than a network with no varying degrees of access, no up-down, front-back orientation, no preferred way of moving, such as moving forward more easily than backward, and no emotional response to its failures and successes."[8] In other words, this research suggests that embodiment inherently conditions thinking. Indeed, in philosophy of cognitive science, much work explores situated cognition, as extended, embodied, embedded, and amalgamated mind—all of these instances acknowledge the integral role of the material circumstances of consciousness.[9] The mind and the body cannot be separated; they are reliant on each other. Hence, to disregard the role of the body in thinking—including thinking about race—in order to explore racism only as a product of thought as conscious or unconscious, does not suffice for understanding the embodied conditions of race and racism.

In feminist theory, even working within a dualistic framework, discussions have flourished focusing on the relation between the materiality of embodiment in regard to the nature of sex and the social construction of the cultural ideas circumscribing gender. Hence, it is not clear why race theory that works within philosophy's dualistic framework has not followed the trajectory of discussing the relation between the material embodiment of race and the constructed significations of race and racism. Instead, in race theory, metaphysical dualism and its prioritization of consciousness primarily leads to the neglect of embodiment.[10] Admittedly, within feminist theory, debate continues as to what exactly constitutes the natural, biological difference that distinguishes the sex of women from men. Interestingly, feminist theory still struggles with demarcating women from men, while simultaneously insisting that women are not determinately reducible to their biological capabilities. In the wake of a history in which women were denied participation in the sphere of public life based on the presumption that they could not develop as thinking beings because of their bodies, feminist theorists have de-emphasized the biological parameters as defining women and emphasized the socially constructed history that isolated them based on the presumed limited capacities of their bodies.[11] Accordingly, early feminist foremothers, such as Mary Wollstonecraft, argued that the education of women—and not their biological makeup—more greatly influences women's development; Simone de Beauvoir succinctly stated, "women are made not born." The early feminists emphasized the role of society in obfuscating the ability to see women's true capabilities. Because of the need to emphasize the role of society in limiting women's development, the role of nature and biology was de-emphasized.

More recently, Judith Butler writes, "'sex' is a regulatory ideal whose materialization is compelled . . . In other words, 'sex' is an ideal construct which is forcibly materialized through time."[12] Her position that socially constituted matrixes of power discursively compel matter including sex into visibility questions the influence and importance of nature. Butler makes explicit the force of social norms not simply to mold nature as sex and subjectivity as gender, but the very parameters of nature and subjectivity. Nevertheless, she also aims to avoid depicting nature as purely passive—because of the common association of nature as the feminine. The success of this latter aim is unclear; Butler's depiction of the materialization of sex has been contested. The most interesting contention addresses Butler's metaphysical stance as not fully recognizing the implications of a metaphysics of process or becoming.[13] Clearly, relying on biology to distinguish between men and women appears to be a challenge.

Of course, if socially constructed meanings compel matter and even construct subjectivity, the most well-known critique of Butler remains the question concerning the location of agency. This particular critique directed at Butler parallels philosophy's treatment of materiality and embodiment. Following dualism's tendency of attributing secondary status to nonthinking things, too much of an association with the matter of embodiment usually has been associated with disabling agency. Letitia Meynell writes, "[t]hough the focus on marked and socialized bodies has been, at the same time, an expression of feminists' deep political commitment to acknowledging and fostering the agency of marginalized political subjects, it is fair to say that much feminist theory has engaged the issue of embodiment with an over-whelming focus on how oppressive practices constrain and damage agency. Although this focus has been indispensable to an adequate analysis of oppression, it has done little to show how the body is the ground for agency more positively conceived."[14] Not only is the function of biology difficult to grasp, but too much of an association with embodiment has been conceived as threatening and damaging the possibilities of agency.

I am not so concerned with settling this debate between essentialism and social constructionism and whether sex or gender is more formidable. Instead, I only want to point out that within feminist theory, at least these two features, nature/materiality and culture/ideality persist as the parameters within which, around which, and against which feminist theory contends. In the aftermath of the eugenics movement, race theorists have wholeheart-edly and eagerly given up that race relies on any biological or natural basis.[15] As such, the discussion around race circumscribes only social construction, meanings, and ideas. Paralleling the framework of feminist philosophy in the discussion between sex and gender, the domain of philosophy of race, in a sense, is narrowed to being only about culture. Of course this makes sense, because as Linda Martín Alcoff explains, race is not a factor in the reproduction of the human species. She writes, "the variable of reproductive role provides a natural infrastructure for sexual difference that is qualitatively different from the surface differences of racial categories."[16] Because race in its natural or biological sense was relegated to the surface, race theory collapses into the misnomer that perhaps race will disappear in a future of brown people. Such a position leaves race theorists with the difficult task of arguing that, although there is no such thing as race (in the natural sense), race still functions because of the meanings of race (in the cultural sense). Philosophy of race is left in the difficult position of arguing for the impor-tance of meanings about something that cannot actually be distinguishable in nature. Firmly situated within a dualistic philosophical tradition that already relegates the body as secondary to consciousness, the position that race has no significant biological basis adds to the difficulties within race theory when addressing the role of the body and the embodiment of race.

Embodiment in its Particularity

Within this theoretical history, the difficulty of addressing race as embodied is not surprising. There is a lack of conceptual space for speaking about the significance of the body in philosophy of race. Because this history confines talking about embodiment in *general*, studying the relevance of embodiment in its *particularities*—the role of the specificities of body features—proves even more difficult.

Contained within this metaphysical framework where the defining aspect of subjects is their status as thinking beings, the social-political solution to understanding racism as conscious intent or as subconscious prejudice emphasizes equal treatment of all members of society and calls for recognizing the sameness of all human beings—hence, the strategy of color-blindness. But this insistence on the commonality of all human beings positions the distinguishing specificities of embodiment—the differences that perceptually distinguish race and sex—as secondary to human beings. This insistence on the identity of all human beings not only conceptually constrains theories of the role of embodiment, it also points to questionable moral and political conclusions—for it denies the possibility of positive, identity-affirming reasons to recognize distinguishable bodily differences. The insistence on commonality and identity of all human beings disregards the very parameters on which the significations of different body features rely. Such dismissal of embodiment in general, and additionally embodiment in its particularities, denies the prevalence and significance of socially constructed meanings about specific body features.

Recall that because of the confluence of body features and meanings, embodiment is central to race. As Michael Omi and Howard Winant argue, we construct and determine which features of the body symbolize race as well as the meanings/significations of the symbols. They write, "race is a concept which signifies and symbolizes social conflicts and interests by referring to different types of human bodies . . . selection of these particular features for purposes of racial signification is always and necessarily a social and historical process."[17] In other words, the history of our society condition and construct the visibility of the differences of embodiment and the meanings of the particular features of the body. Because of these meaning-saturated particular body features and our visual sensibility that is conditioned to focus on these significations, the different racial groups undergo specific experiences. For as I said at the beginning of this introduction, based on particular body features, members of society gauge the appropriate interactions and responses to other people. In this way, the particularities of embodiment construct subjectivity, in all its varied, racialized differences.

Collecting these premises together, the solution of racism emphasizing the sameness of all people inadvertently denies the socially constructed meanings of race. Combining this position of denying the existence and relevance of socially constructed meanings of race with the earlier position of the nonexistence of the biological differences of race results in the rather amazing conclusion that *race does not exist in any sense!*

To get a better sense of the relevance of race in the social construction of subjects, let me evoke Frantz Fanon's difference between externally and internally overdetermined subjectivity. Externally because of the visibility of the different features of one's body, others gauge the appropriate responses to one's embodiment—formatively constructing the experiences one encounters. Internally, an accumulation of such experiences and events builds into a personal history to develop one's sense of self. Heeding the existential dimension, the subject digests, filters, and makes sense of these series of experiences of the world. The essays in this collection elaborate precisely this juncture—illuminating how the meanings circumscribing embodiment constructs the experiences the subject encounters and consequently how the subject develops certain emotions, knowledge, ethical/moral postures, and sense of being-in-the-world. In this way, the specificities of embodiment are primary to subjectivity. Race does not lie as a superficial cover over the primary layer of common humanity; in a profoundly intimate sense, one lives race through the immediacy of the particular differences of one's embodiment.

Ironically, although I have taken pains to explain how philosophy neglects the material and the natural, because of the sedimentation of racial meaning into the very fabric and texture of society, members of society mistake the socially constructed meanings about features of the body as *natural.* One perceives, experiences, and lives the historical, cultural meanings of race as biological, materially real, and natural. Such phrenological impulses demonstrate the difficulty of eliminating the functioning of the specific differences of embodiment, and of sustaining in the social memory that the meanings of race are socially constructed as well as biologically insignificant.

In light of such phrenological impulses, philosophers of race have been arguing for understanding race as an ontological category. As Lewis Gordon explains, "ontology can be regarded not only as a study of what 'is' the case, but also a study of what is treated as being the case."[18] Gordon advocates reconceiving ontology to account for this phenomenon where the socially constructed meanings of race have become so saturated into our being-in-the-world that we mistake the socially constructed as natural/biological. To describe the experience of race in present-day society, where members of society mistake the socially constructed meanings of race as natural (much like gender compels sex), race theorists posit conceptualizing race in onto- logical terms.

Phenomenology

A phenomenological framework facilitates understanding the ontologizing relation between embodiment and race in this confluence between materiality and socially constructed meanings. The phenomenological framework aims to understand precisely the world as a relation between the natural and the cultural, the objective and the subjective, the thinking and the nonthinking beings. This relation, this space that phenomenology explores, is the site of racial meaning. Following the work of Edmund Husserl, Maurice Merleau- Ponty defines phenomenon as a "layer of living experience through which other people and things are first given to us."[19] Attending to the layer of liv- ing experience, the phenomenon of being-in-the-world, a phenomenological framework recognizes that all contact with the world occurs through nego- tiations between the intentions of the subject and the givens of the world, or rather that subjectivity and the world condition each other. This defini- tion of phenomena operates on both the ontologic and the epistemic levels. Merleau-Ponty never separates the ontological and epistemological aspects of the subject and being-in-the-world: "'What do I know?' is not only 'what is knowing?' and not only 'who am I?' but finally: 'what is there?' and even: 'what is the *there is*?'"[20] Although not all of the essays in this text utilize the Husserlian, Merleau-Pontian strain of phenomenology, all the essays explore precisely this interstice between the natural and the cultural, especially in light of how socially constructed meanings have sedimented to now appear mostly, if not purely, natural.

Within this phenomenal framework, let me elaborate a bit on Merleau- Ponty's work because of his now quite famous prioritization of the subject as embodied. For although not all of the essays in this collection explore Merleau-Ponty's theory on embodiment, they do all explore the implications of an embodied subjectivity. One's experience of the world phenomenally occurs through embodiment, as Merleau-Ponty insists, "the alleged facts, the spatio-temporal individuals, are from the first mounted on the axes, the piv- ots, the dimensions, the generality of my body."[21] Moreover, one experiences the body phenomenally. One does not experience the entirety of the body at any one point; different parts of the body enter and exit one's awareness in facing one's various life projects. For example, when I practiced the breast-stroke more regularly in my swimming routine, I started noticing pain in my inner thighs, a section of my body I never paid any attention to before. In new endeavors, one may experience initial disappointment and discouragement with one's body but eventual pleasure and surprise at the new capabilities of one's body.

Merleau-Ponty does not naively situate the body in the world and assume that all bodies see and experience more or less the same thing. Instead, recognizing that all bodies are not exactly and entirely alike, he theorizes how each body's positioning in the world reflects the body's differences. In other words, Merleau-Ponty's attention to embodiment heeds not only the role of the body in general but its particularities. Because of the differences of the body, each individual's position within the world facilitates a unique perspective of the world. The uniqueness of each position does not derive solely from its spatial position; each body occupies a unique position in the world because each body builds up a horizon of immanent personal experiences. As such, each body's optimal distance for perception exhibits the subject's relation with the object of perception in the world. The uniqueness of each perspective has its benefits and drawbacks; Merleau-Ponty writes, the *"person who* perceives is not spread out before himself as a consciousness must be; he has historical density, he takes up a perceptual tradition and is faced with a present."[22] Because of the differences of the body, each subject has her own unique blind spot; the subject cannot possess full self-consciousness of the situations of his or her own body at any moment.

Within a dualistic metaphysics, philosophy had abstracted away the differences among subjects, depicting subjects as replaceable, because the only important aspect of human beings is the status of thinking beings. In highlighting the role of the particularities of embodiment, Merleau-Ponty rescues each person for her unique perspective. Merleau-Ponty writes that each body and each "perception is mutable and only probable—it is, if one likes, only an *opinion*, what each perception, even if false, verifies, is the belongingness of each experience to the same world, their equal power to manifest it, *as possibilities of the same world*."[23] Because of the precariousness of individual perspectives, sole perspectives are at times dismissed as merely opinions. Merleau-Ponty rescues each opinion, by insisting that because of the singular position of each body within the world each body can contribute uniquely to knowledge of the world. Just as a friend in pointing to a specific feature of a scene introduces a new aspect, each body and its perspective holds the potential to further grasp the world.

The phenomenological structure initially depicts the negotiations between the intentions of the subject and the world, but phenomenology conceptualizes more than merely describing the embodied interactions of the situated subject. The phenomenological structure theorizes the possibility of agency, of existentially acting in the world. In contrast to the dualistic metaphysical stance where only thinking beings can act, and where the body as a nonthinking being cannot act, Merleau-Ponty's phenomenology challenges this neat separation by insisting that only embodied subjects act in the world.

The ambiguities of the uniquely embodied subject in the world and the blindness associated with such a position demonstrate phenomenology's focus on situatedness and its constraints and possibilities for knowledge. In the ambiguity and the openness of phenomena lies the possibility of simultaneous separation and union, the particular and the general, multiplicity and unity, or identity in difference. Phenomenology, with Merleau-Ponty's appreciation for the particularities of embodiment, serves as an ideal framework for thinking about the meanings of the embodiments of race.

The Collection of Essays

The essays collected and organized here form a broad definition of phenomenology. More than probing the theoretical parameters of phenomenology, these essays actually do phenomenology by presenting the lived conditions of racialized subjects. In other words, the essays collected here engage in phenomenologically, describing the experience of subjects as the world bombards, coerces, and shapes them, and as they react, respond, and make meaningful their embodied lives. True to the phenomenological endeavor of first capturing one's state of being-in-the-world before making epistemic claims, these essays depict the very real circumstances within which racially embodied subjects negotiate their psychological, emotional, intellectual, and political agency within their social environs. Only by beginning with such descriptions can we endeavor toward knowledge that truly includes these subjects' realities.

This collection of essays attempts to represent a wide variety of racialized bodies, mostly in the United States. Of course, because of the inevitability of exclusion, a complete representation will remain always beyond comprehension. The essays address the embodiment of African Americans, Muslims, Asian Americans, Latinas, Jews, and White Americans. To an extent the choice of these categories represents the members of the discipline of philosophy more than the general population at large. And I stay as close as possible to the author's classifying categories, respecting their rights and their abilities to describe the world and self-express themselves. Moreover, because racial categories change and evolve, I do not attempt to separate between racial or ethnic distinctions. This partly reflects attention to Omi and Winant's arguments against utilizing the idea of ethnicity. They argue that ethnicity and its emphasis on culture as the defining feature of race affiliates too closely with white immigration patterns in the United States. Such modeling after white immigration patterns detracts attention from the particular history of discrimination of racialized subjects, who did not follow traditional more voluntary immigration patterns, but experienced forced transnational moves or subjugation to colonialist practices without immigrating. In other words because ethnicity emphasizes culture, it does not consider the actual reasons for the different treatment of people—their racialized embodiment.[24] Of course, others have disagreed with Omi and Winant's position. But I find their arguments persuasive, especially because they acknowledge the role of the visible differences of embodiment. Each of these essays, with its concentration on a specific form of embodiment, focuses on questions that are urgent to each subjectivity.

The book begins with "Materializing Race" by Charles W. Mills, because it articulates the material basis of race. Mills argues for a particular conception of materiality—a materiality that recognizes the force of the sociopolitical—because of the sedimentation of historical meanings. Drawing from his earlier work in Marxist theory and the notion of subpersonhood, Mills elaborates on the political and economic history as material. Linda Martín Alcoff's book, *Visible Identities*, motivates Mills to insist on this material basis of race. For although Mills concedes a natural/biological primacy to sex because of sex's role in the reproduction of the species, he still insists on the materiality of race. The differences in skin color—in embodiment—originally served as the basis for granting some with personhood and others with subpersonhood. This original divide is not trivial, but rather structures the very material conditions of life in present-day society.

George Yancy's essay, "White Gazes: What It Feels Like to Be an Essence," illustrates the workings of perception, where vision already only occurs through the sedimentation of meanings. In this incredibly honest, present-day illustration of the theme of overdetermination in Frantz Fanon's work, Yancy depicts white racist perception in such mundane events as riding in elevators or watching movies. Clearly, the black subject still experiences what Fanon explains as the fear of "seeing oneself laid out before one as a thing, as an essence." Yancy conveys how present society's history and structures of power produces an epistemology that ontologically conditions black lives. Yancy ends with some speculations on the possibility of the black body conditioning the white body's being-in-the-world.

Turning away from a body mired in meanings, and turning to a body that remains obscure in its abstractness, Donna-Dale L. Marcano, in "Race/Gender and the Philosopher's Body," focuses on the philosopher's body—a body circumscribed by openness and possibilities. Although historically, philosophers have had difficulty acknowledging their bodies, Marcano cleverly points out that such disdain for embodiment does not only reflect the philosopher's absorption with meta-analysis. Rather, such ambivalence for the material conditions of their existence cloaks the social contexts, which delineate only certain bodies as philosophers. The image of the philosopher's body is far from open ended; rather, it is so specifically associated with certain bodies—white males—that our society summarily denies other bodies as capable of intellectual or philosophical work. Marcano draws attention especially to a history of dismissal of the philosophical thinking from black female bodies.

Namita Goswami further explores the role of the embodiment of women of color in her chapter, "Among Family Woman: *Sati*, Postcolonial Feminism, and the Body." Goswami points to women's bodies as the defining feature that historically justified the association of women of color as closer to animality and nature than to humanity. Challenging whether we truly surpassed the colonial period into the postcolonial era, Goswami questions the bifurcation of white women and women of color that results in the homogenization of women of color. Evidence of such homogenization is the static focuses on specific, overdetermined, so-called, third world practices, including *Sati*. Goswami explores Gayatri Spivak's positioning of Bhubhaneswari's *Sati*/suicide as a challenge to the reductive dualistic understanding of *Sati* as only forever caught between the possibilities that "White men are saving brown women from brown men" and "The women wanted to die." In an interesting twist, instead of defending the humanity of women of color, she advocates for a reevaluation of the exceptionalism deemed onto the human and the cultural within the nature/culture divide. Through a focus on the natural remnants and stains of Bhubhaneswari's body, Goswami rethinks humanity's hubristic claim to surpass nature, and the body as natural.

Delving into the practices of the body, from idealization to emotion, David H. Kim, in his article, "Shame and Self-Revision in Asian American Assimilation," examines the phenomenology of the affective dimensions of embodiment. Kim depicts the phenomenology of emotion with the works of Michael Stocker and Peter Goldie. Kim carefully explores affect without reducing the experience of emotion to either solely a cognitive dimension nor to just the surface of bodies. Building from this basis, he applies the affective dimension of embodiment to the specific social political experiences of Asian Americans. Liberal orientalism in American society configures Asian American bodies to experience a distinctive form of racial xenophobia, because Asian American cultural practices are represented as exceptionally positive. More than the dangers of such exceptionalist portrayals of Asian Americans among other minority groups, Kim explains the dangers in the emotional development for Asian Americans. Within this political context, Kim situates Asian American assimilation practices in relation to the self-evaluative emotions of shame and self-contempt.

Alia Al-Saji builds on the phenomenology of affect in "A Phenomenology of Hesitation: Interrupting Racializing Habits of Seeing." Henri Bergson posits that affect is felt when the body hesitates. Affective hesitation delays habitual action by making visible the sedimentation of habit by prefiguring and thus delaying habit into the anticipated future. The body waits before acting; in this waiting, the body remembers the past. Iris Marion Young earlier famously portrayed a hesitation among women as illustrative of the effects of social objectification that result in women's body movements projecting contradictory intentions while performing teleological actions. Al-Saji carefully delineates a second hesitation, a hesitation that undergirds all human activity. Al-Saji evokes Maurice Merleau-Ponty's explanation of an "activity that is not opposed to passivity, an agency that is also powerlessness" to argue that the insistence to see only through recalcitrant structures of racializing vision does not occur simply passively but willfully. The affective body hesitation that allows for a pause to examine the past and the future may disrupt the habituation of racializing vision.

In "Hometactics: Self-Mapping, Belonging, and the Home Question," Mariana Ortega focuses on the multiplicitous subjectivity, a subjectivity whose phenomenological lived experience is divided—specifically Latina lesbians. Edwina Barvosa argues that Maria Lugones draws from the different aspects of herself for strategies to fulfill a self-integrative life project. In contrast, Ortega explores the possibility of a divided subjectivity—one that does not feel integrated and whole, who experiences internal strife, ambiguity, ambivalence, and contestation—exercising agency. Focusing specifically on the context of the home, and the difficulties the multiplicitous subjectivity has in finding safety, comfort, and peace even in this cherished sphere,

Ortega develops a notion of "hometactics" from Michel de Certeau's work on tactics. Ortega posits "hometactics" in place of or in addition to Barvosa and Lugones's emphasis on strategies. In tactics that appear within the temporariness and provocation of situations, Ortega steers clear of "strategies" that cannot quite be disentangled from present systems of power.

Edward S. Casey explains the lines and edges in the body of the nation state in "Walling Racialized Bodies Out: Border Versus Boundary at La Frontera." Casey invites new thinking about this space between the United States and Mexico, by considering this edge through the lens of the difference between borders and boundaries. Borders, as products of human ideas, Casey explains, delineate clearly and crisply; boundaries rarely demarcate with any precision, being more porous in character. Although not immune to cultural machinations, boundaries are more a product of nature. Borders are distinctive from boundaries, but Casey points out that the two are indissociable from each other, while never becoming the other and dissolving their difference. Though the United States concentrates much effort into establishing the materiality of La Frontera, borders, as human-made entities, may function more powerfully in the discursive sense than in the physical material sense. This discursive force of La Frontera especially applies to the racialized bodies along this border.

Returning to the embodiment of people, Gail Weiss calls for carefully heeding the ambiguity of embodiments and subjectivities in "Pride and Prejudice: Ambiguous Racial, Religious, and Ethnic Identities of Jewish Bodies." Focusing specifically on the Jewish subject, and the well-known assignation of Jews as internally overdetermined, Weiss explains that overdetermination does not solely, oppressively eliminate agency but can allow for the free association and cross-fertilization of ideas about Jewish identity. In contrast to Frantz Fanon's and Jean-Paul Sartre's sense of overdetermination that depicts the Jewish subject as only reacting to the negative, reductive, essentializing descriptions of the anti-Semite, Weiss argues that Sigmund Freud's original sense of overdetermination connotes the multiple possibilities of free association. Weiss points to more recent works depicting the Jewish identity for better models of overdetermination that illustrates the ambiguous reactions of both prejudice and pride.

Moving finally toward white embodiment, I, in "Body Movement and Responsibility for a Situation," counter a strong argument against affirmative action, that individuals should not be held responsible for the actions of their ancestors. Hence, whites today should not be punished for acts committed by their forefathers. Lee begins by explaining Maurice Merleau-Ponty's understanding that body movement generates space and time, and his definition of freedom as entailing responsibility for one's entire situation. Lee argues that these two phenomenological insights support the position of the radical whiteness theorists who recognize the ethical responsibility for situations not of one's own making and accountability for the results of more than one's immediate personal conscious decisions and actions. Because of our specific history, whites have developed a particular embodiment and body movement that generates spaces and times that can only be characterized as more comfortable and more enabling to whites.

In the last and final essay, "The Future of Whiteness," Linda Martín Alcoff, examines the conditions for including whites in a future where people of color constitute the majority. In contrast to the facile dismissal of whites as uncomplicatedly untrustworthy because of the historical positioning of whites as the dominant, "master" figures, Alcoff phenomenologically outlines the changing subjective experiences of whiteness now. She insists that, presently, whites experience alienation and a double consciousness that has usually only been associated with people of color. Hence, she does not relegate whites to cluelessness and "vanguardism." Alcoff carefully maintains that the epistemic importance of the alienation of the subjective experience of whites does not arise simply from class divides and class analysis. Alcoff resists determinist assumptions about whiteness, and rather acknowledges ambiguity in whiteness.

Through a phenomenological exploration of various racialized subjectivities, this collection of essays aims to explore the relation between embodiment and race. I hope that it succeeds in highlighting and forwarding this dimension of the philosophy of race.

Notes

1. Patricia Williams, *The Alchemy of Race and Rights* (Cambridge: Harvard University Press, 1991), 256. Similarly, Deidre E. Davis astutely writes that "'[w]e cannot hope to understand the meaning of a person's experiences, including her experiences of oppression, without first thinking of her as embodied and second thinking about the particular meanings assigned to that embodiment.'" ("The Harm that has No Name: Street Harassment, Embodiment, and African American Women," in *Critical Race Feminism*, ed. Adrien Katherine Wing [New York: New York University Press, 1997], 192. She cites Elizabeth V. Spelman's *Inessential Woman:*

Problems of Exclusion in Feminist Thought [Boston: Beacon Press, 1988], 129–130.

2. Feminist theorists have explored the relations between the materiality of the body and gendered meaning more thoroughly. Among the books that discuss this are Dorothea Olkowski and Gail Weiss, eds. *Feminist Interpretations of Maurice Merleau-Ponty* (University Park, Pa.: The Pennsylvania State University Press, 2006); Gail Weiss, *Body Images: Embodiment as Intercorporeality* (New York: Routledge, 1999); and Iris Marion Young, *On Female Body Experience, "Throwing Like a Girl," and Other Essays* (New York: Oxford University Press, 2005). See also chapters in the following books: Elizabeth Grosz, *Volatile Bodies: Toward a Corporeal Feminism* (Bloomington: Indiana University Press, 1999); Shannon Sullivan, *Living Across and Through Skins: Transactional Bodies, Pragmatism, and Feminism* (Bloomington: Indiana University Press, 2001); Linda Martín Alcoff, *Visible Identities: Race, Gender, and the Self* (New York: Oxford University Press, 2006); and Maria Lupe Davidson, Kathryn Gynes, and Donna Dale Marcano, *Convergences: Black Feminism and Continental Philosophy* (Albany: State University of New York Press, 2010).

3. Chandra Talpade Mohanty, "Introduction: Cartographies of Struggle: Third World Women and the Politics of Feminism," in *Third World Women and the Politics of Feminism*, ed. Chandra Talpade Mohanty, Ann Russo, and Lourdes Torres (Bloomington: Indiana University Press, 1991), 23.

4. See Taunya Lovell Banks, "Two Life Stories: Reflections of One Black Woman Law Professor," in *Critical Race Theory: The Key Writings that Formed the Movement*, ed. Kimberle Crenshaw, Neil Gotanda, Gary Peller, and Kendall Thomas (New York: The New Press, 1995).

5. See Chandra Talpade Mohanty, "Defining Genealogies: Feminist Reflections on Being South Asian in North America," in *Making More Waves: New Writing by Asian American Women*, eds. Elaine H. Kim, Lilia V. Villanueva, and Asian Women United of California (Boston: Beacon Press, 1997). See also, Adrien Katherine Wing, "Brief Reflections Toward a Multiplicative Theory and Praxis of Being," *Critical Race Feminism*, ed. Adrien Katherine Wing (New York: New York University Press, 1997).

6. See Karen J. Hossfeld, "Hiring Immigrant Women: Silicon Valley's 'Simple Formula,'" in *Women of Color in U.S. Society*, ed. Maxine Baca Zinn and Bonnie Thornton Dill (Philadelphia: Temple University Press, 1994).

7. Hubert Dreyfus writes, "[i]n opposition to mainline cognitive science, which assumes that intelligent behavior must be based on representations in the mind or brain, Merleau-Ponty holds that the most basic sort of

intelligent behavior, skillful coping, can and must be understood without recourse to any type of representation." (Dreyfus, "Merleau-Ponty and Recent Cognitive Science," in *The Cambridge Companion to Merleau-Ponty*, ed. Taylor Carman and Mark B. N. Hansen, [Cambridge, UK: Cambridge University Press, 2005], 129).

8. Ibid., 135–136.

9. See Mark Rowlands, *The New Science of the Mind: From Extended Mind to Embodied Phenomenology* (Cambridge: MIT Press, 2010); Robert D. Rupert, *Cognitive Systems and the Extended Mind* (New York: Oxford University Press, 2009); and Shaun Gallagher, *How the Body Shapes the Mind* (New York: Oxford University Press, 2005). See also, Henrik Bruun and Richard Langlais, "On the Embodied Nature of Action," *Acta Sociologica*, 46, no. 1 (2003): 31–40.

10. The following three are noticeable exceptions. Frantz Fanon, *Black Skins White Masks*, trans. Charles Lam Markman (New York: Grove Press, 1967). George Yancy, *Black Bodies, White Gazes: The Continuing Significance of Race* (New York: Rowman & Littlefield Publishers, 2008). Linda Martin Alcoff, *Visible Identities: Race, Gender, and the Self* (New York: Oxford University Press, 2006).

11. Interestingly, here we did not need cognitive science to affirm that the body influences the mind.

12. Judith Butler, *Bodies that Matter* (New York: Routledge, 1993), 1.

13. See Linda Martin Alcoff, chapter six, "The Metaphysics of Gender and Sexual Difference," *Visible Identities: Race, Gender, and the Self* (New York: Oxford University Press, 2006), where she discusses Sally Haslanger's critique of Butler via a post-Quinean metaphysics. See also Claire Cole brook, "From Radical Representations to Corporeal Becomings: The Feminist Philosophy of Lloyd, Grosz, and Gatens," *Hypatia* 15, no. 2 (Spring 2000): 76–93.

14. Letitia Meynell, "Introduction to Embodiment and Agency," *Embodiment and Agency*, ed. Sue Campbell, Letitia Meynell, and Susan Sherwin (State College Park: Pennsylvania State University Press, 2009), 9.

15. To be specific, scientists do not utilize the typological conception of race because "[it] is estimated that humans are identical 99.9% of our DNA." (Lisa Gannett, "Racism and Human Genome Diversity Research: The Ethical Limits of 'Population Thinking,'" *Philosophy of Science* 68, no. 3 (Sept. 2001): 487). Instead, race is conceptualized as populations. "Race on this account [typology], was recognized to be a social construct, that would be left to social scientists. For ontological reasons, then, human

genome diversity research is said to be non-racist because it studies populations, not races" (Gannett, 481). Interestingly, Lisa Gannett argues that such population thinking in science still does not avoid racism (see 490).

16. Alcoff, *Visible*, 165. See also 135–136 and 172.
17. Michael Omi and Howard Winant, *Racial Formation in the United States from the 1960s to the 1990s* (New York: Routledge, 1994), 55.
18. Lewis R. Gordon, *Bad Faith and Antiblack Racism* (Amherst, NY: Humanity Books, 1999), 133. See also Charles Mills, *Blackness Visible* (Ithaca, N.Y.: Cornell University Press, 1998), 9–13; Michael D. Barber, *Equality and Diversity: Phenomenological Investigations of Prejudice and Discrimination* (New York: Humanity Books, 2001), 110; Linda Martin Alcoff, "Philosophy and Racial Identity," *Philosophy Today* 41 (Spring 1997): 68–69; and Falguni A. Sheth, *Toward a Political Philosophy of Race* (Albany: State University of New York Press, 2009), chapter 1. They articulate similar positions.
19. Maurice Merleau-Ponty, *Phenomenology of Perception*, trans. Colin Smith (Great Britain: Routledge and Kegan Paul, 1962), 57.
20. Maurice Merleau-Ponty, *The Visible and the Invisible*, trans. Alphonso Lingis (Evanston, Ill.: Northwestern University Press, 1968), 129. Author's italics.
21. Merleau-Ponty, *Visible*, 114.
22. Merleau-Ponty, *Phenomenology*, 238.
23. Merleau-Ponty, *Visible*, 41.
24. Omi and Winant, *Racial Formation in the United States*, 16–20.1.

ONE

MATERIALIZING RACE

CHARLES W. MILLS

The metaphysics of race is by now a familiar topic in philosophy. Philosophers of the last two or three decades interested in the subject of race found themselves presented with two main alternatives, traditional (usually racist) old-fashioned biological conceptions of race (racial naturalism/racial realism/racial essentialism/racial biologism) and a nouveau liberal white color-blindness (racial eliminativism) that urged us to drop the concept from our vocabulary altogether. Either race was natural or, like witches , race did not really exist. Most philosophers of race (the important exceptions being Anthony Appiah and Naomi Zack) chose to reject both alternatives as unsatisfactory and sought instead to carve out a metaphysical space for race as neither biological nor nonexistent, but sociopolitically constructed and existent (antieliminativist constructionism).[1] Indeed—not, alas, primarily because of the work of philosophers, whose cultural influence is quite marginal—the claim that "race is constructed" has long since become an academic cliché. But the consensus in the radical academy on this point conceals deep theoretical disagreements, both because some authors use the language of construction precisely to indicate race's nonexistence ("race is constructed and so doesn't exist": eliminativist constructionism) and because of the divergence even among those who do affirm its existence on what the constituents, the building blocks so to speak, of this "construction" are. Are they discourses, prejudices, culture, performance, legal decisions, social mores? And how might they be related to different theorists' competing views of the workings of sociopolitical causality, and their different framings of the role of the body?

In this chapter, I want to see whether older, now seemingly outdated (and for some, discredited) categories famously associated with the Marxist tradition, specifically *materialism*, can illuminate this debate. Does it make sense to think of race as material? If so how? And what insights might this give us into its dynamics?

"Materialism" in Marxist Theory

Let me begin with a review of the Marxist framework, especially necessary for a readership for whom this is likely to be an obsolete paradigm. In the heyday of Marxist influence in the academy (now long past), materialism was a key term, but with the rise of poststructuralism, it has largely disappeared from sociopolitical theory, except in the work of some feminist writers. Materialism for Marx and Engels has at least two senses, though these are not clearly distinguished, and in fact in the secondary literature on Marx and Engels they are sometimes conflated.

The first sense is the sense familiar to us from introductory courses in metaphysics: materialism as an *ontological* position that contrasts with other ontological positions, such as idealism or dualism.[2] Materialism in this sense claims that the only things that exist are physical entities: there are no souls, no spirits, no minds outside of the thinking brain, no God. Obviously, Marxism is not unique in affirming such a view, and both Marx and Engels saw themselves as part of an older materialist tradition in philosophy that stretched back to ancient Greece. In their opinion, Ludwig Feuerbach was unique among their theoretical adversaries, the Young Hegelians, in being a materialist, though ultimately a materialist who (in their view) did not follow his premises where they pointed. As they write in *The German Ideology*: "As far as Feuerbach is a materialist he does not deal with history, and as far as he considers history he is not a materialist. With him materialism and history diverge completely."[3]

The second, somewhat fuzzier sense could be termed *sociopolitical* materialism: this is not an ontological view of the traditional kind just demarcated, but rather a claim, or set of claims, about patterns of sociopolitical causality. Sociopolitical materialism is asserting that (1) the sociopolitical system can be differentiated into different elements; (2) some of these elements should be thought of as "material" and others as "ideal"; and (3) overall patterns of sociopolitical causality are determined by the "material" elements. The emphasis is on "overall" because materialism in this sense is not (at least in nonreductivist versions) denying that "ideal" elements have *some* causal efficaciousness. What it denies is that they are equally or more important in shaping the overall sociopolitical dynamic. So materialism in this sense is supposed to be an important general truth about the workings of the social world, just as materialism in the ontological sense is supposed to be an important general truth about the nature of the universe.

What were these "material" elements, and why were they so called? Marx and Engels seem to have been working with the following analogy: Materialism as an ontological position affirms the general independence of the material world from the mental. The universe preexisted humanity, other thinking beings, indeed all forms of life. So the universe does not depend on us (or on anybody else). Moreover, when life and the mental (eventually) come into existence, they do so as functions of physical structures, without which they could not survive. So, the reality is that only material entities exist.

The connection with materialism in the second sense is then the supposed analogy between an ontological asymmetry and a causal asymmetry. Materialism as a sociopolitical thesis affirms the differential causal significance of a particular social sector that is also (though not in the same way, obviously) "independent of us." We bring society as a whole into existence by our actions, so it is clearly not an independence of this kind. Moreover, if we were all to perish tomorrow through some catastrophe, society would perish also, so it is not an independence of that kind either. And as long as society exists, it obviously requires our collective participation to function, so this kind of independence is ruled out also.

So what could be left? Marx and Engels's argument is that because we are material creatures, with objective prerequisites for our existence to continue, economic production is necessary. This is independent of our will in the sense that—unless we are willing to die—society *has* to be arranged in a certain way and certain things *have* to be done. But production depends on the level of technological development; we cannot bring into existence a system beyond existing social capabilities. And unless we are able to produce individually for ourselves, our access to social goods will be limited by the power of others. These techno-economic constraints—the level of human technological development and the power relations in which economic production is organized—are thus dubbed by Marx and Engels as the *material*. They set limits on social and individual possibilities and are independent of our will because (1) without access to the means of production, we would not be able to survive; and (2) because of this "material" necessity, the owners of the means of production have differential power over the lives of others, who do not own the means of production. This asymmetrical significance is meta-phorically signaled by designating technology, raw materials, human laboring capacity, and the power relations within which production takes place (the "forces" and "relations" of production in Marxist jargon) as the "base" of society, by contrast with the "superstructure." Class, understood as one's rela-tionship to the means of production, is therefore a more fundamental cat-egory than other social group memberships. So within this taxonomy, class is theoretically privileged as *material*, causally and explanatorily central, in a way that other social groups are not. Class is material, part of the base, while the state, the legal system, morality, and culture are superstructural, "ideal."[4]

Given what has just been said, it is obvious that nature also must be "material" for Marx and Engels. It is, of course, a materiality that (once humans achieve a certain technological level) is increasingly subject to modi-fication by human causality. Marx and Engels are emphatic on seeing human-ity as *part* of nature, rather than lifted above it, but we are natural creatures whose distinctive natural sociality and capacity for technological advance make us capable of reacting back on nature and modifying, within limits, the determinants that shape us. For this reason Marx rejected theories of naturalistic determination, such as biological and geographical determinism, that represented human beings as products of a natural causality unmediated by, or largely impervious to, the social and the realm of social causality. But as the Italian Marxist Sebastiano Timpanaro warned decades ago, the archi-tectural metaphor of base and superstructure needs to take into account that this underlying "base" of nature on which the "base" of the forces and rela-tions of production rests does not disappear, even if its causality is generally mediated through the social.[5] In Marxists' political insistence on discrediting naturalistic materialism, the danger is that the natural is denied efficacious causality altogether:

> Marxists put themselves in a scientifically and polemically weak posi-tion if, after rejecting the idealist arguments which claim to show that the only reality is that of the Spirit and that cultural facts are in no way dependent on economic structures, they then borrow the same arguments to deny the dependence of man on nature. . . . [M]an as a biological being, endowed with a certain (not unlimited) adaptabil-ity to his external environment, and with certain impulses towards activity and the pursuit of happiness, subject to old age and death, is not an abstract construction, nor one of our prehistoric ances-tors, a species of pithecanthropus now superseded by historical and

social man, but still exists in each of us and in all probability will still exist in the future. . . . To maintain that, since the "biological" is always presented to us as mediated by the "social," the "biological" is nothing and the "social" is everything, would once again be idealist sophistry.[6]

What is required, then, is a sociopolitical materialism that does not end up subsuming the natural into the sociopolitical, treating the body as if it simply disappears into the body politic. With the apparent demise of Marxism since the 1970s to 1980s, of course, materialism of any kind has long been seen as refuted, displaced by poststructuralism and a radical constructionism. But Diana Coole and Samantha Frost, the editors of a recent book on what they call the "new materialisms," argue that materialism "is once more on the move after several decades of abeyance."[7] They contend that work across a number of disciplines suggests that "the more textual approaches associated with the so-called cultural turn are increasingly being deemed inadequate for understanding contemporary society," and thus, that "it is now timely to reopen the issue of matter and once again to give material factors their due in shaping society and circumscribing human prospects":

> This means returning to the most fundamental questions about the nature of matter and the place of embodied humans within a material world. . . . [T]heorists are compelled to rediscover older materialist traditions while pushing them in novel, and sometimes experimental, directions or toward fresh applications.[8]

In this materialist spirit (!), then, I want to explore how the "older materialist tradition" of Marxism and political economy could possibly be developed, in the light of more recent scholarship, to theorize race and racial embodiment in materialist terms.

Alcoff on Materialism

The work of Linda Martín Alcoff will be a useful reference point here, since in her essay collection *Visible Identities*,[9] Alcoff stakes out a theoretical position with which I am in fundamental sympathy. Alcoff, too, is trying to recuperate materialism for race and gender identities. Thus, we find her rejecting orthodox Marxism's dismissal of "identity politics" while simultaneously (unlike the post-Marxist theory of the 1980s onward) affirming the importance of Marxist class categories and the need to recognize that "capitalism was a racial and gender system from its inception," so that "The real challenge that identity politics must address in my view is the need to articulate its precise relation to class."[10] She is hostile (as virtually all feminist philosophers are) to a biologistic naturalism about gender while simultaneously warning (as significantly fewer do) that "poststructuralism . . . threatens to deconstruct the feminist subject as well as the female subject" and rejecting Judith Butler's view that "all is culture" and performance.[11] She repudiates (along with virtually everybody else in the radical academy) a class-reductivist or naturalist materialism while simultaneously (along with a smaller number of us) being emphatic on the need to reconstruct a new materialism that is not theoretically handicapped in these ways, which in the case of gender would be "an analysis that maintains the central importance of the material reality of the sexed body."[12] In sum, "gender is both positional and material."[13]

So Alcoff is in agreement with classical Marxism (and contra poststructuralist feminism) on the importance of the material/ideal distinction, while rejecting classical Marxism's restriction of materiality to class. Unlike those theorists who would say that materialism is either false (since in fact it is discourse that determines everything) or meaningless (since this "binary opposition"—idealism versus materialism—is an artifact of a conceptual framework that needs to be transcended and abandoned), Alcoff wants to insist that materialism is meaningful and true.

The question then is: What about race? Alcoff's self-consciously materialist countertheorization of identity politics and identity metaphysics is focused more on gender than on race, but she does say, in her chapter on mixed race, that "any materialist account of the self must take race into account."[14] But what would a distinctively materialist constructionism look like? How do we theorize the social constructedness of race in a theory that prioritizes material determinants as its crucial shaping factors, and, relatedly, how should we understand the materiality of race (if it is indeed material) in relation to these other materialities of class and gender?

Race as Material: Differential Access to Economic Opportunities and Wealth

To start with, of course, it would have to be reemphasized that one would not be arguing for race as material in the naturalistic sense. For contemporary postmodernism, it is virtually axiomatic that the body is constructed and that our reactions to the body are socially mediated. So, in endorsing a materialist anti-post-modernism, I should underline that I am not thereby endorsing the asocial body. In classic racial determinism, race represents natural biological limitations, ineluctable psychological drives, evolutionary laws, and is indeed therefore "material" in this traditional sense. But this would be, as noted in the previous section, unhistorical materialism, the materialism that Marxism claims to have refuted. The whole point of the Marxist critique is that our embodied experience is significantly shaped by the larger social body of the body politic. Marx's discussion of alienation in his early work, as in the 1844 Manuscripts,[15] situates our relation to ourselves and others in the framework of class society. Alienation—from the product of our labor, our productive activity, our species-being, and our fellow-humans—is not intrinsic to the human condition as such. Nor is it a manifestation simply of the externalization of our activity in the world, for then it would be an unavoidable feature of all societies. Rather, Marx is emphatic that it is a consequence of the emergence of class society, as a result of which we are working for others rather than ourselves: "The alien being to whom the labour and the product of the labour belongs, whom the labour serves and who enjoys its product, can only be man himself. . . . If he relates to his own activity as to something unfree, it is a relationship to an activity that is under the domination, oppression, and yoke of another man."[16] Alienation is rooted in "material" processes, and thus requires political economy to elucidate it, but a radicalized political economy which—unlike that inherited by Marx—seeks to explain the origins of private property rather than taking private property for granted.

So this provides us with an overall theoretical starting-point: a materialist account of race, if one can be developed, should somehow be theorized along similar or related lines. But because Marx himself was not concerned with race, his own comments (sometimes racist in fact) offer little guidance. So let us turn instead to one of the most famous treatments of black embodiment in the literature on race, Frantz Fanon's *Black Skin, White Masks*.[17]

In his introduction, Fanon states that he "do[es] not come with timeless truths." Rather, he is diagnosing a phenomenon of a particular historical specificity, arising out of the history of colonialism: "The architecture of this work is rooted in the temporal." Race, no less than class and class society, must be historicized, rather than treated as eternal. Fanon explicitly repudiates the vocabulary of "ontology" to represent this situation: "Ontology . . . does not permit us to understand the being of the black man." But this, I would suggest, is because he is associating the "ontological," in Aristotelian fashion, with the timeless and necessary, whereas the reality is that "not only must the black man be black; he must be black in relation to the white man." So this insight, I would claim, can be readily accommodated by the category of a *social* ontology.[18] Blackness is not a timeless category and the origin of blackness is not natural but "sociogenic," the result of social forces. Thus, it does make sense to regard this racialization as ontological, but of a social "nature," which, for blacks involves an "inferiority complex" that "is the outcome of a double process: primarily, economic; subsequently, the internalization—or, better, the epidermalization—of this inferiority."[19] As with the Marxist concept of class alienation, then, race and racial alienation arise out of our relations to our fellow-humans, as a result of exploitative economic processes and their psychological consequences.

Can this social ontology be regarded as *material*, though? For the orthodox Marxist tradition, the answer has generally been no. It would certainly be agreed that racism as an ideology (as with all ideologies) is the product of material forces, here expansionist capitalism, and the need to justify slavery, colonial conquest, and aboriginal expropriation. But that does not make race *itself* material. This refusal of material status could be seen as a distinctively Marxist version of the more familiar liberal brand of racial eliminativism, that is, a Marxist racial eliminativism. In the orthodox base/superstructure taxonomy, race would be located at the superstructural level, in the form of racist *ideologies* that rationalize genocide, superexploitation, and the differential treatment, in seeming violation of liberal norms, of people of color. But the material base itself would be composed of classes and class fractions. *Racism* would be acknowledged, but it would be denied that *race* as such has any social reality that cannot be expressed in the familiar vocabulary of left theory—for example, races as subordinated national minorities or subproletarianized sections of the working class. Orthodox Marxists refuse the status of the (sociopolitically) material to race because the (sociopolitically) material is exhausted by class: classes as the main kind of social group, around which the structuring of society is organized; class relations of production as the material girders of this structure; class exploitation as central; and class interests as the material interests that different classes try to advance in a struggle with each other which, in tandem with technological advance, is the main dynamo of history. But race, it would be claimed, cannot be conceptualized this way. The white working-class is misled by bourgeois ideology, in the service of capitalist interests, into thinking of themselves as white, thereby ignoring their "true" class interests. But they are not seen as having *racial* interests. Rather, the theoretical emphasis is on how *all* workers are disadvantaged by racism. So the claim was that white workers did not really benefit from racism; they only thought they did. Correspondingly, the barriers to be overcome in developing a multiracial anticapitalist political movement were primarily ideological in nature. In reality white workers' interests would best be served by a nonracist socialist society.

So the first step in challenging this denial of materiality to race is to point out race's material payoff for whites and material handicapping of non-whites—the "material" as signifying economic advantage and disadvantage. Instead of working simply with the categories of capitalism (as a social system) and racism (as an ideology), we would expand our theoretical framework to incorporate the concept of white supremacy as itself a social system.[20] So we would be recognizing the socio-institutional reality of race, not just racism as idea, belief, prejudice, antagonism, ill-will. White supremacy itself should be seen as a system of domination, structured by exploitative relations between races, and thereby constituting "racial" interests as stakes in respectively maintaining and overturning the system. These interests are multidimensional in character, including social status, differential political input, cultural hegemony, and somatic normativity. But at their core, arguably, is economic privilege and economic disadvantage, a sense of the "material" completely uncontroversial in everyday discourse as well as Marxist theory.

It is just this issue which has become the focus, in far greater detail and theoretical sophistication than ever before, of a growing body of the recent social-science literature on race. Earlier treatments of black/white racial disparity tended to concentrate one-dimensionally on income differentials. The primary metric was the respective incomes of median white and black households, and patterns of progress and retreat in narrowing the gap between the two. But the severe limitedness of this theoretical approach has now been realized. From different disciplinary perspectives—legal theory, sociology, economics, political science—and with different emphases, the significance of whiteness as property, whiteness as ownership, whiteness as enhanced access, whiteness as wealth, has now been made theoretically central. George Lipsitz's "possessive investment in whiteness," Cheryl Harris's "whiteness as property," Melvin Oliver and Thomas Shapiro's contrast of black wealth and white wealth, Linda Faye Williams's "white skin privilege"—can all be seen as exploring and highlighting the importance of material white advantage as superior opportunities for accumulating wealth.[21]

For it turns out that *wealth* differentials are far more important than income differentials in determining the long-term prospects for racial equality. In a capitalist country such as our own, wealth provides a cushion against medical catastrophe or employment layoff, can be used to start a small business, make a down-payment on a mortgage, secure a comfortable retirement, and be transmitted as an inheritance to one's children to give them a head-start in life. And whereas income differentials between the median white and the median black household have, over the last half-century, been generally in the 50 to 65 percent range, wealth differentials between the median white/ black households have been far greater. Moreover, in recent years they have gotten worse rather than better (so one cannot even speak optimistically of long-term trends closing the gap), reaching a ratio of 20 to 1 in 2007.[22] As the authors of a 2010 Brandeis study conclude: "With greater numbers of families struggling with ever-growing debt, that far outstrips their income and savings, many low-income and minority households must turn to costly lending products because they have no other option."[23] Material constraint, in other words. Nor can it be retorted that this is really just class, since the authors make the point that black households at *all* income levels are far poorer than their white counterparts. Race is a crucial variable in itself. Indeed, as another set of statistics reveal, it is precisely at the working-class level—where the white left historically claimed that race was just a matter of ideology, "ideal" rather than "material"—that the differential is the greatest of all. According to 2004 statistics, for example, the bottom quintile of the white population had a dizzying 400-plus times the wealth of the bottom quintile of the black population, $24,000 to $57.[24]

So the critique is not that class is not material whereas race is, nor that the white working-class is not exploited. The critique is that capitalism, as it develops in the modern world, is generally racialized, so that white supremacy as a system of advantage and disadvantage interlocks with it, and white workers are both the victims of capitalist exploitation and the beneficiaries of racial exploitation. The materiality of race can be straightforwardly cashed out—appropriate metaphor—in terms of differential likelihoods of material advantage and disadvantage for privileged and subordinated races, R1s and R2s, linked to material structures of racial domination (residential and educational segregation, diminished chances of home value appreciation, unequal educational access, the racial division of labor, employment and market discrimination, racialized transfer payments from the state, and so forth). Obviously it is not the case that all nonwhites are poor and that all whites are rich, unlike a class metric of workers and capitalists. Rather one compares corresponding positions (deciles, quintiles) on overlapping wealth distribution curves. But insofar as race is probabilistically linked to significant differential probabilities of access to opportunities and wealth, it would seem that—in this not-insignificant sense—it can indeed be seen as material.

However, consider the following objection. Class is likewise material in enhanced/diminished access to wealth. But this is because power over the means of production and exclusion from power over the means of production directly advantages or handicaps one in the economy. Yet insofar as race also advantages/handicaps one, it is not because "race" itself has such a material power. Your white or dark skin, your straight or kinky hair, your "Caucasian" or "non-Caucasian" features have no such intrinsic capability, and as such are ontologically different from economic powers. Possession of, say, land in a peasant economy directly enables one to grow things; nonpossession of land directly forces one to work for landowners. But possession of a particular "racial" morphology does not, absent particular social categorizations, directly enable one to do, or prevent one from doing, anything. The constraint here arises *indirectly*, through being categorized a certain way in a certain kind of social order (a racialized one). If one is categorized as a member of the privileged race, material opportunities are opened up; if one is categorized as a member of the subordinated race, material opportunities are blocked. So it is the social categorization that is doing the work. And the problem is that other social indicators, which it would be difficult to regard as material in any sense, could also play such a role.

Imagine, for example, a theocracy that privileges members of religion F1 (F for faith) and discriminates against members of religion F2. Then it could well be the case that being a follower of F2 means that your chances of getting social opportunities and attaining wealth will be far less than for followers of F1. So F-membership will not merely be correlated with wealth, but will actually have a causal connection with wealth. By this criterion, then, we should consider one's religious beliefs as also being material, which seems like a *reductio* of the argument.

How could this objection be blocked? The obvious reply is that while one can always change one's religious faith, or pretend to change one's religious faith (concealing one's true beliefs), one cannot—cases of "passing" aside—change one's race. So insofar as the morphology of the body is crucial, whether as itself determinant for biological racism or as epistemic indicator of racial membership for cultural racism, race is an ineluctable part of the self which, independent of one's will, is going to significantly shape one's fate and access to material opportunities, and is thus material in a way that religious faith is not. Indeed, the fifteenth-century Spanish introduction of the criterion of *limpieza de sangre*, purity of blood, against *conversos*, Jews who converted to Christianity to escape religious persecution, is standardly cited as a paradigm example of the shift from religious to racial anti-Semitism, and as one of the first clear-cut examples of racism in the early modern period.[25]

Race as Material: A (Social) Ontological Indicator

However, I now want to explore the possibility that race signifies an additional and deeper level of materiality than just economic advantage/disadvantage.

Let us return to Linda Alcoff's book. In a section of chapter 6 called "Is Sex Like Race?" Alcoff points out a crucial difference between the two: there is no racial entity or physiological structure correspondent to "the variable of reproductive role": "Gender identities in some variation seem to be, unlike race, historically ubiquitous, hardly recent, and based in a set of biological features with more morphological substance" than "biologically insignificant physical attributes such as skin color, the shape of the nose or eyes, or hair type." Gender is embedded in the history of the species in a way that is far deeper than race is, which most theorists in the field argue only comes into existence in the modern period. Thus, as Alcoff observes: "[I]n regard to race it makes much more sense to look at the global political economy and the history of colonialism for an understanding of why and how skin shades gained such ontological significance in recent centuries."[26]

What I want to ask is how we should think of this political economy, and this "ontological significance," especially given the obvious difference between race and sex. I think the socialist-feminist attempt to theorize gender might be useful here. Before the rise of poststructuralism in the 1980s, when Marxism was still seen as a live theoretical option, socialist feminism attempted to bring together the insights of Marxist feminism and radical feminism into a synthesis that would correct the weaknesses of both. Marxist feminism, the orthodox Engelsian feminism of *The Origin of the Family, Private Property and the State*,[27] was judged by many left feminists of the "second wave" of feminism to be theoretically inadequate, which is why they came up with the separate category of socialist feminism.[28] Socialist feminists argued that in *The German Ideology*, Marx and Engels in effect retreat from their original perception that gender relations should be considered part of the base, and thus be material. Contra such a retreat, these feminist theorists contended that we should see the base as consisting not merely of the relations of production but of the relations of *reproduction*, in that a society would not be able to perpetuate itself unless the human population was being reproduced. This was a "material" necessity also.

The imperative of daily survival requires natural appropriation, which leads to technological development and the constraints of the techno-economic. But it is also the case that the species needs to reproduce, and women were the ones with the biological capacity to have children. It is not that women's reproductive capacity (natural/material) dictated female gender subordination. Rather, this was a set of reproductive relations imposed by male power (sociopolitical/material).[29] So whereas orthodox Engelsian Marxist feminism saw only class relations and class power as material, socialist feminists argued that gender relations and gender power needed to be seen as material also. Not only did capitalists dominate and exploit workers, but men dominated and exploited women. The social "base" was in fact a complex entity incorporating both class and gender relations of domination. There was a political economy of class, but there was also a political economy of gender, which were intertwined in a "dual system" of "capitalist patriarchy."

Now obviously, as sketched earlier, I would claim that this should really be expanded into a "triple system" that also incorporates the political economy of race. But the problem, as the Alcoff quote indicates, is in trying to determine the material significance of race given its biological superficiality. There is no equivalent in the raced nonwhite body to the different genitalia of the gendered female body. The fact that women are the ones who conceive children is not itself an artifact of gender ideology. This is a material (natural) reality, even if it has been used as the foundation for false normative and sociopolitical claims about who should have the burden of raising the children conceived. That women are naturally and appropriately to be confined to the domestic sphere is a (doubly false) descriptive and normative sociopolitical claim that reflects male interests and can be challenged by feminist theory. But that women at our current stage of technological evolution are naturally the ones who bear children is a biological claim that is true. (*Brave New World* scenarios are coming perhaps sooner than we think, but obviously for most of human history they have been materially impossible.[30]) And the problem is that the morphological features taken to be racially defining for racism—skin color, facial topography, hair texture—have no such biological role. Unlike the case of gender, where there is a genuine natural biological base of reproductive significance on which sex roles are superimposed, there is no comparable natural biological racial base. There are no genuine differences between "races" of the biological import of the genuine differences between the sexes. If people of color are characterized as natural slaves awaiting transportation to the plantations, as savages incapable of ownership rights over the land they occupy, as barbarians to be subjugated by superior civilizations, it is on the grounds of mythical racial differences. There is no physical property of their bodies that can actually be identified as justifying these regimes.

So again, we can see why it is far easier for the political economy of race to be assimilated to a class political economy than it is for the political economy of gender to be so assimilated, and why it has been easier to deny race a distinct "materiality" of its own. The orthodox Marxist will argue that there is nothing to play the role of the "relations of reproduction," which is what socialist feminists claim embed gender materially. If one replies by pointing out that black slave labor in the prebellum United States, in a hybrid economy where capitalism is articulated to slavery, is clearly differentiated from "free" white wage labor, or that after Emancipation, blacks were largely confined to subproletarianized sections of the working class, this (it would be retorted by the orthodox Marxist) is just to concede the point by falling back on class categories. One is claiming to be differentiating a distinctively *racial* political economy, but in fact no such deep difference can be demonstrated. To the extent that race exists and is material, the orthodox Marxist will insist, it is really just class in disguise, class in a different skin.

In other words, absent class ideology and class power, it would still be the case that access/nonaccess to the means of production will determine your survival. Absent gender ideology and sexist practices, it would still be the case that women are the half of the species capable of bearing children. These are physical facts about human beings in the *biologically* materialist sense on which *social* materialism builds. But absent racial ideology and racist practices, "phenotypically" black traits such as dark skin, curly hair, everted lips, and so on have no such socially shaping causal power. The same body physically would have a different social significance in an alternative racial system; the phenomenology of racial embodiment is not biologically based. How then can race be "material" in any deep way?

What I am going to suggest is that the category of personhood might be developed in such a fashion that its "material" dimension is revealed, and that "relations of personhood/subpersonhood" could play for race the role played by these other kinds of material relations.

On the face of it, this is an unpromising category. After all, the whole discourse of personhood is an *ethical* discourse, to be associated with, say, Kantianism (whose noumenal/phenomenal divide would seem to make him a paradigmatically *anti*materialist theorist!), not the tradition of political economy. Moreover, Marxism has been interpreted by many commentators as a fundamentally amoralist or antimoralist body of theory.[31] So how could such divergent theoretical foundations be brought together?

Here is my argument. (In the following I will assume, without argument, the truth of moral objectivism: that morality is objective.[32]) I propose that we should see personhood as a category that is *both* ethical and political-economic. It is ethical (socially independent and objective) in that it expresses the moral standing of human beings (and intelligent aliens, if they exist), and the rights, freedoms, and duties they should have. But it is also political-economic (socially determined and socially relative) in that the norms for its application are determined not simply by the intrinsic features of human beings, but by their social recognition/nonrecognition as moral equals. In other words, even if all humans are objectively persons (setting aside the complications of newborn infants, the brain-dead, and so forth), they will not be intersubjectively recognized as such unless they have a certain status within the political economy. So we could differentiate objective personhood and intersubjective, socially recognized personhood. And the reality historically and currently is that not all persons (by objective moral standards) have in fact been seen as persons.[33]

The failure to acknowledge and theorize this reality is itself, I would claim, an artifact of the whiteness and Eurocentrism of mainstream philosophy. Overtly or tacitly focusing on the white Western experience, it tells a narrative of populations who are class-divided but nonetheless recognized as equally human, so that the contingency of this recognition, and its original denial to people of color, is omitted from the historical account. Modernity removes the traditional formal class barriers dividing different groups of Europeans, whether in Europe or the world they colonize, so that personhood emerges as the central social category. But at the same time it constructs barriers of a new kind, "racial" barriers, between the European/Euro-implanted population and the rest of the world, so that the latter are relegated to the status of subpersonhood. As George Fredrickson summarizes things in his *Racism: A Short History*:

> What makes Western racism so autonomous and conspicuous in world history has been that it developed in a context that presumed human equality of some kind. . . . If equality is the norm in the spiritual or temporal realms (or in both at the same time), and there are groups of people within the society who are so despised or disparaged that the upholders of the norms feel compelled to make

them exceptions to the promise or realization of equality, they can be denied the prospect of equal status only if they allegedly possess some extraordinary deficiency that makes them less than fully human.[34]

In other words, I am suggesting that, with the advent of modernity, both the relations of production highlighted by (white) Marxism and the relations of reproduction highlighted by (white) feminism—that respectively structure class positions in the market economy and gender positions in the domestic economy—come to be established on a groundwork so foundational that it is not even seen as sociopolitical by white sociopolitical theory: relations of personhood/subpersonhood, that structure the positions of (official white) humanity in relation to the rest of the world. White Marxism educates us to the fact that class should be denaturalized, that it is not because of God's will or innate superiority and inferiority that some are rich and others poor. White feminist theory educates us to the fact that gender should be denaturalized, that it is not because of their genitalia that half are in the public sphere while the other half are in the private sphere. But both of these bodies of theory, centered on the white experience, take for granted as natural the personhood of the humans that are their theoretical units, failing to see that this (recognized) personhood is *itself* a historical product that likewise needs to be denaturalized, and that is not extended to the other humans on whose exploitation these class and gender systems rest. The political economy of personhood comes to underpin the political economy of class and gender.[35]

Once such a theoretical shift is made, it can be appreciated that from the modern period onward (when race comes into existence), race is indeed material in that it is because of race that one is entitled to or debarred from the "normal" treatment extended to white humans. The categories of capitalist and worker, male and female, are in a sense secondary to the more fundamental categories—appearing "natural," the result of biological law—of human/subhuman. That the latter do not, on their face, *appear* to be categories of political economy is because the political economy is so foundational to the new racial world order that it is not even recognizable *as* a political economy. So we now have a principled rather than ad hoc theoretical foundation for locating and understanding the distinctive historical significance of race.

Nonetheless, it may be objected that the earlier criticism still holds valid. If moral standing, inclusion in the category of the (fully) human, is supposed to be the demarcator of status, linked to race, surely this is radically different from (Marxist) class and (socialist feminist) gender categories, where a material foundation—power over the means of production, reproductive capacity—can be identified independently of the social decision to recognize. Independently of what human beings, or a privileged subset of human beings, choose to give status to, it will still be the case that access to the means of production is necessary to survive and that women's bodies are the ones that reproduce the species. But here there is no comparable "material" fact about the subordinated races. If it is just a matter of how they are classified, how can this be part of a "materialist" theory, when the initial claim was that for Marxism, "materiality" had to do with "independence of the will"? Surely a social decision is precisely the kind of thing that *is* dependent on the will!

The reply I would offer is the following. The (sociopolitical) materiality of race is different from the (sociopolitical) materiality of class and gender in, admittedly, lacking their (naturalistically) material foundation. At all times, we are constrained—"independent of our will"—by the facts of natural necessity and human reproductive capacities in ways that we are not by the peculiar set of features that come to be designated as "racial." Indeed, a world without race once existed and may one day exist again. But once—for contingent reasons having to do with the history of European expansionism—the Euro-social decision to introduce racial categories into the world and structure a new system of social domination accordingly *is* made, this system then takes on a life of its own precisely because the demarcation (fully human/ not fully human) is so fundamental to the world thereby created. We are not talking about social intrahuman status distinctions of class, gender, ethnicity, and so forth among those we recognize as human; we are talking about the far more basic, initial ground-floor distinction between the "us" (whites) and the "them" (nonwhites) not seen as fully human in the first place. Obviously, this demarcation becomes crucial to the structuring of "our" (white) lifeworld, especially when it is massively reinforced by social institutions, mores, practices, spatial segregations that locate us (whites) as settlers over against natives, as free over against the enslaved, as the colonizers over against the colonized, as colorless over against coloreds. Bodies that in a different world would be neutral now acquire an immense racialized significance, insofar as their physiognomy bespeaks their membership/nonmembership in the ranks of the fully human. A decision once made is not so easily unmade, especially when the formal rejection of several hundreds of years of racial ideology has not been accompanied by a correspondingly radical institutional change, so that the original racialized topography of the world, with its divergently racialized experience, continues largely intact, thereby continuing to reinforce officially repudiated categories and perceptions.

Drawing on Maurice Merleau-Ponty, Linda Alcoff writes:

> Because race works through the domain of the visible, the experience of race is predicated first and foremost on the perception of race, a perception whose specific mode is a learned ability. . . . The perceptual practices involved in racializations are then tacit, almost hidden from view, and thus almost immune from critical reflection. . . . This account would explain both why racializing attributions are nearly impossible to discern and why they are resistant to alteration or erasure. Our experience of habitual perception is so attenuated as to skip the stage of conscious interpretation and intent. Indeed, interpretation is the wrong word here: we are simply perceiving.[36]

Very similarly, but utilizing John Dewey and the American pragmatist tradition, Shannon Sullivan in her recent book *Revealing Whiteness*, explores the role of "unconscious habit" in making race, where habit is to be thought of as "as an organism's subconscious predisposition to transact with its physical, social, political, and natural worlds in particular ways." Habits are thus "manners of being and acting that constitute an organism's ongoing character." The result, in a racialized world, is racial habits, "raced predispositions [that] often actively subvert efforts to understand or change them, making themselves inaccessible to conscious inquiry [so that] race often functions unconsciously as well." Sullivan concludes that race is thus properly characterized as ontological—"one's race indeed has the status of ontology"—not in the "static" sense of "fixed racial essences" but reconfigured as "historical and malleable" rather than "eternal and immutable."[37] Though Sullivan does not herself use the language of "materialism," her account is obviously congruent with a social materialist analysis that recognizes how the social ontology of a racialized body politic becomes incarnated in the material bodies of its members, fleshed out in their reactive behaviors, incorporated in their perceptions and conceptions:

> Given that human beings are composed of habits formed in transaction with a white privileged world, their very being has been shaped . . . by race and racism. . . . The ontological roots that white privilege

puts down are bodily as well as psychical, or rather, engage a person's physicality and mentality in their co-constitution. White privilege is not just "in the head." It also is "in" the nose that smells, the back, neck, and other muscles that imperceptibly tighten with anxiety, and the eyes that see some but not all physical differences as significant. A person's psychological disposition toward the world can be found throughout her body, in her physical comportment, sensations, reactions, pleasures, and pains. . . . And all of this, including the "properly" bodily aspects of white privilege, can function unconsciously. The body, in fact, often serves as a prime site of nonreflective resistance to the transformation of habits of white privilege. It can actively thwart conscious attempts to dismantle a psychosomatic sense of white superiority.[38]

We can thus see how a case can be made for the materiality of race, even though there is no racial physiological entity corresponding to the general bodily requirements of human survival or the sexually differentiated requirements of human reproduction. The materiality of race (apart from the economic dimensions earlier sketched) inheres in the reflexes of, and associations evoked by, particular bodies in a world where the body politic is normed by the white body. Socialized from birth to discern race, the marker of full and diminished personhood, we learn to apprehend this world through a sensory grid whose architecture has been shaped by blueprints still functioning independent of our will and conscious intent, and resistant to our self-conscious redrawing. To return one last time to traditional historical materialism and its possible (nontraditional) Fanonian rethinking: in the *1844 Manuscripts*, Marx writes that in class society, the human senses become "inhuman," reflecting, transmitting, and reproducing the alienation of the social order.[39] A new, nontraditional historical materialism sensitized to race as well as class would recognize, similarly, how alienating material structures of white domination originally created by human causality now, in reified and coercive ways, distort the senses. Fanon writes: "All I wanted was to be a man among other men."[40] But alienated cognition—an alienation "not an individual question" but to be "sociodiagnostically" analyzed as "a massive psychoexistential complex"—prohibits such an egalitarian pattern of perception: "There will be an authentic disalienation only to the degree to which things, in the most materialistic meaning of the word, will have been restored to their proper places."[41] Racial cognition affects both blacks and whites, since "Consciousness of the body . . . is a third-person consciousness" and "a racial epidermal schema" displaces the "sensations and perceptions" of a preracial world by the "thousand details, anecdotes, stories"[42] woven by the white man:

> "Dirty nigger!" Or simply, "Look, a Negro!" . . . I found that I was an object in the midst of other objects. . . . I was responsible at the same time for my body, for my race, for my ancestors. I subjected myself to an objective examination, I discovered my blackness, my ethnic characteristics; and I was battered down by tom-toms, cannibalism, intellectual deficiency, fetishism, racial defects, slave-ships. . . . My body was given back to me sprawled out, distorted, recolored, clad in mourning. . . . The Negro is an animal, the Negro is bad, the Negro is mean, the Negro is ugly; look, a nigger . . .[43]

Racial demarcators thus trigger responses of which we are not even consciously aware, shaping our perceptions in processes completed in fractions of a second, and largely recalcitrant to intervention at the conscious level. Our bodies—(biologically) material—have learned to see other bodies—also (biologically) material—through a nonbiologically materially originating but sociopolitically materially originating normative cognitive apparatus established hundreds of years ago to differentiate full persons from those less than full persons, that has now become (doubly) materially embedded and which continues, through a fused physical and sociopolitical corporeality, to influence us today. Race is indeed material.

If this analysis is plausible, it shows not just how historical materialism would need to be rethought but how complex materiality is as a category, and how its different (class, gender, racial) incarnations would have to be related to one another for any comprehensive anatomy of our individual and social bodies to be drawn up.

Notes

1. Appiah's famous judgment was that "The truth is that there are no races": Kwame Anthony Appiah, *In My Father's House: Africa in the Philosophy of Culture* (New York: Oxford University Press, 1992), 45. Similarly, in a 1997 article, Zack rejected the idea that races are natural kinds, but did not explore the possibility that they might be "social" kinds, stating:

"Race is a social construction imposed on human biological differences which are not in themselves racial—because nothing is racial which is not 'in the head'": Naomi Zack, "Race and Philosophic Meaning" [1997], in Bernard Boxill, ed., *Race and Racism* (New York: Oxford University Press, 2001), 54. (However, in recent years she has claimed that the widespread interpretation of her position at the time as an eliminativist one was mistaken, and that she never meant to deny the social reality of race.)

2. I am using *ontological* here in the original technical philosophical sense to refer specifically to *global* claims about what the fundamental kinds of metaphysical entities in the universe are, whether solely material, solely mental, or both material and mental. So the aim is to set up the contrast with "materialism" in the sociopolitical sense pioneered by Marx. However, with that distinction having been drawn, I do then go on later in the essay to use *ontological* in the looser way that has become standard in critical sociopolitical philosophy, and which does not normally carry this significance. In context, I hope the distinction will be clear. (Thanks to one of the referees for pointing out this ambiguity, and the need for clarifying my usage of the term.)

3. Marx and Engels, *The German Ideology*, excerpted in David McLellan, ed., *Karl Marx: Selected Writings*, 2nd ed. (New York: Oxford University Press, 2000), section II, "The Materialist Conception of History 1844–1847," 192.

4. See my "Is It Immaterial That There's a 'Material' in 'Historical Materialism'?" in Charles W. Mills, *From Class to Race: Essays in White Marxism and Black Radicalism* (Lanham, Md.: Rowman & Littlefield, 2003), chapter 2.

5. Sebastiano Timpanaro, *On Materialism*, trans. Lawrence Garner (London: Verso, 1980).

6. Timpanaro, *On Materialism*, 44–45.

7. Diana Coole and Samantha Frost, "Introducing the New Materialisms," in Coole and Frost, ed., *New Materialisms: Ontology, Agency, and Politics*, 2 (Durham, N.C.: Duke University Press, 2010).

8. Coole and Frost, "Introducing," 2–4.

9. Linda Martín Alcoff, *Visible Identities: Race, Gender, and the Self* (New York: Oxford University Press, 2006).

10. Alcoff, *Visible Identities*, viii, 18–19.

11. Alcoff, *Visible Identities*, 142, 157–158.

12. Alcoff, *Visible Identities*, 163.

13. Alcoff, *Visible Identities*, 289.

14. Alcoff, *Visible Identities*, 278.

15. Karl Marx, *Economic and Philosophical Manuscripts*, excerpted in McLellan, *Karl Marx*.

16. Marx, *Manuscripts*, 92.

17. Frantz Fanon, *Black Skin, White Masks*, trans. Charles Lam Markmann (New York: Grove Weidenfeld, 1967).

18. Here and below, as I warned in note 2, above, I am using *ontology* in the familiar sense of critical theory.

19. Fanon, *Black Skin, White Masks*, 11.

20. See my "White Supremacy as Sociopolitical System," in Mills, *From Class to Race*, chapter 7.

21. George Lipsitz, *The Possessive Investment in Whiteness: How White People Profit from Identity Politics* (Philadelphia: Temple University Press, 1988); Cheryl I. Harris, "Whiteness as Property," *Harvard Law Review* 106, no. 8 (June 1993): 1709–1791; Melvin Oliver and Thomas Shapiro, *Black Wealth/ White Wealth: A New Perspective on Racial Inequality*, 10th anniversary ed. (New York: Routledge, 2006); Linda Faye Williams, *The Constraint of Race: Legacies of White Skin Privilege in America* (University Park, PA: Pennsylvania State University Press, 2003).

22. Institute on Assets and Social Policy, Brandeis University, May 2010, "The Racial Wealth Gap Increases Fourfold, 1984–2007," by Thomas M. Shapiro, Tatjana Meschede, and Laura Sullivan.

23. Shapiro, Meschede, and Sullivan, "Racial Wealth Gap,"3.

24. Linda Faye Williams, "The Issue of Our Time: Economic Inequality and Political Power in America," *Perspectives on Politics* 2, no. 4 (2004): 684.

25. George Fredrickson, *Racism: A Short History* (Princeton: Princeton University Press, 2002).

26. Alcoff, *Visible Identities*, 164–165.

27. Karl Marx and Frederick Engels, *Collected Works*, vol. 26 (New York: International Publishers, 1990), 129–276.

28. See Zillah R. Eisenstein, ed., *Capitalist Patriarchy and the Case for Socialist Feminism* (New York: Monthly Review Press, 1979); Alison Jaggar, *Feminist Politics and Human Nature* (Lanham, Md.: Rowman & Littlefield, 1988 [1983]).

29. The question still needs to be answered, though, of why organized male power developed rather than organized female power. The origins of patriarchy are still theoretically contested.

30. Aldous Huxley, *Brave New World (P.S.), with "Brave New World Revisited"* (New York: Harper Perennial, 2010). The novel was first published in 1932.

31. Steven Lukes, *Marxism and Morality* (New York: Oxford University Press, 1985).

32. See, for example, Russ Shafer-Landau, *Moral Realism: A Defence* (New York: Oxford University Press, 2005).

33. See my contribution to the online National Humanities Center symposium, "On the Human": Charles W. Mills, "The Political Economy of Personhood," posted April 3, 2011.

34. Fredrickson, *Racism*, 11–12.

35. This is somewhat of an oversimplification, since white women are not full persons either. However, I would claim that they attain a virtual personhood through their relation to white males that is denied people of color.

36. Alcoff, *Visible Identities*, 187–188.

37. Shannon Sullivan, *Revealing Whiteness: The Unconscious Habits of Racial Privilege* (Bloomington: Indiana University Press, 2006), 23, 25, 32, 128.

38. Sullivan, *Revealing Whiteness*, 188–189.

39. Marx, *Manuscripts*, 100.

40. Fanon, *Black Skin, White Masks*, 112.

41. Fanon, *Black Skin, White Masks*, 11–12.

42. Fanon, *Black Skin, White Masks*, 110–112.

43. Fanon, *Black Skin, White Masks*, 109, 112–113.

TWO

WHITE GAZES

What It Feels Like to Be an Essence

GEORGE YANCY

Introduction

Frantz Fanon writes, "I want my voice to be harsh, I don't want it be to beautiful, I don't want it to be pure."[1] Fanon's desire that his voice be harsh, not beautiful and not pure, has particular relevance when it comes to discussing the reality of white racism. Indeed, his desire resonates with my own preferred attempt "to voice," to articulate, the past and contemporary realities of white racism and how Black bodies have suffered, and continue to suffer, under such a regime. Because many of my students are white, they are particularly desirous, specifically when discussing the theme of whiteness, of a voice that is "beautiful" and "pure," one that does not relentlessly point to the ugliness and terror of past and present forms of white racism. They prefer that I offer a metanarrative account of white racism that shows how North America has become a place standing on the historical precipice of unburdening itself of the last vestiges of white racism. They are often surprised and taken aback by my candidness regarding past and present instantiations of white racist brutality. My sense is that they never expected philosophy to be so candid, so blatantly descriptive. Some of them, particularly in the one introductory philosophy course that I regularly teach (Basic Philosophical Questions), come with little or no understanding of philosophy. Yet, when we begin to think philosophically about race and raise personal questions about race, they sense that something has gone awry. In fact, some of my white students, who are no doubt angered by my lack of philosophical "purity," have expressed doubt about whether or not I am even teaching philosophy: "I thought that I took this course to study philosophy, not race." My sense is that they would rather that I speak a form of "philosophicalese" that is abstract and detached. Yet, this opens the door to forms of bad faith regarding the fundamental links between how one thinks about the world philosophically and how one's historical specificity, with all of its attendant biases, shapes precisely how one thinks. By bad faith, I mean the various ways in which these students encourage modes of self-deception regarding the assumption that to philosophize is to do so from nowhere; where to do philosophy is an intellective process unrelated to social practices. However, philosophy is fundamentally a social practice. My students remind me of many contemporary philosophers who apparently understand the sole purpose of philosophy to be about supersensible realities and forms of ontology that are "unsullied" by the embodied existence of race and racism. Perhaps many students think that philosophy will offer a way to escape, a way to engage in abstract reflection, removed from the existential funk of everyday life. Perhaps like many, they think of philosophy as a form of highfalutin conceptual bullshit, something that they can learn about without any deeply personal demands made on them.

I have been known to ask my white students, "So, who in here is a racist?" Some mouths open wide. Many faces look confused. Some white students manage to express a nervous laugh, perhaps a giggle. One white student shared with me how another white student was bewildered and angered by my question: "Did you hear what *he said*?" Unlike many of my white philosopher colleagues, I am not only working hard to get my white students to engage a subject (whiteness) that is deeply volatile and calls forth some of the most vicious forms of psychological defensiveness, but I am also contesting various metaphilosophical assumptions about what constitutes a philosophical problem. In some sense, by introducing whiteness and race into my philosophy courses, I am already deemed a troublemaker, something of a renegade philosopher. My penchant for an "impure" voice and one that refuses to be "beautiful" does not help. Then again, there is also that "nagging problem" of my Black body, a body that is often perceived as always already invested in "white bashing." In short, as a Black philosopher, every moment in the classroom is one filled with specific *racial* challenges, contestations, and risks—all marked by that heightened sense of uneasiness when it comes to engaging race seriously and unflinchingly.

For many of my white students who at least attempt to engage whiteness and race as legitimate subjects for philosophical analysis, they still often approach whiteness, its power and privilege, as something "out there," as a reified *je ne sais quoi*. They still resist suggestions that white power and privilege are expressed in ways that are mundane, that is, that whiteness saturates everyday modes of perception, modes of physical movement, modes of discourse, modes of aspiration and expectation, modes of desire, modes of relationship formation—friendships, conjugal partnering, and so on. Indeed, many of my white students engage in forms of discourse that obfuscate their complicity with white power and privilege. In this way, they attempt to render white power and privilege as foreign to their own everyday practices. Some whites will declare, "My friend [another white] always uses the *N*-word and I just get sick of hearing this." I have witnessed many variations of this white "distancing strategy,"[2] or ways that whites avoid being implicated in forms of anti-Black racism. Indeed, many of my white students engage in such public declarations of anger or frustration regarding white racism. Whether consciously or unconsciously, such strategies often function to mark the ways in which they are different from "those white racists," those who use, for example, the *N* word. Indeed, some of my white students engage in such public racist disavowals as ways of "confirming" their own postracial and postracist subject-formations and liberal political sensibilities. However, as Zeus Leonardo notes, "whites invest in practices that obscure racial processes."[3] One such practice is precisely the act of public displays of "white virtue." And while such whites might be sincere and might indeed find overt white racist acts to be despicable, this does not exempt them from various ways in which they are white and therefore continue to be invested in the structure of white power and white privilege. After all, white power and privilege are fundamentally linked "to a constellation of societal, institutional, and cultural factors."[4] Calling out and marking "nasty" white racists "let's the 'good whites' off the hook at the same time that it dilutes a critique of the multiple ways that white people perpetuate, and benefit from, white racism."[5] The above point is not to argue against all forms of antiracist agency on the part of whites. Rather, my point is that "undoing" whiteness is complex. There is no attempt to deny that there are white allies in the struggle against white supremacy and white privilege. To do so would be blatantly false. My aim, within the above context, is to point out the sheer complexity of whiteness and how it manifests itself within white psyches and white institutional structures—sites that can function as forms of white racist entrapment. This, of course, points to the importance of vigilance on the part of antiracist whites as they attempt to undo white power and privilege in their daily lives.[6] In short, antiracist agency does not magically undo the complex ways in which whites are both complicit with systemic forms of white supremacy and the ways in which they harbor white racism in their bodies, thoughts, and affects. Indeed, my sense is that whites are fundamentally opaque to themselves vis-à-vis their own racism. This opacity is partly a function of the profound ways in which anti-Black racism has become etched into white bodies and white psyches.[7]

Engaging in forms of discourse regarding race and racism that refuse to be beautiful and pure is my way of resisting romanticizing the present or the past of white racism. It is my way of calling into question the existence of dry and boring discourse, the sort that often confers "brilliance" on those of the professoriate. It is my way of avoiding collusion with the obfuscatory efforts of "white talk"—"talk that serves to insulate white people from examining their/our individual and collective roles (s) in the perpetuation of racism."[8] "White talk," on this score, is incompatible with Parrhesia (or fearless speech). When it comes to discussing issues of racism and racial embodiment, we mustn't be like Odysseus who dared to be adventurous *and* yet remained safe. We must allow the Sirens to sing to us without the safety of a mast, without plugging up our ears with wax.[9] We must be fearless. When it comes to intimate and courageous discussions regarding race, how it is lived and how it is experienced, we ought to valorize the aleatoric, allow for the strength of unpredictable openness to fracture calcified norms and the unproductive sedimentation of white racist practices. Along with fearless speech, though, we need fearless listening. Both are indispensable. I understand fearless listening as an openness to have one's assumptions regarding race and racism shattered, though for the better, where one sees with greater vision and comprehension; it involves, in the case of white people, having one's white self-identity challenged and fissured, even as that process of fissuring will require a constant refissuring. Fearless listening is reminiscent of the risk of erotic passion. While I am not claiming that fearless listening is the same as erotic passion, there is something to be said about the importance of risk and vulnerability involved in each. For example, Drucilla Cornell writes, "In erotic passion, the boundaries of selfhood yield to the touch of the other."[10] Here I only wish to pick up on the dynamism of fearless or courageous listening as a profound site of risk and vulnerability. Such listening is a process where the boundaries of white selfhood yield to the dialogic touch, as it were, of people of color. In other words, people of color possess critical epistemic perspectives on the complexities of whiteness and how whiteness functions to obfuscate greater self-understanding on the part of white people and how whiteness reinforces insidious ontological and spatial boundaries that sustain white insularity.

If it is true, as Attorney General Eric Holder reminds us, that we are "a nation of cowards"[11] on matters of race, then, fearless speech and fearless listening are absolutely essential for transforming this nation into a courageous nation on matters of race. Yet, Holder's indictment is specifically relevant to white people in terms of the issue of race. And while it is true that President Obama has been elected for a second term, and that he "won a clear popular vote victory—with a majority of his total vote nationwide coming from white voters,"[12] having become president again is not incompatible with the existence of anti-Black racism. Just because whites voted for Obama for a second term does not mean that those same whites are willing to engage their white privilege and their anti-Black racism critically. White cowardice and active resistance to engage such issues is a reminder that the existence of a Black person as commander-in-chief does not radically alter the structure of whiteness, its privilege, power, and maintenance.

My Black students, who are often very few given the overall racial composition of my university, are, quite frankly, tired of talking about race, especially when it comes to talking to white people about *their racism*. Cowardice in terms of discussing race is not the same as impatience about discussing race. Within our contemporary moment, the former is born of a refusal to see just how deeply one's white self is embedded within the fray of white racism. The latter, however, speaks to the weight of dissatisfaction and anger stemming from whites' denial of their white power and privilege and how these negatively impact the lives of Black people and people of color more generally. After all, Black people and people of color already see how white racism functions; they know how it impacts their lives, their psyches, their bodies. They have learned how to see and mark whiteness. Marking whiteness for Black people and other people of color is and has been a question of existential survival. As Sara Ahmed notes, "Whiteness is only invisible to those who inhabit it."[13]

As suggested above in terms of the epistemic insights into the subtle structures and practices of whiteness, Black people and people of color see whiteness in the nooks and crannies of everyday North American life. Black people see it "in the casualness of white bodies in spaces, crowded in parks, meetings, in white bodies that are displayed in films and advertisements, in white laws that talk about white experiences, in ideas of the family made up of clean white bodies."[14] As such, I understand Holder's indictment as a form of fearless speech, one that specifically asks white people to be courageous in the act of examining, as best they can, the multiple ways in which they continue to perpetuate white racism. However, because whites inhabit the normative structure of whiteness, there are ways in which the casualness of white power and privilege will escape being rendered visible. Hence, the socially situated epistemic insights of people of color are indispensable.

Clicking Sounds

The sounds of car doors locking are deafening: *Click. Click. Click. Click. Click. Click. Click. Click. Click. Click. Click. ClickClickClickClickClickClickClick.* I have experienced these *clicks*. The *clicking* sounds are always already accompanied by white nervous gestures, and eyes that want to look, but are hesitant to do so. The *click* ensures their safety, effectively resignifying their white bodies as in need of protection vis-à-vis the site of danger, doom, and blackness. In fact, the *clicks* begin to return me to myself as this dangerous beast, a phantom, rendering my Black body the site of microtomy and volatility. The *clicks* attempt to seal my identity as a dark savage. The *clicking* sounds mark me; they inscribe me, rematerializing my presence, as it were, in ways that I know to be untrue—in ways that are not me. Unable to stop the *clicking*, unable to stop white women from tightening the hold of their purses as I walk by, unable to stop white women from crossing to the other side of the street once they have seen me walking in their direction, unable to stop white men from looking several times over their shoulders as I walk behind them minding my own business, unable to establish a form of recognition that creates a space of trust or liminality, there are times when I want to become their fantasy, to become their Black monster, their bogeyman. In the case of the *clicks*, I want to pull open the car door and shout: "Surprise! You've just been carjacked by a ghost, a fantasy of your own creation. Now, get the hell out of the car!" But, of course, this act of agency, this act of protest might simply reinforce the racist stereotype of the Black male as brutal and violent. This act of agency, of taking a stand, might simply reinstall the Black body as a site to be feared.

The *clicks*, within the context of white fear and trembling, can be said to function "metonymically": *Click* (nigger). The *clicking* sounds begin to fragment my existence, cut away at my integrity, depicting me in the form of an essence, a solid type, in ways that dehumanize me. *Click* (thug). *Click* (criminal). *Click* (thief). *Click* (sullied). *Click* (hypersexual). *Click* (savage). I am on the receiving side of the *clicks*. And yet, those whites in their cars, through the sheer act of locking their doors, perform their *white* identities as in need of safety, as in need of protection. The *clicks* mark multiple ways in which they see *their* identity. *Click* (prey). *Click* (innocent). *Click* (pure). *Click* (morally respectable). *Click* (better than). *Click* (civilized).

Not only are the bodies that initiate the *clicks performing* their *white* identities through the *clicks*, but the *clicks* themselves install white identities, hail white identities, and solidify white identities. The *clicks* happen within a social space of meaning constitution. The *clicks* are signifiers of regulated space, forms of disciplining bodies, and part of a racial and racist web of significance that bespeaks the sedimentation of racist history and racist iteration. Yet, as suggested, the *clicks* misidentify me, they distort who I am. The *clicks* "dematerialize" me, only to "rematerialize" me in a form that I do not recognize. Fanon argues that under colonialism, the colonized are forced to ask themselves constantly, "In reality, who am I?"[15] Du Bois argues that Blacks who have given thought to the situation of Black people in America will often ask themselves, "What, after all, am I?"[16]

Through an uneventful, mundane act of white index fingers locking their car doors (*click, click*), the Color Line is drawn. After so many *clicks*, on so many occasions, I am installed as a stranger to myself, forcing a peculiar question: Where *is* my body? The question itself makes sense once the body is theorized not as a brute *res extensa*, but as a site of confluent norms, as something whose meaning is a function of a complex interpretive and perceptual framework. The question points to the power of racist interpellation and how one is often left with the experience of having been disjointed, of having been mistaken, repeatedly, for someone else or for *something* else.

I am *not* a criminal, a beast waiting to attack white people. Hence, their sense of safety is a false construction. They have constructed a false dichotomy: an outside (the Blacks) as opposed to the inside (the whites). But what if that inside, that feeling of safety, that fabricated space, is a construction that is parasitic on the false construction of the Black body as dangerous? If so, then their sense of themselves as "safe" is purchased at the expense of the possibility for a greater, more robust sense of human community or *Mitsein*. They have cut themselves off from the possibility of fellowship, of expanding their identities, of reaping the rewards of being touched by the Black other and thereby shaking the boundaries of their white selves. To live a life predicated on a lie often requires more lies to cover it over. Black bodies, then, function to conceal the truth that so many whites lead lives that are constructed around a profound deception—namely, white people need protecting from Black people, the wretched/damned of the earth. The need for this lie bespeaks a (white) self that is on the precipice of ontological evisceration.

Race as Lived

There has been a great deal of important work that argues that race is semantically empty, ontologically bankrupt, and scientifically meaningless. In short, there are many philosophers who argue that race is an illusion, that there is no factual support for a racial taxonomy. Since race has no referent and does not cut at the joints of reality, so to speak, it is said to be a fiction. From this, we are advised to abandon the concept of race just as the concepts of phlogiston and spontaneous generation were abandoned. Like the concept "witch," race is said to have no real referent in reality. On this score, a physicalist's rejection of race is logically compatible with the acceptance of eliminativism. According to the eliminativist, the concept of race is empty, and does not specify human differences that are deemed fundamentally distinct. The problem with this, however, is that the phenomenological or lived dimensions and reality of "race" exceed what is deemed "real" within the framework of a physicalist ontology. It is also important to note that to believe that there is no more to be said about race because it is impossible to reduce it to a naturally occurring object in the spatiotemporal world is to engage in a form of disciplinary hegemony.

The fact is that whiteness qua race continues to exist within the socially and existentially *lived* space of our everyday experiences. The "reality" of race, then, though not a natural kind, is purchased within the framework of a *social ontology* that recognizes the very serious persistence and implications of race beyond what has been called its ontological vacuity. "Race," in other words, is a social category. But even here we need to be careful. After all, as the mantra goes: "What's the problem? Race is only a social construction. In fact, I don't even see race; I see people." This mantra is another instance of "white talk," another way of avoiding the *lived* reality of race and the ways in which the rhetoric of white color-blind antiracism installs a problematic universalism, a rhetorical site where whites continue to reap inordinate power and privilege. This universalism has the result of rendering nugatory the deep political, existential, and embodied impact of race/racism. As Joel Olson writes, "The white political imagination persists in the color-blind ideal through a conception of race in general and white in particular as a politically neutral identity that simply refers to a set of [benign] physical or social characteristics."[17]

In my view, to say that whiteness as racially embodied is the site of a social category is *not* meant to overlook the *relationally lived* phenomenon called whiteness, its dynamic structure, its semiotic and political currency, and its privileged status in the everyday world. To overlook the *relationally lived* dimension of whiteness and how it impacts the experiences of people of color is to risk reducing the epistemic content of the latter's experiences to self-inflicted delusions. There is the necessity, then, to give philosophical attention to the Black body in an anti-Black world, a world that is relationally constituted by whites, and to explore the "fiction" of race, a fiction that continues to take itself as real. Hence, it is important to theorize whiteness as *lived* and how whiteness gets performed within the context of the interstitial and the quotidian, and to explore the complexities involved in undoing whiteness, even as whites are complicit and embedded within systemic racialized contexts that continue to confer power and privilege.

I am specifically concerned with theorizing Black embodiment within the context of white everyday power or hegemony, that is, to describe Black *Erlebnis* within the context of an anti-Black world. It is important to note that an analysis of Black *lived* experience is dialectically linked to an account of whiteness and how whites construct Black bodies, how the latter are experienced as problematic bodies, as problem people. Hence, within this context, such concepts as invisibility, "corporeal malediction," and the phenomenological or *lived* reality of Black bodies under tremendous existential duress are foregrounded. This approach places emphasis on how the Black body was/is subjected to powerful discursive regimes that historically rendered the Black body as "docile" and as the site of "evil," bestiality, "criminality," and "inferiority." The power of the white gaze, which is a *structured* way of "seeing," which is mediated by certain racist norms and values, interpellated the Black as that which is epistemologically and ontologically "given." On the one hand, epistemologically, the Black body's moral turpitude is deemed a state of affairs that whites claim to know independently of their own white racist constructions of the Black body. On the other hand, ontologically, the Black body is assigned the status of that which is always already fixed; its being is truncated in its meaning vis-à-vis a superimposed meaning produced through the white imaginary. In short, then, how the Black body *is*, is how it is *known*, and how it is *known* is how it *is*. Here we have a collapse of ontology and epistemology without much slippage. What the Black "is" and how the

Black body is "known" are constructed through gazes, bodily gestures, and discursive practices that have overdetermined its being and constructed it as a denigrated *thing*.

Black Body as "Thing"

Treated as a "thing" within the context of white anti-Black racism, Blacks were/are reduced to their bodies, bodies without subjectivity, without *Geist*. Referring to the Black body as a "thing," then, is more than a tropological reference. Think of the lynched Black body—a thing in need of discipline. For example, in 1934, twenty-three-year-old Claude Neal[18] was accused of killing a white woman and it is said that a confession was wrung out of him, meaning that it was forced, twisted, or strained out of him. Neal was first castrated. His penis was cut off and stuffed in his mouth, and he was made to say that he liked it. His testicles were then stuffed in his mouth, and he was forced to say that he liked them. Now and then someone would slice off a finger or a toe. He was eventually killed. Parts of his body were cut off and sold as one might sell pieces of precious minerals.

Or think about the rape of enslaved Black women who were said to be always sexually available, indeed, hypersexual essences ("things") and thereby could not be raped. Such Black bodies were metaphorically open, always desiring to be taken. Black women's bodies might be said to be holes without bottoms, or perhaps just bottoms with holes. The point here is that Black bodies were deemed "objects" of white desire, mutilation, and control. They constituted, along with the wild flora and fauna of distant lands, raw material to be exploited. One might argue that Black women constituted/constitute a different kind of "strange fruit."

Or think of Bill Bennett, former secretary of education under Reagan, who, in 2005, remarked: "I do know that it's true that if you wanted to reduce crime you could, if that were your sole purpose, you could abort every black baby in this country, and your crime rate would go down."[19] He then goes on to say how impossible, ridiculous, and morally reprehensible this would be, but yet true. So, while he clearly disagrees with the statistic that crime is down because abortion is up, he has no problem using the epistemic operator "true" vis-à-vis the apparent necessary connection between aborting *Black babies* and the decrease in crime rate. Note that he says "I do *know*." In short, Bennett *knows* that it is *true* that the category of Blacks who are still in the womb will *necessarily* commit crimes, and he knows this prior to their birth.

Hence, in the name of a future that we cannot possibly predict, little Jamal, let us say, has already committed a crime, his body is already against the law, because Bennett knows that it is true that if he is aborted our crime rate will go down. Here is a case where the Black fetus is always already the essence (a "thing") of criminality, prior to its birth. This is not a case of three strikes and you're out or even one strike and you're out. Presumably, all that is required for one to be out is to be a *Black thing/Black essence*. At the moment of conception, then, Black life is already out.

Or what about being a Black philosopher within a country and within academic contexts where Black intelligence is denied, where, for example, I become an oxymoron as a Black philosopher standing before my white students only mimicking speech. As David Hume said of Negroes, they are parrots.[20] Worse off than the poets critiqued by Plato, Blacks even lack inspiration; they have no inner creative spirit. Indeed, Black bodies are just surfaces lacking depth. One might say that Black bodies are ontologically flat, mere things awaiting on the will of white people, that is, those possessing the only true power of transcendence and the true capacity *to know*. As Sartre notes, "For three thousand years, the white man has enjoyed the privilege of seeing without being seen; he was only a look—the light from his eyes drew each thing out of the shadow of its birth; the whiteness of his skin was another look, condensed light."[21]

Or think of philosopher Cornel West who was stopped by a police officer who accused him of trafficking cocaine. West retorted that he was a professor of religion and the officer said, "Yeah, and I'm the Flying Nun. Let's go Nigger."[22] If you've seen the Flying Nun, played by Sally Field, you know that it was a fantasy about a nun who could fly. On this score, the white police officer is saying that West, like the Flying Nun, is a fantasy. After all, how can a Black body be a professor of religion or a philosopher? As a Black body, West always already constitutes the *essence* of criminality. The white gaze of the white police officer has foreclosed any other profile. And even if it was granted that West was indeed a professor, from the perspective of the white gaze, West would constitute something fit for teratology; perhaps Frankenstein's monster. If not a freak, then perhaps a white man *only* in disguise.

One defining and central feature of Sartrean existentialist philosophy is the thesis that existence precedes essence. According to Sartre, "It means that, first of all, man exists, turns up, appears on the scene, and, only afterwards, defines himself."[23] In short, for Sartre, there is no pregiven essence that defines human reality. We are thrown forward, always already ahead of ourselves. He writes, "I am suspended in midair between the self that I have been until now and the self that I will be, and this state of suspension is my present, my characteristic being; this self is always 'postponed.'"[24] For Sartre, he is not what he was/is and not yet what he will be/become. What it means to be human is that what and who we are is forever deferred. This is captured by Sartre's deployment of the term *postponed*. To postpone (etymologically, *postponere*, "to place after") captures the dynamic sense in which we are, ontologically, never fully given, but always *placed after* (that is, placed behind) any particular current manifestation of ourselves. There is always more to come. Yet, when theorized within the context of the racial Manichean divide, Sartre's ontology of the human person, particularly when it comes to the *lived* experiences of Black people, must concede (and be challenged by) the specific *racial* ways in which Black people are perceived as and made to feel like things/essences. To live one's life within a raced and racist context where one undergoes the experience of being fixed like a thing/essence is to undergo the experience of being *placed before* or placed in advance of, not after. There is no suspension or deferral. In short, within the context of white anti-Black racism, the so-called essence of Black people precedes their existence; they appear on the stage of existence ready-made, ontologically inferior, and subordinate.

The Elevator Scenario

Given that the construction of the Black body is linked to the historico-ideological construction of the white body, it is important to turn (or return) the gaze on the constitutional acts of white racist intentional consciousness. However, to theorize whiteness in terms of its self-conscious claims to supremacy would leave un-theorized the various ways in which whiteness gets expressed in very subtle and insidious ways. Unlike Black bodies physically confiscated from Africa, Black bodies are confiscated within social spaces of meaning construction and social spaces of transversal interaction that are buttressed by a racist value-laden episteme, an episteme that constructs the Black body as ontologically denuded. It is a peculiar experience to have one's body confiscated without physically being placed in chains. This form of confiscation is demonstrated in the following scenario, one that is pregnant with philosophical meaning.

Well dressed, I enter an elevator where a white woman waits to reach her floor. She "sees" my Black body, though not the same one I have seen reflected back to me from the mirror on any number of occasions. She sees a Black body "supersaturated with meaning, as they [Black bodies] have been relentlessly subjected to [negative] characterization by newspapers, newscasters, popular film, television programming, public officials, policy pundits and other agents of representation."[25] Her body language signifies, "Look, *the* Black!" On this score, though short of a performative locution, her body language functions as an insult. Over and above how my body is clothed, regardless of the fact that I wear a suit and tie, she "sees" a criminal. Indeed, she does not really "see" me. Rather, phenomenologically, she might be said to "see" a Black, fleeting expanse, a peripherally glimpsed vague presence of something dark, forbidden, and dreadful. Despite what I think about myself, how I am for-myself, her perspective, her third-person account, seeps into my consciousness. I catch a glimpse of myself through her eyes and just for that moment I experience some form of double consciousness, but what I see does not shatter my identity or unglue my sense of moral decency. After all, from the perspective of white hegemony, hers is deemed the only real point of view. One might say that the white woman's consciousness of the meaning of my Black body coincides with the meaning of the Black body *as such*, and that from her perspective there is no meaning that the Black body possesses that is foreign to her, that is, a meaning that is capable of enlarging her field of consciousness/"seeing." As Patricia Williams might say, I occupy "a space of the entirely judged."[26] When she "sees" me, the symbolic order of "Blackness *as* evil" is collapsed: I *am* evil. My Blackness *is* the stimulus that triggers her response. "The Negro," as Fanon notes, "is a phobogenic object, a stimulus to anxiety."[27] Her gaze is "not a simple seeing, an act of direct perception, but the racial production of the visible, the workings of racial constraints on what it means to 'see.'"[28]

As Black, I am the "looked at." As white, she is the bearer of the "white look." In this regard, it is also the *white woman*, not just the white man, who has enjoyed the privilege of seeing without being seen. Indeed, for the Black male to see her, to dare to look, had its own racial and specifically gendered dangers. As the bearer of the white look, the reader will note that I have not given my consent to have my body transformed, to have it reshaped, and thrown back to me as something I am supposed to *own*, as a meaning I am supposed to accept. And while it is true that all of us are subject to the gaze of others without giving our consent, that is, in our bodily constitution we are "being-for-the-others," the white gaze might at any moment entail a heinous, *racially* inflected form of violence on the Black body. For Black women, the violence is multiple.

The white woman clutches her purse, eagerly anticipating the arrival of her floor, "knowing" that this Black predator will soon strike. As she clutches her purse, I am reminded, as explored above, of the sounds of whites locking their car doors as they catch a glimpse of my Black body as I walk by (*click, click*). She fears that a direct look might incite the anger of the Black predator. She fakes a smile. By her smile she hopes to elicit a spark of decency from me. But I don't return the smile. I fear that it might be interpreted as a gesture of sexual advance. After all, within the social space of the elevator, which has become a hermeneutic transactional space within which all of my intended meanings get falsified, it is as if I am no longer in charge of what I mean/ intend. What she "sees" or "hears" is governed by a racist epistemology of certitude that places me under erasure. Her alleged literacy regarding the semiotics of my Black body is actually an instance of profound illiteracy. Her gaze on my Black body might be said to function like a camera obscura. Her gaze consists of a racist socio-epistemic *aperture*, as it were, through which the (white) *light* of "truth" casts an inverted/distorted image. It is through her gaze that I become hypervigilant of my own embodied spatiality. On previous occasions, particularly when alone, I have moved my body within the space of the elevator in a noncalculative fashion, paying no particular attention to my bodily comportment, the movement of my hands, my eyes, the position of my feet. On such occasions, my "being-in" the space of the elevator is familiar; my bodily movements, my stance, are indicative of what it means to *inhabit* a space of familiarity.

The movement away from the familiar is what is also effected vis-à-vis the white woman's gaze. My movements become and remain stilted. I dare not move suddenly. The apparent racial neutrality of the space within the elevator (when I am standing alone) has become one filled with white norma-tivity. I feel trapped. I no longer feel bodily expansiveness within the elevator, but constrained. I now begin to calculate, paying almost neurotic attention to the proxemic positioning of my body, making sure that this "Black object," what now feels like an appendage, a weight, is not too close, not too tall, not too threatening. So, I genuflect, but only slightly, a movement that feels like an act of worship. My lived-body comes back to me like something onto-logically *occurent*, something merely *there* in its facticity. Notice that she need not speak a word to render my Black body "captive." She need not scream "Rape!" She need not call me "Nigger!" Indeed, it is not a necessary require-ment that she hates me in order for her to script my body in the negative ways that she does. White America has bombarded me and other Black males with the "reality" of our dual hypersexualization: "you are a sexual trophy and a certain rapist."[29] Fanon, aware of the horrible narrative myths used to depict Black bodies, notes that the Negro *is* the genital and *is* the incarnation of evil, being that which is to be avoided and yet desired. Ritualistically enacting her racialized and racist consciousness/embodiment, she reveals her putative racist narrative competence. "One cannot decently 'have a hard on' everywhere," as Fanon says, but within the white imaginary, I apparently fit the bill. To put a slight interpretive inflection on Fanon here, as the insatiable, ever desiring Black penis, a walking, talking, hard-on, I am believed eager to introduce white women into a sexual universe for which the white male "does not have the key, the weapons, or the attributes."[30]

I am often reminded of my purpose, my inner *racial* teleology, that is, my essence, through popular culture. I sit in movie theaters waiting for "me" to appear on screen, waiting to see "my body" appear before me. I saw myself in the movie *The Heartbreak Kid* (2007), where a white woman who plays Ben Stiller's wife pleads with him while having sex. She shouts, "Fuck me like a Black guy!"[31] One, of course, feels sorry for Stiller's character as he really tries, with pronounced gyrations, "to have sex with her like a Black guy." But he does so to no avail.

The white gaze has fixed me. Like looking into Medusa's eyes, I have been made into stone, stiff, forever erect. It is as if Viagra runs naturally through my veins. In fact, I have become a phantasm. So fictive has the Black body become, that its very material presence has become superfluous. There are times when the Black body is not even needed to trigger the right response. All that is needed is the imago. Fanon observed, "A [white] prostitute told me that in her early days the mere thought of going to bed with a Negro brought on an orgasm."[32] While actual Black bodies suffered during the spectacle of lynchings, one wonders to what extent the *Black body* as phantasmatic object was the fulcrum around which the spectacle was animated.

Within the *lived* and consequential semiotic space of the elevator, the white woman has "taken" my body from me, sending an extraneous meaning back to me, an extraneous *thing*, something *foreign*. So, here I am—a philosopher trying my best to live my life as an abstract thinking substance. I reside in the clouds. I try to leave my body behind, like many of my white male colleagues. Yet, within this elevator, my body is being sliced as she adjusts her microtome. As Fanon writes, "I am being dissected under white eyes, the only real eyes. I am *fixed*. Having adjusted their microtomes, they objectively cut away slices of my reality. I am laid bare."[33]

In terms of the elevator scenario, my body, through the white woman's gaze, manifests a particular modality of volatility. Fanon, in *Black Skin, White Masks*, while undergoing the process of having his body phenomenologically returned to him, stated that he existed triply[34]—that is, he existed in three places. In terms of the elevator effect, I exist ontologically quadrupled. I appear to be in four places. For example, I am "here," taking up space outside the elevator before its arrival. I am also "ahead of myself." In other words, "being-ahead-of myself" suggests the sense in which I am always already *fixed, complete, given*—in short, *I am placed before*. Before I enter the elevator, I exist in the form of a static racial template. My being is known by whites before my arrival. I reside, as it were, in a fixed place, always already waiting for me. Once on the elevator, though physically separated from the white woman, I am "over there," floating as a phantasm in her imaginary, a kind of thought-bubble. Yet, I am also "alongside" of myself as I catch a glimpse of myself through her gaze. It is as if I carry myself around in the form of an appendage. Hence, I experience myself as "here-ahead-of myself-over-there-alongside-myself." It is an experience that forces me to ask about the where-abouts of my body. Not only am I the object of white microtomes (etymo-logically, "to cut"), but my body has become volatile (from *volare*, meaning "to fly"). Hence, I have become, under the white gaze, "immaterial" and "vaporous," neither here nor there, yet, both here *and* there.

The space within the elevator has become a microcosm of some of the dynamic processes of a larger, systemic form of colonial invasion. Just as the colonial presence attempts to deplete the power of the colonized, I feel as if my power to script my own identity, my agency to disrupt the constel-lations of meaning imposed from without, has been/is being depleted. On this score, my agency to act-in-the-world, to assert how I understand/nar-rate my own identity, appears reduced to a form of knowledge regarding my actions of which I am restricted to having privileged, epistemic access only. In other words, I feel forced within an epistemic *solipsistic* position because her interpretive hegemony displaces my intended meanings with her own set of interpretations.

What then am I to do? Within this racially saturated field of visibility, I have somehow become this "predator-stereotype" from which it appears hopeless to escape. The white woman thinks that her act of "seeing" me is an act of "knowing" what I am, of knowing what I will do next, that is, hers is believed to be simply a process of unmediated/uninterpreted per-ception. However, her coming to "see" me as she does is actually a cultural achievement. It is an achievement that not only distorts my body, but also distorts her white body. Historically, think of those Black bodies that felt alien to themselves, feeling their understanding of their own bodies slip away from them, perhaps even pushing them ever closer toward the precipice of epistemic violence, ever closer to living in a state of self-hatred. Phenomeno-logically, it is as if I *become* "Black" anew within the context of each encounter with the generative dimensions of the white gaze/imaginary. I am, as it were, a phantom, indeed, a "spook," that lives between the interstices of my physical, phenotypically dark body and the white woman's gesticulatory performances. *She performs, ergo, I become the criminal.* Within the dynamic racialized space of the elevator, I have become the externalized figure, the fantasized object, of the white woman's own white distortion. It is this distortion that carries an existential and ontological surplus, providing her with a sense of positivity vis-à-vis my negativity.

Conclusion: Being in Crisis

What am I to do within this racially charged space? How do I "desegregate" the experienced space within the elevator? Do I enact a disruptive, counter-white racist performance? If so, what would this look like? And what if such a performance gets reinterpreted within her racial schema? I could always turn around and state contemptuously: "Frankly, I don't give a damn about you or your kind!" In short, I would speak with the sort of contempt spoken by Fanon where he said, "Kiss the handsome Negro's ass, Madame!"[35] But this would only confirm her fears of the mythical raging, angry Black male. In other words, my action would only increase her feelings of trepidation. I could also strike up a conversation: "I am a philosopher, with a PhD, and I also attended Yale University." There is the possibility, though, that her white gaze is so fixed that this newly discovered information would not shake her framework. Her head would say yes, but her body would say no. I could also attempt to trigger a sense of shame: "Miss, I assure you that I am not interested in your trashy possessions and I especially have no desire to humiliate you through the violence of rape, nor are my sexual desires outside my control." In this case, I position my moral subjectivity in such a way that she relationally comes to take up the position of a particular kind of subject, one who feels shame. In other words, this shame is "a constituted effect" produced through the effective positioning of myself as a moral actor within this dyad. Perhaps as I leave that elevator I have gained a victory, affirming my dignity and sending her on a journey of discovery regarding the layers of her whiteness. Then again, she could be thinking, "'Nigger,' just who do you think you're talking to?" This would function as a way of eliding the truth that she felt threatened by what she and other whites daily construct as the "Black monster," while still maintaining a sense of "superiority" by questioning that I spoke to her in such an "uppity" fashion.

Then again, what if I have indeed positioned her to feel shame? What if she leaves the elevator feeling bad about what she did, feeling bad about her whiteness? What happens when this feeling gets quickly transformed into a *positive* sense of white self-regard? As Sara Ahmed writes, "The very claim to feel bad (about this or that) also involves a self-perception of 'being good'"[36] Perhaps she will now make a point of remaining with her shame, wallowing in it. As the "shamed-one," she may come to feel a sense of white pride precisely through her feelings of shame. Thus, the issue of Black pain and suffering gets set aside and transformed into a process of focusing on white narcissism, which is a reinscription of whiteness as the center of discourse and concern. It is *her* pain, *her* guilt, *her* need to feel good, pure, and ethical that gets foregrounded. What appeared to be a movement toward challenging whiteness is reinscribed as a place for precisely preserving whiteness.

And what if I'm mistaken about her? What difference does this make *for me*? Given the prevalence of white racist history and its construction of the Black male body as a body to be feared, especially within the context of the myth of the Black male rapist, being epistemologically mistaken does not make a difference in terms of the *lived* experience of what it means to undergo the experience of being stereotyped. Is she off the proverbial racist hook? What if her purse strap was simply broken and instead of securing it from my "imminent act of thievery," she is simply attempting to prevent it from falling? She may then shout, "How dare you think I'm racist?" In this case, history is on my side, that is, it is reasonable to assume that she enacted racist behavior in the form of pulling on her purse. Moreover, there is nothing logically inconsistent with her attempt to support her broken purse and the accompaniment of racist fears, albeit unconscious. How do I know racist behavior when I see it? I would argue that the answer to this question has to do with a larger socially shared space of reasons. In other words, my knowledge is not indubitable. It is not as if her behavior constitutes an incorrigible state of affairs about which there is absolute certainty. Rather, my knowledge that her behavior is racist is a warranted assertability claim that gets its epistemic purchase within the context of a larger epistemic community of people of color who have undergone precisely the everyday, concrete experience endured on the elevator. Hence, "knowing" that her behavior was racist is not guaranteed by a subjectivist (i.e., Cartesian) turn inward, one that invokes serious problems regarding skepticism. Rather, "knowing," within the context of the elevator, has to do with the larger community of intelligibility within which people of color come to understand white ways of being, white ways of stereotyping, and modes of white racist comportment. Indeed, it is not as if she engages in a *sui generis* form of behavior about which I need to guess. Rather, it is a racist dance all too familiar to Black people. The racist practices of white people, micro and otherwise, are not phenomena about which Black people are epistemologically skeptical. Black people always already share a familiar world, a shared integument, as it were, where white people and the ways of whiteness are *known*.

More intriguingly, how does she know racist behavior when she sees it, including her own? Is it my responsibility to put her at ease? What if I'm simply tired, *like many of my Black students and other students of color*, of alleviating white fears? What is *her* responsibility?

And what if the elevator broke down for six hours? Would this create a space for her "death" or perhaps her salvation? Or perhaps this is a distinction without a difference. Indeed, perhaps the "death" of whiteness, that is, the death of its existence as hegemonic and narcissistic, will have important philosophical anthropological implications for how we begin to reconceptualize humanity in ways that are not defined through the axiological and ontological framework of whiteness. What if she got to know me differently during those six hours? What if she got to see through the surface of things? What if we got to discuss, with some level of *real* intimacy and risk, what had occurred on the elevator just hours ago? What if she got *to see me*? "To see me," though, would also entail that she sees me as "raced," that is, as a *Black* man whose narrative and concrete experiences are shaped through the stream of racial discourse and racial experiences, a raced form of being that has had real effects in defining me, though not totally. In other words, she would fail *to see me* if by doing so she were to see me only through the lens of an abstract humanism. My point here is that I do not want her to misconstrue who I am yet again. Yet, in coming "to see me," would I become the exceptional Black and thereby not really "Black" at all? What if her perceptual practices began to crack? Then again, what will happen when the elevator starts up again? As racially embodied as white, she will soon enter into the larger social world where her whiteness will get cited, where her power and privilege will continue to operate in her favor (and the disfavor of people of color), despite the lessons that she had learned on the elevator. Indeed, she returns to a world in which white skin privilege is systemic, where her whiteness is complicit with white norms and the perpetuation of white privilege and power. She returns to a white world, white spaces, where intimacy and risk vis-à-vis critical discussions about race are rendered unnecessary and indeed militated against, perhaps resulting in her punishment by a parent, spouse, or friend. What we need are more moments of breakdown—something analogous to the elevator, but it must be sustained. And it must remain so without the assurance that things will get better, where "getting better" means something like the certainty that the elevator will begin moving again shortly and we will be out of harm's way, saved from a temporary moment of inconvenience. Yet, collectively we need moments that are precisely *unfavorable* to our comfort. For whites in particular, they need to be put into *crisis* vis-à-vis their whiteness.[37] Etymologically, the word *crisis* means "to decide." "To decide," in this case, points to something momentous. Within this context, "to decide" also raises the theme of temporality, the sense of urgency. For the most part, white people are not in crisis vis-à-vis their whiteness; they are under constant therapeutic reprieve, assured that there is nothing problematic about whiteness, about their *white selves*. We need more social encounters that place white people in a state of crisis regarding their whiteness, social encounters where immediate retreat is not an option, where the security of gated communities is not an option, and where getting away with living in bad faith or self-deception is off the table. We need a place where *we* get to dwell near and where *you* get to be in crisis—a fundamental turning point, a site of uncertainty, off-centeredness, and within a space too close to hide. In conclusion, perhaps there should not be any place called white innocence. White innocence, after all, is another place to hide, another place to be safe, to be free of crisis. It is another place where whites get to, as Richard Wright might say, "dream and fix their eyes upon the trash of life,"[38] the shadows of life.

Notes

1. Frantz Fanon, *Toward the African Revolution* trans. Haakon Chevalier (New York: Grove Press, 1969), 49.
2. Barbara Applebaum, *Being White, Being Good: White Complicity, White Moral Responsibility, and Social Justice Pedagogy* (Lanham, Md.: Lexington Books, 2010), 42.
3. Zeus Leonardo, *Race, Whiteness, and Education* (New York: Routledge, 2009) 83.
4. Alice McIntyre, *Making Meaning of Whiteness: Exploring Racial Identity with White Teachers*. Foreword by Christine E. Sleeter (Albany: State University of New York Press, 1997), 99.
5. McIntyre, *Making Meaning of Whiteness*, 99.

6. See George Yancy, *Black Bodies, White Gazes: The Continuing Significance of Race* (Lanham, Md.: Rowman & Littlefield, 2008), esp. chapter 7.

7. See George Yancy, *Look, a White! Philosophical Essays on Whiteness* (Philadelphia, Pa.: Temple University Press, 2012), esp. chapter 6.

8. McIntyre, *Making Meaning of Whiteness*, 45.

9. Drucilla Cornell, *Transformations: Recollective Imagination and Sexual Difference* (New York: Routledge, 1993), 44.

10. Cornell, *Transformations*, 103.

11. Pelikan. "U.S. Attorney General Eric Holder Remarks on Black History Month, 'Nation of Cowards'" (February 18, 2009). http://www.clipsandcomment.com/2009/02/18/full-text-us-attorney-general-eric-holder-remarks-on-black-history-month-nation-of-cowards/ (accessed June 2, 2011).

12. Chris Cillizza and Jon Cohen, "President Obama and the White Vote? No Problem" (November 8, 2012). http://www.washingtonpost.com/blogs/the-fix/wp/2012/11/08/president-obama-and-the-white-vote-no-problem/ (accessed December 9, 2012).

13. Sara Ahmed, "Declarations of Whiteness: The Non-Performativity of Anti-Racism," *borderlands* e-journal 3, no. 2 (2004). http://www.borderlands.net.au/vol3no2_2004/ahmed_declarations.htm (accessed June 2, 2011).

14. Ahmed, "Declarations of Whiteness" http://www.borderlands.net.au/vol3no2_2004/ahmed_declarations.htm.

15. Frantz Fanon, *The Wretched of the Earth* (New York: Grove Press, 1963), 250.

16. Du Bois, "The Conservation of the Races," in *W. E. B. Du Bois: A Reader*, ed. David Levering Lewis (New York: Henry Holt and Company, 1995), 24.

17. Joel Olson, *The Abolition of White Democracy* (Minneapolis: University of Minnesota Press, 2004), 97. I had the wonderful opportunity of meeting Joel only once before he passed on March 29, 2012. The honor was my mine. He will be missed.

18. Walter White, "A Report from Walter White on the Lynching of Claude Neal," *ChickenBones: A Journal for Literary & Artistic African-American Themes.* http://www.nathanielturner.com/lynchingclaudeneal.htm (accessed on June 4, 2011).

19. Andrew Seifter, "*Media Matters* Exposes Bennett: '[Y]ou Could Abort Every Black Baby in This Country, and Your Crime Rate Would Go Down'" (2005), Video. http://mediamatters.org/mmtv/200509280006 (accessed on June 4, 2011).

20. David Hume, "Of National Characters," in *The Philosophical Works of David Hume*, ed. T. H. Grose (London: Longman, Green, 1882), vol. III, 252n.
21. Jean-Paul Sartre, "Black Orpheus," in *Race*, ed. Robert Bernasconi (Malden, Mass.: Blackwell Publishers, 2001), 115.
22. Cornel West, *Race Matters* (Boston, MA: Beacon Press, 1993), x.
23. Jean-Paul Sartre, *Existentialism and Human Emotions* (New York: The Wisdom Library, 1957).
24. Justus Streller, *To Freedom Condemned: A Guide to the Philosophy of Jean-Paul Sartre*, trans. and with an Introduction by Wade Baskin (New York: Citadel Press, 1960), 51.
25. Robert Gooding-Williams, "Look, a Negro!," in *Reading Rodney King, Reading Urban Uprising*, ed. Robert Gooding-Williams, 158 (New York: Routledge, 1993).26. Patricia J. Williams, *Seeing a Color-Blind Future: The Paradox of Race* (New York: Farrar, Straus and Giroux, 1997), 74.
27. Frantz Fanon, *Black Skin, White Masks*, trans. Charles Lam Markmann (New York: Grove Press, 1967), 151.
28. Judith Butler, "Endangered/Endangering: Schematic Racism and White Paranoia," in *Reading Rodney King, Reading Urban Uprising*, ed. Robert Gooding-Williams, 16 (New York: Routledge, 1993).
29. Jane Lazarre, *Beyond the Whiteness of Whiteness: Memoir of a White Mother of Black Sons* (Durham, N.C.: Duke University Press, 1999), 81.
30. Fanon, *Black Skin, White Masks*, 165.
31. *The Heartbreak Kid*, directed by Peter Farrelly and Bobby Farrelly (Universal City, Calif.: Dreamworks Pictures, 2007, (Movie), sec. 44:30.
32. Frantz Fanon, *Black Skin, White Masks*, 158.
33. Frantz Fanon, *Black Skin, White Masks*, 116.
34. Frantz Fanon, *Black Skin, White Masks*, 112.
35. Frantz Fanon, *Black Skin, White Masks*, 114.
36. Ahmed, "Declarations of Whiteness," http://www.borderlands.net.au/vol3no2_2004/ahmed_declarations.htm.
37. I would like to thank Amber Kelsie, a graduate student from the University of Pittsburgh's Department of Communication, who took my course "Phenomenology of Race" in the fall of 2012. It was Amber who spoke of and encouraged a discourse of crisis vis-à-vis whiteness. Her suggestion helped the majority of white students to understand exactly what was at stake.
38. Richard Wright, "The Man Who Went to Chicago," in *Eight Men*, introduction by Paul Gilroy (New York: Harper Perennial, 1996), 214.

THREE

RACE/GENDER AND THE PHILOSOPHER'S BODY

DONNA-DALE L. MARCANO

In *The Alchemy of Race and Rights*, Patricia Williams, a law professor, tells the story of an incident in 1988 at Stanford University involving two students and Beethoven. In the fall of 1988, two students identified as Fred and QC, one White and the other Black, had an argument over the racial identity of Ludwig van Beethoven. QC, the Black student insisted that Beethoven had "black blood,"[1] a claim that, given the history of the one-drop rule in the United States would very likely make Beethoven not just mulatto or mixed but Black. The next night, Fred along with some other White students got drunk, and finding the notion that Beethoven might indeed be Black or "have black blood" not merely implausible but a "preposterous" one, decided to color a poster of Beethoven to represent his alleged blackness and posted it outside of QC's dorm room.[2] In other words, the students colored Beethoven black, which the official campus investigation and report described vaguely as an act done in the service of representing "a Black stereotype."[3] Two weeks later the word nigger was written on a Black fraternity's poster, which eventually yielded no information about the identity of those who wrote the word on the fraternity's poster but did yield information regarding Fred and his peer's action to blacken Beethoven in the vision of a Black stereotype.

The following months included an investigation of the Beethoven defacement, at which time Fred was identified as the primary agent of coloring of Beethoven left at QC's room. In the resulting report, Fred offered some reasons for his action, including that he was troubled by all the talk of race and on blackness. He felt the emphasis on race denied one's humanity by being racial.[4] Fred also explained that as a descendant of German Jews, he had been used to humiliating teasing, which he eventually learned to "not to mind," and felt that Black students took race too seriously; therefore, he did not understand why they could not respond to the issue in the spirit it was meant, that is, "nothing serious." He wanted to send the message "to stop all this divisive black stuff and be human."[5] Fred explicitly articulated the question thusly: "Why can't we all just be human? I think it denies one's humanity to be 'racial'"[6]

Fred's response to what he considered the pervasive and unintelligible "focus" on race as one that denies humanity is quite compelling for many reasons. Race has been one of the most salient factors utilized to deny the humanity and citizenship of individuals arbitrarily grouped into a racial hierarchy that took on epic social and political proportions. Denying that we notice race or take race seriously is one solution to the historical oppression based on race. It is indeed for many of us the ultimate solution to seeing the humanity of individuals as individuals. Indeed, Fred was not and is not alone in understanding an emphasis on race, racial grouping, or racial identity to be divisive, a way of representing the world as divided between them and us. Nonetheless, Fred's reaction to the possibility that Beethoven might be Black or mixed with Black blood is just as compelling. Why, if Fred saw only humanity did this possibility, this tidbit of information, lead him to actually color Beethoven a more apparent Black, a black previously unnoticed or unsuspected by him? Again for Fred, the assertion of the blackness of Beethoven was not merely implausible; it was "preposterous." One may not know of the historical presence of Africans in Germany, and thus find the assertion implausible, but the word *preposterous* provides a tone of irrationality, illogicality, outrageousness, craziness, incredulity, and the unthinkable to the claim. As Williams points out in her reflection, she was struck by how "the word boxes in which race, blackness, and humanity were structured as inconsistent concepts."[7] Thus, the universality that undergirds the concept of humanity seems to be challenged by race, and blackness in particular.

The story continues that in the wake of Fred's experience of the possibility of Beethoven being Black he was assigned to do some reading on the subject. Upon discovering that Beethoven's assumed racial designation as White, or more precisely "pure" White, was not only up for debate but it did indeed appear that Beethoven had a close Black ancestor, Fred became even more upset. Williams recounts the report in which Fred claimed that "The discovery upset him, so deeply in fact that his entire relation to the music changed: he said he heard it differently."[8] Let me restate this: *Fred heard Beethoven's music differently*. We must then ask what changed, if not the assumed race of Beethoven. What changed about Beethoven's humanity that Fred heard his music differently?

I find this phenomenon interesting. Discovering Beethoven as not-White clearly resulted in a phenomenological impact so jarring that it could not be reconciled by a return to the "humanity" of Beethoven but by "seeing" Beethoven differently, by seeing the blackness of Beethoven and thus hearing Beethoven differently. Fred's act of defacing a poster of Beethoven by blackening the representation of him appears to be an act of making real the ridiculousness of this representation. In other words, Fred brought forth both the reality of the possibility of Beethoven's blackness and, in doing so, also brought forth the irrationality of such a possibility to the concrete by darkening Beethoven's face. He needed to see both the reality and its impossibility and he needed others to see it as well. Whether he wanted to recognize it or not, for Fred, Beethoven's humanity or universal appeal as a renowned world-class composer was tied to not only his Europeanness but to his presumed Whiteness.

The phenomenon of reinterpreting or reenvisioning a text, an event, a phrase, or music once we've discovered someone's gender or race or nationality is not necessarily unusual or peculiar to Fred. We probably do this often and unconsciously when we look at a book, a book title, and look for the name that may tell us if this is a female or a male author. We may look for a picture on the back cover or obtain further knowledge if we are unable to detect the author's sex, race, or nationality. We may hear a quote or phrase and wonder who is the person quoted and determine a meaning of such a quote by the person's race, sex, nationality, or political leanings. Just as frequently, behind the desire to know or behind the reinterpretation are assumptions held and then recalibrated to fit our discovery. In this chapter, I will examine the way in which the representation of the philosopher's body, and thus who does philosophy, is always tied to White men. This representation of the philosopher and the philosopher's body often goes unnoticed, because philosophy is often understood as a way of thinking or a way of being in the world that transcends race and gender. We would be confounded by the idea of Black logic: there is only logic. We would be distressed at a Black metaphysics: there is only metaphysics. We would question what it would mean that a female ethics is articulated: there is only ethics. All of these notions would be highly questionable, not because we now know that race and gender are not biological essences that determine how one structures reality or entities of that reality or because we now know that essential racial and sexual or gendered characteristics do not exist and therefore there cannot be essential characteristics of the structures of thought or the structures of right and wrong. Instead we would be confounded by the existence of a Black or a female metaphysics, because philosophy transcends the body and thus it transcends race and gender. The often unspoken but certainly still articulated premise is that philosophy with its dependence on argumentation and rationality transcends race and gender, whether they be deemed biological or social constructs. To be sure, prominent philosophers throughout the canon have rejected the possibility of a raced or gendered philosophy or philosophers, because they just did not believe that certain people—women and non-Whites—could actually do philosophy. In the United States, up until 1970s or 1980s, the woman or Black who was encouraged to engage philosophy was considered exemplary, and subsequently there has been the need not only to argue for a feminist philosophy or a Black philosophy but also the need to challenge the assumption that Blacks, women, or both could not do philosophy or the notion that they had not been writing and thinking philosophically all along, despite the social and political forces that intentionally denied them access to book learning, as they say.

No, we would not be confounded because we now know that sexual or racial essences do not exist, but rather because philosophy continues to be understood as always having transcended race and gender and thus the body: philosophy is tied to the mind. In other words, philosophical engagement lends itself to the conception that once engaged the individual transcends the lived experience of a body enmeshed in historical conditions, interpretations of those conditions, and especially identifying constructs such as race and gender. However, I will argue that philosophy and thus the philosopher are indeed tied to the body, and how we represent the philosopher's body. Because of this, Black women's intellectual work has been neglected as philosophical and thus philosophy because of their bodies. More importantly, the tale of Fred's response or rather inability to imagine a Black Beethoven reveals a significantly disorienting experience that, I argue, obtains as well for imagining real philosophy done by real Black women. To put this another way, I contend that the interlocking and multiple oppressions faced by Black women in American history acts to inhibit the inclusion of their intellectual work as philosophical and philosophically relevant because they are Black and women. The history of Black women's role, and thus because of the imaginary of Black women's bodies, the phenomenological impact of connecting philosophy with Black women is experienced as disjunctive and disorienting. The proof I suggest to you is that few of us, including those who identify as Black women, are ever taught Black women's intellectual work, which is now assigned to the confines of literary works. Though literary works, specifically here I mean novels, can certainly contain philosophical content or reflect specific philosophical tenets or methodologies, literary works by Black women are often used in conjunction with the supposition that one reads to find out only about Black women or that one must be a Black woman herself, and thus the interest is natural, so to speak. Philosophy courses that include discourses on rights, critiques on capitalism, and the nature of oppression are remiss when excluding the works of Black women, who have a 200-year history of arguing, critiquing, and explaining oppression in a society in which the constructs of race, gender, class, and sexuality create an interlocking network of oppression and distortion of individuals. Additionally, I will question whether the position of returning to no race, no gender is the solution to confronting this history of neglect. Ultimately, I contend that we must see diverse philosophers in our midst, who we do not merely perceive as the neutral palette for the accurate imitation of White philosophers, clothed in Black skin or female genitalia.

Understanding the History of the Particularities of Race, Gender, and Philosophy

My argument here should be separated from arguments that may admit the history of discrimination present in philosophy as elsewhere in the social and political realms of women and people of color. I am not arguing that professional institutions of philosophy like academia have previously discriminated against minorities of men and women. While true, this fact in and of itself states little in regard to the metaphilosophical position I pose regarding the relationship of bodies to philosophy. What is striking about the aforementioned story of the reaction to Beethoven's possible race is not founded in any explicit discriminatory notions. Rather, the story is striking because of the inconceivable prospect of rethinking the universality of genius in a body now visible for the first time as particularized by race. Indeed, in the history of women philosophical writers, women privileged to be trained philosophically, including Mary Wollstonecraft and Simone de Beauvoir, have argued that despite modernity's claim of equality for all men, women were nonetheless conceived as the Other, inferior, incapable or unwilling of fully rational comportment necessary to vote, follow ethical principles, or transcend concerns beyond the private realm. Feminists since de Beauvoir have shown that the foundational logic of philosophy operates in such a way that feminine difference undergirded the fully rational, fully human male. In *The Man of Reason: Male and Female in Western Philosophy*, Genevieve Lloyd carefully combs through philosopher's tracts from Plato, Aristotle, Augustine, and Bacon to Descartes, Hume, Hegel, and Rousseau to show that the "man" in the Man of Reason is no abstraction, and that "our trust in a Reason which knows no sex has been largely self-deceiving," but in fact secures maleness to Reason.[9]

> What exactly does the maleness of Reason amount to? There is more at stake than the fact that past philosophers believed there to be flaws in female character. . . . But the maleness of Reason goes deeper than this. Our ideas and ideals of maleness and femaleness have been formed within structures of dominance—of superiority and inferiority, "norms" and "difference," "positive" and "negative," the "essential" and the "complementary." And the male-female distinction itself has operated not as a straightforwardly descriptive principle of classification, but as an expression of values. . . . Within the context of this association of maleness with preferred traits, it is not just incidental to the feminine that female traits have been construed as inferior—or, more subtly, as complementary—to male norms of human excellence. Rationality has been conceived as transcendence of the feminine; and the feminine itself has been partly constituted by its occurrence within this structure.[10]

As a result of rethinking and revisiting the philosophical canon in an effort to unloosen the footnotes, asides, allegories, and images dedicated to the feminine, a diverse group of feminists have responded in diverse ways to address the fact of difference employed in the philosophical, social, and political arenas. Thus, understanding the philosophical role in the constitution of social and political particularities of sex and gender advanced a critical examination of powerful discriminatory values existing at the very heart of philosophical method, analysis, and imaginary.

Already by the 1940s, Beauvoir remarked that "conceptualism has lost ground. The biological and social sciences no longer admit the existence of unchangeably fixed entities that determine given characteristics, such as those ascribed to woman, the Jew, or the Negro."[11] Indeed it is affirmed by philosophies of rationalism, enlightenment, and nominalism that "women are merely the human beings arbitrarily designated by the word woman."[12] And yet, Beauvoir points out that man represents both the positive and the neutral in opposition to woman, which is defined by limiting criteria, and without reciprocity.[13] Linking the conceptual opposition of masculinity and femininity to the body, Beauvoir claims that women's body, the impossible fact of the existence of ovaries and uterus, appears to imprison woman in her subjectivity.[14] Thus, the male body, despite having glands that impact subjectivity, and is therefore a testament as well to the relationship of body and mind, "thinks of his body as a direct and normal connection with the world which he believes he apprehends objectively, whereas he regards the body of woman as a hindrance, a prison, weighed down by everything peculiar to it."[15]

Beauvoir conveys the sense that even the ready acceptance of equality which at minimum intends to wreak havoc on a metaphysic of essentialism, the body of women remains an object situated and marked with social and political meanings that limits its existence only to particularity and inhibits its access to universality. This body is unable to reciprocate in the articulation of the human condition that defies claims to rationalism, nominalism, equality, or humanism.

We may also understand that discriminatory history in philosophy regarding race exists. Though many of us would refuse to believe that philosophy departments across the country actively limited access of Blacks and White women to graduate philosophical classrooms at one time, we may be more inclined to admit that racist footnotes attributed to well-known philosophers exist and are therefore an unfortunate flaw of generally intelligent White men attributable only to the historical context in which they live. Nonetheless, Black philosophers, mostly men, have had to contend with unspoken racism and neglect of Black intellectuals such as W. E. B. Du Bois and others who used philosophy to analyze systems of colonial oppression. One of the first concentrated efforts highlighting the work of Black philosophers occurred in 1977.[16] In response to arguments that suggested Blacks had heretofore no examples of philosophical thinking and that philosophy specifically linked with the issue of race or blackness undermined the universality of philosophy, Black men privileged to be trained philosophically and well aware of the intellectual work of men who preceded them, began the work of advancing Black philosophy, Africana philosophy, and rereading the canon with an eye to the often ignored conceptual role of race in philosophy.

A History of the Black Woman's Body and Mind

In 1995, Beverly Guy-Sheftall published *Words of Fire*, an anthology that chronicles Black women's intellectual work, primarily essays and speeches given by Black women as early as Maria Stewart, in the 1830s. Guy-Sheftall aimed "to document the presence of a continuous feminist intellectual tradition in the nonfictional prose of African-American women going back to the early nineteenth century when abolition and suffrage were urgent issues."[17] In the last thirty years, Black female scholars have worked to uncover, discover, and recover the story of diverse Black women's lives and writings that have historically been left out of the visions and versions of feminism as well Black social and political thought. The first impact at reading this anthology, one recognizes right away that the very problems affecting Black women—the woman problem and the race problem—generates complex and diverse accounts of locating Black women in a society in which their very existence was invisible, even as they played a necessary role in constituting the imaginary of "all the black people" and "all the women" in the overturning of American racism and sexism. But this was the least of their problems. Many of these Black women understood themselves to be uniquely located in the American system of interlocking constructs of race, gender, class, and sexuality—all tied to the body—in such a way that any critiques of American oppression would fail to capture the depth, breadth, and stubbornness of oppression unless they started with looking at the condition of Bblack women. This could be perceived as an extremely exceptionalist account in which Black women's condition of multiple oppressions cause them to be so uniquely placed in regard to a particular social identity that various analyses of oppression cannot help but offer only an addendum. But Black women writers and speakers, even as early as the nineteenth century, were unable to disconnect their unique position from that of the various collectives to which they belonged. Belonging to categories often spun as distinct, they were women and Black, slave and free, reproductive commodity and domestic worker, laborer and unpaid worker, sexually free and sexually coerced, powerful matriarch and blameworthy as powerless in the success of a whole race. Black women understood that their position could be linked to the poor, the weak, the disenfranchised women and men of color, women in general, men in general, in other words, all people.

In the early 1800s, while Maria Stewart lamented conditions of oppression facing free Northern Blacks as little better than the much-stated horrors of southern slavery, Stewart and others like Sojourner Truth, critiqued

American society and a relentless White supremacy and nativist patriarchy, which demanded Black women to be useful and perceived as merely laborers, possibly domestic servants at best, barely paid if at all. Desiring to be paid for their labor, access the benefit of some kind of early education for Black women, or the right to vote, speakers like Stewart and Truth were two of many Black women writers who looked on optimistically at the possible positive moral influence of Black women on all segments of society if they were offered at least an education. By the late nineteenth century, Anna Julia Cooper in "The Status of Woman in America" had observed the extravagance connected to what we now call the "gilded age," and wrote that while America was developing millionaires, relishing in the assurance of wealth and dogged by money-getting and dollar-worshiping, women had an important role to play in challenging a society that valued greed and self-ishness.[18] In this respect, Cooper argued, Black women occupied a unique position in an unsettled and transitional period in which her status seems to be the least ascertainable and definitive of all the impactful forces of society because she was confronted by both the woman question and the race problem.[19] Despite being "as yet an unknown or unacknowledged factor in both," Cooper writes that as Black women have been forced at the periphery of political life,

> it may be woman's privilege from her peculiar coigne of vantage as a quiet observer, to whisper just the needed suggestion or the almost forgotten truth. The colored woman, then, should not be ignored because her bark is resting in the silent waters of the shelter cove. She is watching the movements of the contestants none the less and is all the better qualified, perhaps to weigh and judge and advise because not herself in the excitement of the race.[20]

Mary Church Terrell cites the achievement of Black women only a little more than three decades removed from slavery, who worked tirelessly in their communities for the education of young women:

> When one considers the obstacles encountered by colored women in their effort to educate and cultivate themselves, since they became free, the work they have accomplished and the progress they have made will bear favorable comparisons at last with that of their more fortunate sisters, from whom the opportunity of acquiring knowledge and the means of self culture have never been entirely

withheld. Not only are colored women with ambition and aspiration handicapped on account of their sex, but they are almost everywhere baffled and mocked because of their race. Not only because they are women, but because they are colored women are discouragement and disappointment meeting them at every turn.[21]

Always confronted by the accusation of sexual misconduct and immorality, Black women like Terrell found it necessary to defend the purity of Black womanhood as well as their advancement and charitable and activist work in their communities around the country, when "the immorality of colored women is a theme upon which those who know little about them or those who maliciously misrepresent them love to descant."[22] Terrell notes that the tremendous effort of young Black women in obtaining education: "The intellectual progress of colored women has been marvelous. So great has been their thirst for knowledge and so Herculean their efforts to acquire it that there are few colleges, universities, high and normal schools in the North, East, and West from which colored girls have not graduated with honor."[23]

By the 1920s women like Sadie Mosell Alexander increasingly analyzed Black women's location in terms of wage labor, class, and economic dependency. While wartime demand for their wage labor in sought after manufacturing jobs alleviated their confinement to domestic service or agricultural labor, Black women were forced to stay in the lowest skill positions and were paid less than both White women and Black men. White supremacy, sexism, and class exploitation combined to maintain Black women as not only laborers but often the primary or sole laborer in the family. Understanding Black women's social position as "workers, as Negroes, and as women," Claudia Jones, in her 1949 essay "An End to the Neglect of the Problems of Negro Women" argued that "Negro women were the most oppressed stratum of the whole population."[24] Postwar unemployment found many Black women forced to return to domestic work in urban areas and increased exploitation in agricultural labor, both of which confined women to barely paid labor. Jones found that the superexploitation of Black women was attributed to their special oppression as Negroes, women, and workers. The exploitation of Black women's bodies as a marginal underpaid labor force, states Jones, "is directly related to her almost complete exclusion from virtually all fields of work except the most menial and underpaid, namely, domestic service."[25] Victimized by "the white chauvinist stereotype as to where her place should be,"[26] Black women's bodies as body in service to the land and homes of others were reinforced in discourses of film, radio, and press, not as Jones concluded, "in her real role of breadwinner, mother, and protector of the family, but as traditional 'mammy,' and Negro slave mother who puts the care of children and families of others above her own."[27]

With sharp insightful critiques of capitalism, the Black liberation movement, the socialist/Marxist movements, and women's movement dominated by White women, Black women with diverse backgrounds declared that they were in an adversarial position to mainstream society because of the multiple oppressions they experienced. But as Patricia Hill-Collins points out, the rich intellectual tradition of Black women have remained virtually invisible due to the suppression of their knowledge claims and is neither accidental nor benign.[28] Owing the continued suppression of Black women's intellectual work to three long-standing interdependent dimensions of African American women's oppression, Hill-Collins cites the exploitation of Black women's labor, and thus bodies, the political dimension of their oppression and controlling images of Black women as mammies, jezebels, breeders, and welfare mothers, as a highly effective system designed to keep African American women in an assigned, subordinate place, as well as suppress the ideas of Black women intellectuals in addition to protecting elite White male interests and worldviews.[29]

As Fannie Barrier Williams states in 1905, "The colored girl . . . is not known and hence not believed in; she belongs to a race that is best designated by the term 'problem' and she lives *beneath the shadow of that problem* which envelops and obscures her"[30] (my italics). Living beneath the shadow of a problem, Black women's embodiment is enmeshed in a history of oppression and suppression that denies and refuses their philosophical and intellectual contributions. Living beneath the shadows suggests that Black women are both underdetermined, even as their bodies are overdetermined by a history that relegated them to only labor and sexual deviancy.[31] Nonetheless, historically, Black women have fought to define themselves, move beyond the shadow and argue that their distinctive social location, history, activism are necessary to an understanding of the relationship between self, economy, polity, and community.

Beethoven and the Philosopher's Body

Those of us whose philosophical work takes race and the racist history of philosophy seriously would agree with Robert Bernasconi when he notes that recent historical research has highlighted the extent to which enlightenment philosophers were not only champions of racist views but that, in addition, few of them opposed racist practices:

> The abolition of slavery, for example, owed more to a rereading of the Bible than to arguments proposed by philosophers, even philosophers appealing to the Bible, and those philosophers who did argue against slavery, like Granville Sharp, are, in any event, largely forgotten by mainstream philosophy today. Things are not much better when we move to recent history, or even the present: Philosophy has lagged behind other disciplines in reconceiving its cannon in an effort to address its own racist history.[32]

Indeed, it is my belief that philosophy has lagged behind in addressing its racist, sexist, and classist history, despite its lofty aims of truth, ethical values, transformation, progress, freedom, universality, and enlightenment. More importantly, we should continue to question the nature of philosophy as we have known it, such that it continues to underwrite its exclusions of some social locations as qualifiers rather than others. For instance, why are the qualifiers "African American" or "feminist" as particular locations of and relations to philosophy still often viewed as additional to "real" philosophy, while we continue to take French or Greek qualifiers of philosophy as real?

I have argued elsewhere that the relationship between Socrates and Alcibiades portrayed in Plato's *Symposium* is a good example of who is the traditional conception of the philosopher in contrast to who is not. Socrates, the exemplar of "the philosopher," drinks but never gets drunk, desires beautiful boys but never submits to that desire, is a soldier but one whose head is always in the sky thinking lofty thoughts. Socrates is the gadfly of Athens society, but never attached to his family, clan, or community. Socrates transcends the body. In contrast, Alcibiades, long held as the example of one who is not the philosopher, desires philosophy and desires philosophy through the body of Socrates, desires connection and praise from his community; he drinks and gets drunk. While Socrates desires beautiful boys but never has sex, Alcibiades desires philosophy and finds that expression in the sensual relationship with Socrates. In the end, Alcibiades is characterized merely as the handsome seducer of the philosopher, but one whose desire for Socrates and for politics is the story of the pursuit of mere physical appearance of Eros and not a love of wisdom—that is, philosophy. This story told over and over again is offered sometimes subtly, sometimes forcefully as a critique of the nature and state of being Alcibiades. What is often missed is that Alcibiades is offering a critique of Socrates as well.

Like the story regarding Beethoven's blackness, the philosopher's body presents itself conceptually as without race and transcending race, without sex and transcending sex, without oppression and transcending oppression. The philosopher's body is human without the limiting criteria that designate the variety of bodies and thus relations to knowledge. In other words, the philosopher's body presents itself as universal, until, that is, it is challenged as particularly White or particularly male or particularly sexualized. At that point, like Fred, the philosopher must be "blackened" in order to concretize it as other than the universal. And even given this opportunity, the preposterousness of the blackened, genitalic body forces a disjunctive experience because some bodies are tied more closely to the body than others. To insist on an approach that maintains a neutrality or invisibility of embodiment, to insist only on the "human" as a solution to the problem of race and racism, sex and sexism denies the history of philosophy that necessarily transcends the body, only to maintain and sustain the suppression of intellectual thought of Black women and women of color.

Notes

1. Patricia Williams, *The Alchemy of Race and Rights* (Cambridge, Mass.: Harvard University Press, 1991), 110.
2. Ibid., 111.
3. Ibid., 110.
4. Ibid.
5. Ibid.
6. Ibid.
7. Ibid, 111.
8. Ibid, 112.
9. Genevieve Lloyd, *The Man of Reason: Male and Female in Western Philosophy* (University of Minnesota Press, 1984), x.
10. Ibid., 103.
11. Simone de Beauvoir, *The Second Sex* (New York: Vintage Books; [1952]1989), xx.
12. Ibid.
13. Ibid., xxi.
14. Ibid.

15. Ibid.
16. I am thinking here of the volume on "Philosophy and the Black Experience," published by *The Philosophical Journal* in 1977.
17. Beverly Guy-Sheftall, *Words of Fire: An Anthology of African-American Thought* (New York: The New Press, 1995), xiii.
18. Ibid., 44–45.
19. Ibid., 45.
20. Ibid., 47.
21. Ibid., 64–65.
22. Ibid., 65.
23. Ibid.
24. Ibid., 109.
25. Ibid., 110.
26. Ibid., 111.
27. Ibid.
28. Patricia Hill-Collins, *Black Feminist Thought: Knowledge, Consciousness, and the Politics of Empowerment* (New York: Routledge, 2000), 3.
29. Ibid., 5.
30. Patricia Hill-Collins, *Black Feminist Thought: Knowledge, Consciousness, and the Politics of Empowerment* (New York: Routledge, 2000), 3.
31. I want to thank Kristie Dotson, PhD (Michigan State University) for the insight that Black women's presence is just as accurately characterized by underdetermination as it is by overdetermination, the latter of which is often used in relation to the Black body in philosophical literature.
32. Robert Bernasconi, "Sartre and Levinas: Philosophers Against Racism and Anti-Semitism," in *Race After Sartre: Anti-Racism, Africana Existentialism, and Postcolonialism*, ed., Jonathan Judaken (Albany: State University of New York Press, 2008), 113.

FOUR

AMONG FAMILY WOMEN

Sati, Postcolonial Feminism, and the Body

Namita Goswami

The political question is how to understand the difficulty of detaching from lives
and worlds that wear out life, rather than sustain it.
—Lauren Berlant, *The Female Complaint*

She has handed down respect of the possibilities—and the will to grasp them.
—Alice Walker, *In Search of Our Mothers' Gardens*

Introduction

In her widelyread and anthologized essay, "Under Western Eyes: Feminist
Scholarship and Colonial Discourses," Chandra Mohanty examines what
she terms "third world difference." According to Mohanty, third world difference is that "stable ahistorical something" that ostensibly oppresses a majority of women in "third world" countries. This stable, ahistorical difference
also produces a peculiar logic or consistency of effects that elide historical,
cultural, and material heterogeneities. A composite image of the "third world
woman" displaces the irreducible complexities of the lives of women in the
"third world." By virtue of being a signature feature of Western humanist
representations of the "third world," this image stands in for the heterogeneous realities of women in the "third world."[1] Mohanty examines the analytical presuppositions and discursive methods of feminist scholarship that
produce, maintain, and re-present "third world difference."

For example, exclusive focus on gendered subordination and a preconsti-
tuted class or category of women has led to an impoverished understanding

of power. Reliance on universal models of women's oppression reinforces global gendered subordination, that is, a global divide between those who suffer gendered subordination. Nonetheless, these universal models also codify stereotypical and overdetermined differences between the "West" and "non-West."[2] As a result of these theoretical frameworks and analytical presuppositions, which rely on and reinforce "first world" privilege, "Western" women emerge as the true subjects of feminism while "third world" women are relegated to perpetual object-status.[3] Ontologically bound to her absence and disfigurement, the singular, monolithic "third world woman" becomes the recipient of a benevolent maternal imperialism. As empty sign of sheer victimhood, she enables the implicit self-representation of Western women as progressive and politically astute in the face of universal oppression. Nonetheless, her (stable, ahistorical) "third world difference" enables Western feminism to extol the virtues of Western culture.

Uma Narayan's influential text, *Dislocating Cultures: Identities, Traditions, and Third World Feminism* (1997), similarly criticizes the presumed superiority of "Western" culture in feminist frameworks that seek universal models of women's oppression but reinforce stereotypical differences between the West and non-West.[4] The presumed superiority of Western culture reinforces a "colonialist stance"[5] toward heterogeneous third world realities. Such feminist frameworks rely on representations of non-Western cultures that emerged during colonialism, which characterize third world cultures as inherently oppressive and violent toward women. According to Narayan, rather than reinforce the chauvinistic notion that feminism is indigenous to Western culture, feminists ought to examine the social, cultural, and economic contexts that indelibly implicate their own histories with those of third world women.

The problems she identifies that lead to this colonialist stance include: (1) lack of specific historical contexts and time frames for the various problems that are strung together as "problems effecting Indian women" (such as dowry, *sati*, and domestic violence); (2) third world contexts are represented as uniform and monolithic spaces that have no important internal cultural differences, complexities, and variations; (3) problems that affect particular groups of third world women are often presumed to be primarily, if not entirely, results of an imagined and unitary complex called their traditions/religions/cultures, and as a result of this "multiple metonymic blurring," these phenomena become virtually synonymous with each other; (4) totalizing representations of Indian culture and traditions contribute to an ongoing practice of blaming or scapegoating culture for problems in third world contexts and communities, a practice that sharply contrasts with noncultural accounts of problems where mainstream Western subjects bear culpability; (5) third-world contexts emerge as places without history and as suffused by unchanging religious worldviews (6); third world women are either victims of patriarchal practices or objects of compassion for white "Western" women; and (7) such analytical presuppositions and representations perpetuate the belief that a critical stance toward Western patriarchy makes one immune to every form of participation in problematic aspects of Western culture.[6]

Both Mohanty and Narayan criticize how hypervisible and overdetermined practices or rituals, such as *sati* (widow burning), clitoridectomy, and foot binding, are used to symbolize the lives of women in the third world. As mentioned earlier, such stereotyping ontologically binds third world women to their victimhood while enabling Western feminist discourses to relegate women as such (both Western and non-Western) to a universal class of victims. Postcolonial feminism, therefore, examines how first world feminism both presupposes and perpetuates a belief in the third world's innate cultural difference from the first world. As a result of our stable, ahistorical difference from Western liberalized women, our culture becomes our stable, ahistorical nature; nature is fixed as that stable, ahistorical something that signifies human exceptionalism as well as third world difference; and nature itself disappears from view. In this essay, I use Spivak's concept of subalternity and her analysis of Bhubaneswari's *sati*/suicide to further dislocate the (global and transnational) cultural imperative to see our culture through Western eyes. Such cultural overdetermination perennially displaces the heterogeneity of the third world, renders the female body the transparent textual effect of social, political, historical, and cultural realities, and relegates postcolonial feminism to the task of redeeming third world culture by way of an ostensibly universal feminist humanism.

As Spivak's examination of Bhubaneswari's *sati*/suicide demonstrates, however, the female body of *sati* gestures to the *heterogeneity* of culture precisely due to its cultural overdetermination. While Spivak does not provide explicit details for this story about a young woman in her extended family, her concept of subalternity enables us to think about culture metaphysically. Spivak alludes to the concrete details of Bhubaneswari's suicide, which she pieced together through hearsay among family women. Such allusions demonstrate precisely how the heterogeneity of the "female subject *in life*" is irretrievable.[7] Yet, as the difference that lives on the other side of the subject/object divide, she allows us to think of gender ontologically. In other words, as Spivak argues, any attempt to plot her history is necessarily how we *appropriate* a role in (her) gendering.[8] Yet, her irretrievable heterogeneity may allow us to dismantle the cultural prejudice that has come to stand in for culture per se. If the female body of *sati* gestures to the *heterogeneity* of culture precisely due to its cultural overdetermination, could subalternity allow us to think of (a) culture that does not require separation from an ill-understood and stereotypically posited nature?

As a result of the cultural prejudice that is the nature/culture dichotomy, third world women are often marked by their ostensible affinity to nature. Such stereotyping has paradoxically led postcolonial feminism toward greater cultural overdetermination in so far as certain strands of postcolonial feminism presuppose the anthropomorphic nature/culture dichotomy in their analysis of culture. At those moments, however, when *sati* disrupts or exceeds the tropes, allegories, and analytical frameworks that seek to render it intelligible, a vibrant, living feminist inquiry can discern other interpretive gestures. Such interpretive gestures allow us to criticize the victimization of the female body without reinforcing reductive identity-based hierarchies. Postcolonial feminist inquiry can bring the heterogeneity of culture into view such that (our) culture is no longer, under Western eyes, that stable, ahistorical perennially different something that causes us to die. Instead, a living, vibrant postcoloniality, in this time of consequences, attempts to dismantle the nature/culture dichotomy that renders nature the signifier of irreducible human difference. Nature, in fact, as "all on planet Earth that has no need of us and can stand alone," refuses its consent to our historic demand for planetary exceptionalism and, as we must recognize, is coming back for us.[9] Thus, historical responsibility for our common culture perhaps requires recuperating an alternative history of our cultural relationship to nature.

To this end, I conduct an analysis of *sati* in the interest of a paradoxical postcolonial feminism that foregoes "human" bodily exceptionalism in order to privilege our (only possible) lives as animals. Anthropogenic climate change demands an undoing of gender and, hence, an undoing of culture, by rejecting the "human" body as signifier of our separation from nature. The human body is the site of nature, but denied as such, stands in for culture, that is, for human exceptionalism. In other words, according to our cultural prejudice, to have a human body is to be different from all there is. Thus, if gender is culture, and culture is the human body, then undoing gender is undoing the human body. Upholding ersatz vertical secession from nature renders nature nothing more than a façade to be maintained through our unquestioning occupation of a cultural niche. Postcolonial feminism, however, may embody the possibility for facing up to the very real consequences of not acknowledging that we are animals. This paradoxical postcolonialism naively reconstructs as historical privilege the socially, culturally, and politically maligned worlds signified by the female body of *sati*. A naive reconstruction of debasement as historical privilege may create the possibility of interrupting the repetition of nature in culture as nothing.

Such a shift in perspective—nature is culturally constituted so that culture can *seem* natural—allows for a postcolonial feminist reimagining of the inexorable logics of the anthropomorphic nature/culture dichotomy. This simplistic dichotomy evacuates our historical nature as animals to render separation from nature as the only possibility of being in a world. Acknowledging this animal life, which lives beyond yet remains intrinsic to our over-determined cultural formation, enables us to gain a meaningful, hopeful, and fundamentally proportional presence in our world. We are not *here* because of an ultimately delusional and hubristic separation from nature; as body, we are the *repetition* of nature,[10] and, as such, the body *is* our world. A theory of culture, therefore, ought to deliberate on the body as a telescoped, condensed, standing-in for the meaningful world in which we already live.[11] Such a theory of culture can perhaps enable us to see an alternative archive of culture, one in which the female body of *sati* is not already *there*, in the beginning, determining all else that follows.

In other words, thinking the threshold of this age, lest we who are the historical other of nature are left out/side of history, means going even further back than the paradoxically postcolonial archive of antiquity argued for by Spivak.[12] I emphasize, instead, that we must look toward an/other time frame: where it "all" began, in the beginning. If the female body of *sati* represents a history of violence justified by our cultural and, hence, natural failure to separate from nature, then a living postcoloniality renders this history meaningful by refusing our reified consumption of an increasingly inhospitable planet. Such consumption can function as an alibi for further mutilation in the name of postcolonial development and antiracist progress. This living perspective, instead, affirms the potency of culture by reminding us to *see* the heterogeneity of nature, which has been boxed "in" and cut "off" by the concept/category of "nature." Thus, the utopia we seek should be presupposed rather than proposed as the ever-unattainable "post" in "postcolonial," because we are already in/of nature and nature is here—and always has been. Postcolonial feminism demands that the traditional historical archive, where nature is already presumed to have no history,[13] be historically adequate such that this archive is no longer simply an exclusionary system (which we *call* culture, nation, or history). This demand, however, should also call into question the cultural and, hence, natural, difference that we assume to be the cause of our victimization. Given that colonialism has been justified by a rendering of the vanquished as indistinguishable from nature, *we* are the memory of *how* culture appears as a "self-evident force of nature."[14]

The concept of an archive of nature, therefore, is an achievement that recognizes how we share this planet with others beings. As such, this culturally different archive of nature may be the possibility of making the body "be" the repetition of nature rather than merely "be" the repetition of culture.[15] This history (in the making), which is long overdue, renders emphatic or insistent the substantive heterogeneity of nature that our cultural category of "nature" keeps at bay. Yet, this threshold is *where* analyses of *sati* often curiously stop, and thus forego their negativity, because they accept that the body, in the beginning, is nothing until it is outside/in history. Therefore, I propose for the dissolution of this body, which is perennially in the beginning of postcolonial feminism, to achieve a paradoxically long view of our lives as animals: the blood beyond the culturally saturated body. This paradoxical form of embodiment—to be blood without the body—is our possibility to *see* nature's heterogeneity. Culture writes over this heterogeneity to literally *take* place by consolidating the past-ness of the past; this is *where* nature was marked, separated out, and kept. Yet, nature cannot go somewhere else. It *is* what's *there*. The living body, therefore, constitutes what is properly real.

Postcolonial feminism can refuse ersatz vertical secession from nature by unplugging the female body of *sati* to let the blood gush forth. At the impasse in our conceptual systems where a reference to "life" must be created, postcolonial feminism can embody that leap of faith which imagines into being the very ground beneath our feet, such that our culture is not our dying a second time.[16] This postcolonial native informancy of what the loss of nature means at ground level is the negativity that emerges from behind the overdetermination of the female body of *sati*.[17] Thus, postcoloniality can mean something as both historical era and distinct conceptual contribution if we privilege a different understanding of embodiment. By refusing to stop short at the rupture with an ill-understood and stereotypically posited nature, postcolonialism can reveal the bloody brutality that makes the nature/culture dichotomy real. Culture is that stable, ahistorical difference that turns the ground beneath our feet into the killing floor of a factory/farm. *Those* chickens are coming home to roost as the possible impossibility of self-preservation that is global warming.

Undoing Culture

In the following, I read Sandhya Shetty and Elizabeth Jane Bellamy's "Post-colonialism's Archive Fever" by looking out for slips of the tongue in the cultural propaganda that is the "original mother tongue of history."[18] Postco-lonial feminisms may interrupt the repetition of nature in culture as the signi-fier of irreducible human difference. They dismantle this cultural prejudice by embodying that peculiarly felicitous circumstance of postcoloniality that enables us all, we postcolonials, gathered together,[19] to call a bluff at ground level: we must beg the question of nature in order to use nature historically.[20] Yet, where nature is assumed to have no history, that is, in that place where the immediacy of virtual reality is sublimated as culture with universal valid-ity, issues regarding the most "backward" areas of the world may provide the most sophisticated understanding of our current global predicament.[21]

Shetty and Bellamy argue against reading Spivak's 1987 essay "Can the Subaltern Speak?" as an exercise in her own class-based consolidation within "first world" academic structures.[22] Instead, they return to Derrida's notion of the archive, in particular to Spivak's question regarding the possibility of a postcolonial archive, to argue that "Can the Subaltern Speak?" can be approached in a more productive manner as the attempt not to recuperate "lost voices" but rather "lost texts."[23] Spivak's "highly motivated" use of the term archival becomes the impetus for a salient and "long overdue" reading of the unread portions of her text, that is, of those portions where she reads the texts of antiquity: the *Rg-Veda* and the *Dharmasastra*.[24] Shetty and Bellamy aim to restore this essay to a canonical or foundational status in postcolonial theory. They recognize that this task of establishing postcolonial canonicity or tradition necessarily entails recuperating her brand of deconstructive fem-inism from its crude identification with the political failures of deconstruc-tion. To follow through on this doubled charge of foregrounding the critical postcolonial viability of Spivak and Derrida, Shetty and Bellamy privilege an examination of the concept of the archive. This examination creates the pos-sibility for a more sympathetic postcolonial feminist stance towards Spivak's reading of the gendered subaltern in the archives, that is, of the subaltern woman as textually produced within the archive of antiquity. In other words, as Shetty and Bellamy emphasize, Spivak reads the silence of the widow as a "distinctly textual moment."[25]

While colonial power/knowledge pits the two sentences—"White men are saving brown women from brown men" and "The woman wanted to die"—at semantic odds, Shetty and Bellamy argue that Spivak (by way of Derrida) undoes this fatal dialectic between victim and agent by "'thinking' of the law . . . ontologically."[26] Thus, Spivak labors to reveal how the widow's silence is written-in into the archive of antiquity as that loss of memory that renders antiquity an "unnegotiated nonfactor"[27] in postcolonial theory's exclusive focus on colonial modernity. Against this foreshortened history of female victimhood, Spivak reinstates the production of the gendered subaltern as a "diachronic 'palimpsest.'"[28] Spivak's archive for postcolonial studies, which paradoxically grasps at and attempts to reach out to antiquity, becomes that place at the archaic origin that, in a certain sense, already writes the palimpsestic narrative of imperialism and nationalism (and now postcolonial studies) as the widow's *legendary* silence. When read in this way, the archive becomes the bridging *movement* between "Hinduism" and "Britain," which almost seamlessly turns "ritual" into "crime." As a result, the widow's silence is that place from where the two seemingly opposite sentences—"White men are saving brown women from brown men" and "The woman wanted to die"—are granted semantic content by their respective *archons*.

For Shetty and Bellamy, the unread portions of Spivak's essay signal how postcolonial criticism seems to automatically begin from colonial discourse analysis.[29] According to Spivak, this repeated (traumatic) loss of antiquity has led to postcolonial theory's failure to formulate radical questions because of the lack of value attributed to classical learning.[30] As Shetty and Bellamy note, Spivak examines how Sanskrit as a specific language became susceptible to "strategic misinterpretations" that date back to antiquity to textually produce that seemingly seamless reconfiguration of *sati* as "ritual" into "crime."[31] Spivak's highly motivated recovery of antiquity, therefore, is interested in archival violence, that is, the violence of the archive. This violence of/in the archive structurally pivots the *smriti* and *sruti* traditions ("that which can be remembered" and "that which can be heard," respectively) from polymorphous polyvalence to the strict letter of the law in order to do "real political work":[32] *turning* "ritual" into "crime." As such, because the widow's silence is (already) written-in into these texts of *sati*/suicide, Spivak's concern with the writing of antiquity "backdates the 'origin' of colonial subject formation from modernity to antiquity."[33]

To Derrida's list of European prejudices—theological, Chinese, and hieroglyphist—Spivak adds a fourth that is able to locate or place postcolonial criticism of imperialism "within the West's 'science of writing.'" Spivak's attempt to locate the geopolitical Derrida, as Shetty and Bellamy put it, is less to be cartographically specific than to preserve the vitality of textuality as a political pragmatics or type of political activity.[34] What does this mean for Spivak's reading of the archive of antiquity and the widow's written (in) silence? In Spivak's deconstructive feminism, *this* relay (between Derrida and Spivak) becomes a dismantling of the "imperialist prejudice"[35] that writes us into the archive/text as already geopolitically determined—and (consequently) silent. If the archive is that place where prejudice is written (in) and made (real), then this postcolonial concept of the archive enables writing for difference. In other words, writing for that difference from where Spivak's sustained investment in deconstruction fulfills or follows through on the active "complicity between writing and the opening of domestic and civil society."[36] The concept of the postcolonial archive, therefore, is not so much an additive or corrective gesture as a (re)figuration of what being in (a) domestic outline (Derrida's term) looks like. The postcolonial archive that paradoxically goes from colonial modernity to antiquity, as "*this place* from which [that] *order* is given,"[37] reorients postcolonial criticism by rewriting the ground beneath our feet.

This textual and ideological shift in perspective in Spivak's deconstructive feminism, writes (us) into the world by taking us to the threshold[38] of the postcolonial archive—the Sanskrit archive of antiquity—to look for a "(sexually) subaltern subject . . . lost in an institutional textuality at the archaic origin."[39] Thus, if "[*t*]*hat* word," that is, the subaltern, is set aside for, or means, the "sheer heterogeneity" of dubiously decolonized space, and the subaltern as subject is "irretrievably heterogeneous,"[40] then this postcolonial archive commands us into the world as *archons* tending an impossible because foreclosed genealogy—at the archaic origin. Subalternity, therefore, does not mean, nor does the (sexually) subaltern subject stand-in for, stable, ahistorical (cultural) victimhood. Instead, this form of sanctioned suicide or self-immolation that is truth-knowledge of the insubstantiality of the self (*tatvajnana*) as well as of piety of place (*agré* or, rather, "first" place) takes place in full view of our irreducible heterogeneity. As our passage in/to antiquity, this sanctioned suicide or self-immolation becomes our proper ancestral rite for the dead: we give ourselves over to that place, that is, to *her* place, which is "lost in an institutional textuality at the archaic origin" for the postcolonial archive. As such, this acting out of both truth-knowledge and piety of place, which is all that the woman is allowed, is that "performative displacement"[41] that violates that which can be remembered and heard (*smriti* and *sruti*, respectively). In other words, in this transposition, our geopolitical determination becomes the dubious place of a properly political or legendarily postcolonial criticism, which repeats the loss of heterogeneity in the very act of redeeming third world cultures by way of locating signposts and traces of the woman's "voice." *Her* absent body marks the spot.

Such a transgression of the letter of the law of our disciplines is that distinctly textual moment that writes our desire in excess of the general rule of conduct prescribed by our geopolitical determinations and disciplinary boundaries. Thus, the paradoxically postcolonial archive of antiquity signals a structural violence which overwrites/writes over that which can be remembered and heard (*smriti* and *sruti*, respectively)—to *take* its place. In Spivak's deconstructive feminism, the lost texts/voices of/for deconstruction and postcolonialism, as two seemingly opposing versions of political practice, find common ground. They are commanded by that "place of mutual untranslatability and irreconciliation"[42] that is the widow's (written-in) silence and, hence, her displacement as female subject *in life*. Thus, if any attempt at her replacement is necessarily how we appropriate a role in gendering, then can one think (the law of) gender ontologically? Is this question of gendering the memory of (another) time/frame from within rationalized gender, which gives third world women two cultural choices: either we are already gendered females in the process of development, or development is another (truer) form of gendering that frees improperly or prohibitively gendered women; in other words, capital frees gender?[43] Spivak's reading of the text of *sati*/suicide as parable enables us to *see* that the possibilities for interpretation are not perennially caught in the dubious semantic oddity of the two sentences— "White men are saving brown women from brown men" and "The woman wanted to die"—but are really absolutely vertiginous.[44]

Given how these possibilities remain "scandalously" unread, Spivak is able to make her much-publicized claim regarding the silence of the subaltern; her silence is that ontological command of the law of postcolonial studies that says, "for postcolonialism, 'in the beginning' is *sati*."[45] Spivak's opening out of the hermeneutic horizon of inquiry turns the question of gendering into the memory of another time/frame. The remarkable discovery that the subaltern woman cannot be located *textually unlocatable*,[46] that is, the subaltern cannot speak, allows us to move beyond the narrow sense of postcoloniality toward postcoloniality in the general sense, which privileges the "palimpsestic layers"[47] that bring antiquity into view. We are no longer caught, like the subaltern woman, between two semantic oddities—"White men are saving brown women from brown men" and "The woman wanted to die"— perennially shuttling between subject and object status. Thus, the overdetermined dialectic of free will—she was forced to die or she wanted to die—that is fixed into place and, hence, fixes us into place, by colonial modernity, appears at the cost of antiquity, that is, our sheer and irretrievable heterogeneity.

The relay that Spivak creates is as follows: If *satt* means the True, the Good, and the Right; and *sati* (the feminine form of *satt*) means "the good wife." The British turn *sati* (the good wife) into *suttee* (rite of widow self-immolation). These "slippages, mistranslations, and corrupt phrasings" of Sanskrit sacred texts constitute the *history* of *sati* as good wife and as rite of burning. Within this history, which fixes the woman's being as being a good wife (by burning), lies the volatile and troubling space of the widow's *non*agency.[48] Yet, *sati* as synecdoche for the colonial encounter, for *that* movement between "Hinduism" and "Britain," which when examined by the long-term view that the concept of the postcolonial archive is meant to carry forward, reveals a history of repression. This postcolonial archive reveals repression not just of Sanskrit as a specific language available for violation but also of what Spivak terms "women's time"[49] and what Shetty and Bellamy term "an ultimately pregendered time."[50] This long-term view takes us to Bhubaneswari's *sati*/suicide by a curious temporality that paradoxically reaches (back) into antiquity. As a result, we can *see* the actual, rather than simply psychological or individual ("willed"), reinscription of the social and ritual text of *sati*/suicide whose "moot" decoding or interpretation we call the "voice" of the subaltern woman.[51]

Shetty and Bellamy conduct their reading of the postcolonial archive's doubly unread portions—the archive of antiquity and Spivak's reading of this archive's antiquated documents—in the interest of an understanding of postcoloniality as a form of "cultural melancholia." In other words, for Shetty and Bellamy, the concept of a postcolonial archive impels us to reach out to antiquity; in fact: "we cannot *not* want antiquity."[52] Their use of a double negative does not mark a desire for antiquity, but protests the trauma of colonial modernity that (repeatedly) forecloses antiquity. Thus, in the postcolonial moment, that is, belatedly, antiquity becomes what we must necessarily dissociate from and what we must call on.[53] The postscript of Shetty and Bellamy's essay curiously embodies this fort/da, as they interject a reply ("But we are not finished yet") to the one who they see as the mother/founder of postcolonial studies: Gayatri Spivak—*en famille*.[54] This conversation among "family women,"[55] which is a story of disciplinary convention and its gender troubling, took place during a conference where the authors presented their work. Spivak was present on the occasion and asks Shetty and Bellamy whether they can create a relationship between the "riddling 'story'" of Bhubaneswari's *sati*/suicide (she is a member of Spivak's extended family) and founding a discipline.[56] What would Bhubaneswari's death mean when linked to the question of disciplinary identity? At this moment, perhaps due to misremembering and mishearing this public conversation among family women, I pick up on the moment of relay, to respectfully add to the archive a fifth prejudice that commands (us) into the world—at the archaic origin, *en famille*: the cultural prejudice.

Shetty and Bellamy read Bhubaneswari's *sati*/suicide as that failure of "family memory" and, hence, of "postcolonial memory," that turns her menstrual blood into a history or story not (to be) passed on by family women. Shetty and Bellamy cast Spivak's reading of this legendary family *sati*/suicide as the "real payoff" at the end of "Can the Subaltern Speak?"[57] They emphasize that Spivak's unread passages regarding Bhubaneswari's *sati*/suicide constitute the place where family memory is disrupted; that is, Bhubaneswari becomes the "'crypt'-ic secret of family shame." These passages in Spivak's text comprise a "gift" to postcolonial studies. They serve as a reminder, on the basis of Bhubaneswari's rewriting of the *shastric* prohibition of *sati* during menstruation, that this displaced place of the female as subaltern makes the discipline possible.[58] Yet, such an inscription of Bhubaneswari's reinscription of the law of *sati*/suicide does not see precisely *what* Bhubaneswari leaves behind: her menstrual blood. Far from being merely psychological, as Shetty and Bellamy seem to suggest, this reinscription of the law of *sati*/suicide is set in motion by a young woman who waits for the onset of menstruation, that is, who *times* her act of truth-knowledge (*tatvajnana*) and piety of place (*agré* or, rather, "first" place) in women's time by refusing (unlike the hero Arjuna of the Hindu epic the *Mahabharata*) to be persuaded by (the promise of) the *Time* of the nation/state through killing kin.[59]

Her menstrual blood signals that place in view of which Bhubaneswari makes impossible the passage between colonizer and nationalist ("Britain" and "Hinduism") because she cuts herself out (cuts bleed), unplugs the system, and leaves behind a trace for an alternative genealogy. Thus, Bhubaneswari paradoxically inserts the body into genealogy-as-history by way of removing her body. This (Good, True, Right) act speaks the lie of the semantic oddity that perennially shuttles the woman between subject- and object-status. Even though both cultural statements ("White men are saving brown women from brown men" and "The women wanted to die") posit an ostensibly natural difference between "Britain" and "Hinduism," both statements actually mean the same thing: the good wife. Thus, Spivak moves the "example" of Bhubaneswari from the domestic enclosure known as the family into the public space by writing her into the text of postcoloniality.

Indeed, her text-that-is-a-classically-learned-radical-question—Can the Subaltern Speak?—inserts "the body (via menstruation)"[60] into the general question of founding a discipline as a questioning of disciplinary identity. Bhubaneswari's menstrual blood was already cast as the signifier of the lack of
an "illicit" pregnancy in a young woman of sixteen or seventeen, who is "*no
doubt* looking forward to good wifehood." Bhubaneswari's rewriting of how
sati/suicide is commanded into the social space, however, takes (a) place by
waiting for the onset of menstruation.[61] According to Spivak, Bhubaneswari's
act of waiting turns her body into a vehicle with which to protest this body's
gendered dimension; literally: her physiology is meant to serve the passions
of a single male. The death of this not-an-unsanctioned-mother is explained
away as either the result of her taunting by a brother-in-law because she is too
old to be "not-yet-a-wife" or due to her failed mourning for her dead father.
A letter found ten years after her *sati*/suicide in 1926 revealed that male
nationalists called on Bhubaneswari as an incarnation of the "blazing, fighting, familial Durga" (a goddess).[62] They then commended Bhubaneswari-as-
Durga by giving her the responsibility to commit a political assassination.
Bhubaneswari's gendered overdetermination—she is unable to face up to the
mission but is aware of the necessity for keeping this secret—leads ultimately
to her killing herself.[63]

Spivak learns of Bhubaneswari's death through family rumors and
pressed a fellow Bengali woman for more details. This Bengali woman, who
is a philosopher and an expert in Sanskrit texts, expressed incredulity at Spivak's desire to learn more about the "hapless" Bhubaneswari (rather than her
two sisters that led fulfilling lives). This incredulity was *no doubt* due to her
distrust of diasporic interests that command, from that (first world) place
of postcolonial reason, that Indian women stand-in for timeless universal
female victimhood. A (post- or neo-) colonialist stance uses "third world difference" to justify postcolonial migration to the West as well as the neoimpe-
rial complicity of this postcolonial elite in exploiting "third world" nations.
Such migration and complicity are re-presented as escape from this culture's
preternaturally oppressive qualities. Spivak learns from this Bengali woman
that Bhubaneswari's suicide was a situation involving a secret and forbidden
love. Spivak notes that her "inadvisable remark" regarding the silence of the
subaltern, which was made in the accent of passionate grief and mourning,
bespeaks her failure to plot a history of how Bhubaneswari attempted to
"speak" by transforming her own body into women's writing—a text that
is written not from within culture but from that other place that is women's
time. Yet, in little more than fifty years after independence, her attempt at

writing (with/out) her (own) body is "silenced" by what we would consider to be her more liberated granddaughters, who turn her into a "scapegoat."[64]

Instead, the (postcolonial, liberated-by-capital) feminist *ought* to plot a history of what it means to be beyond the overdetermined subject-object dialectic and, hence, on the other side of a difference that reinforces mutually implicated identity. This plotting seeks to create a rupture in how we know such a subject such that this *sati*/suicide can make a difference rather than being the "dead letter" of antiquity that never ends up in/at its proper place/ address. Thus, if the word subaltern is reserved for sheer heterogeneity, and the subaltern is irretrievably heterogeneous, then Bhubaneswari did fight for national liberation by her refusal to assassinate in view of that metaphysical vision signified by her menstrual blood. If woman can only enact the truth-knowledge (*tatvajnana*) and piety of place (*agré* or, rather, "first" place) that is the purview of the male, then Bhubaneswari displaces the patriarchal register onto pregendered time by hanging herself. This means that she takes herself out of the gendered, cultural equation and leaves behind her menstrual blood as sign (like a pyre) of sacred place and truth-knowledge—to which she per-haps returns.

Bhubaneswari's *sati*/suicide, while transformed into a legend by Spivak's examination of the writing of this text, in fact signifies, given Spivak's despair, the necessary failure of knowing and, hence, preserving heterogeneity. Shetty and Bellamy reread Spivak's despairing passages as a commemoration of the female as subaltern who *is* the space from which the discipline emerges: Bhu-baneswari's dissent cannot be decoded and remains institutionally illegitimate because the subaltern cannot speak. Yet, as Shetty and Bellamy note, Spivak refuses the "gift" that would name her as the founder of the field of post-colonial studies because she does not "*see* anything called postcolonial*ism*."[65] They end their essay with a question regarding the pragmatics ("how") of giving an unwanted gift to someone whose name they posit as the name of the discipline. Spivak's refusal of this gift of death, however, renders/pre-serves postcoloniality that subaltern space of sheer and irretrievable hetero-geneity from where the contemporary moment of critique is commanded as violence to that which can be remembered and heard (*smriti* and *sruti*, respec-tively). In other words, although Bhubaneswari's *sati*/suicide takes place ("but not too loudly") in that decidedly women's time of menstruation, due to the subaltern's irretrievable heterogeneity, she becomes, in a certain sense, the "arena" of judging or testing our explanations of culture as we attribute meanings to this act.[66]

Thus, if we cannot not want antiquity, then *what* we cannot not want is that heterogeneity at the site of the violence of the archive where postcoloniality becomes an encounter with nothing (in the archive), since the (sexually) subaltern subject is textually unlocatable.[67] Bhubaneswari naively leaves behind her blood without the culturally saturated body and attempts to provide the textual ingredients for a countersentence that can convey the proper language of our life (Derrida's phrasing). Bhubaneswari's first and final cut is destined to be misheard and misremembered. Yet, her menstrual blood is the possibility of thinking *through* the culture that commands that we lose our mother/nature, always, to perhaps come out on the other side.[68] This essay, therefore, adds cultural prejudice to the list of prejudices, as the (m)other of all "posts," *after* Spivak's addition of the imperialist one, as the possibility for movement from feminist tradition to exegesis of sacred texts. This highly motivated (feminist) ancestral rite returns, yet again, to antiquity—*en famille*, for the sake of the very heterogeneity that lives inside us—fundamentally; hence, as a well-kept but nonetheless open secret of family shame, the subaltern precludes us from claiming what we understand to be our genealogy.[69]

I attempt, therefore, to pass female blood right/rite on by moving beyond the repertoire of symbols enabled by traditional understandings of gender. This space-clearing gesture is meant for a different cultural subject who experiences the ground beneath her feet as the essential and historical claim of that Mother whose disavowal condemns us all to blindness. In other words, any projection of kinship (family women) that structures itself against a damaged and maligned nature remains fundamentally bound to what it claims to have transcended.[70] To be family women, therefore, requires undermining the presumption of essential debasement that attaches to cultural inheritance from the (female) animal. According to this cultural prejudice, the body is meant to be written over by an exclusive, violent, and hegemonic cultural project that effaces nature. As *archons*, by undoing this project of culture and, hence, this project of gender, we may perhaps interject a renewed semantic field/fold to the palimpsestic narrative of human life. This narrative of human life can perhaps describe our actual historical situation of embodiment rather than uphold the cognitive dissonance of ersatz vertical secession. Our historically different cultural interest in non-Eurocentric ecological justice,[71] therefore, enables us to see *how* the (gendered, not bloody/real) body is written-in into the record. Postcolonial feminisms can become the historical opportunity to understand nature as the signifier of irreducible heterogeneity because they allow us to *see* the "human" as the odd man out.

In this archive of antiquity, we may notice how by using nature to signify irreducible human difference, and by presupposing culture to be the principle of vertical secession from nature, we mime nature as nothing. In other words, nature as written-in into the archive is textually unlocatable. Miming nature as nothing creates a "rupture" so that the body can become an implement. This body/implement allows us to signify that immediacy on which we can then stage a self.[72] Bhubaneswari's legendary postcoloniality or act of truth-knowledge (*tatvajnana*), by leaving behind her menstrual blood, perhaps enables all (of us) to *see* the insubstantiality of (this) self and the piety of (this) place: that is, (of) the "first" (and only) place (*agrè*). One could perhaps also say that Bhubaneswari turned the rays of light emitting from the palm of the goddess in the heavens above, which signify *satt* in popular iconography of *sati*, into a rope around her neck. The True, the Good, and the Right literally leave no room for the (sexually) subaltern subject, who is lost in an institutional textuality at the archaic origin, to breathe.[73]

There is no (dead) husband whose truth-knowledge (*tatvajnana*) of the insubstantiality of the self she only perennially mimes, or whose funeral pyre is her piety of place, that is, her "first" (and only) place (*agrè*). She does not kill herself where her husband is burning, for she has no husband (to be), but where her menstrual blood is. This menstrual blood remains. In her paradoxical reinscription of the text of *sati*/suicide, her substantial menstrual blood is (her) truth-knowledge of the insubstantiality of the self and is her piety of place. There is no wood that destroys a/the body and, hence, conveys the insubstantiality of self and piety of place. There is only blood, that is, blood without the culturally saturated body, which conveys both women's time and the proper language of our life. This legendary postcolonial reason, by reinscribing the text of *sati*/suicide, attempts to disrupt rather than uphold stable, ahistorical difference (nature/culture or animal/body). Such an archive of antiquity may enable a passage to an ecological rather than calculating frame of mind because a living, vibrant feminist postcolonialism does not automatically turn the heat of archive fever into the reasonable, itemized, objective, and self-interested bases for our continuing survival.[74] Thus, the discursive folly and ideological power of homogenizing third world women is that violence of the archive that writes us into the archive as (our) stable, ahistorical nature. The subaltern's irretrievable heterogeneity, which is signified by Bhubaneswari's menstrual blood in this palimpsestic reading, undoes the culture that signifies human exceptionalism by way of third world difference. As a result of this cultural prejudice, the culturally saturated body is no longer bloody; instead, *our* embodiment is our difference from all there is. Bhubaneswari's menstrual blood allows us to see the living heterogeneity that makes any/body real because her blood overwrites/writes over that archive of antiquity that makes nature nothing. Her paradoxical undoing of gender reinscribes the subject of *sati* not as good wife but as that utopian understanding of the project of culture in which *all* mothers are important.[75]

Notes

1. Chandra Mohanty, "Under Western Eyes: Feminist Scholarship and Colonial Discourses," in *Third World Women and the Politics of Feminism*, ed. Chandra Talpade Mohanty et al. (Bloomington and Indianapolis: Indiana University Press, 1991), 53.
2. Mohanty, "Under Western Eyes," 52.
3. Ibid. 71, 74.
4. Narayan also points out that nationalists have also been involved in reinforcing these static images of third world culture, in their endeavors to establish independence as well as in postindependence communitarian politics.
5. Uma Narayan, *Dislocating Cultures: Identities, Traditions, and Third-World Feminism* (New York: Routledge, 1997), 48.
6. Narayan, *Dislocating Cultures*, 41–80.
7. Gayatri Spivak, *The Critique of Postcolonial Reason: Toward a History of the Vanishing Present* (Cambridge: Harvard University Press, 1999), 235.
8. Spivak, *Critique of Postcolonial Reason*, 227.
9. E. O. Wilson, *The Creation: An Appeal to Save Life on Earth* (New York: W. W. Norton, 2006), 15.
10. Gayatri Spivak, *Outside in the Teaching Machine* (New York: Routledge, 1993), 20.
11. For Spivak, the archives are a "crosshatching of condensations, a traffic in telescoped symbols." They give texture and zoom in and/or focus/ bridge distances across space and time. It is the process of archiving, the constitution of an archive that interests her (Spivak, *Critique of Postcolonial Reason*, 205). Later on she discusses overdetermination, that is, the telescoped and intense image the term calls to mind, which persuade and are based on figuration on the ground; while determination refers to defining/fixing/determining, overdetermination, for Spivak, is not the repeated use of a definition but about quality, that is, the intensity of a telescoped image. She argues, the "*mechanics* of the constitution of these

'facts' are dissimulated in the official historical record" (226; emphasis added). We can think of these mechanics as effected difference (self-determination) dissimulated through overdetermination to constitute "facts" and the "record" or "proceedings" of "history."

12. Sandhya Shetty and Elizabeth Bellamy, "Postcolonialism's Archive Fever," *Diacritics* 30, no. 1 (Spring, 2000): 36.

13. Gayatri Spivak, "Harlem," *Social Text* 81 22, no. 4 (Winter, 2004): 134.

14. Paul Gilroy, *Postcolonial Melancholia* (The Wellek Library Lectures) (New York: Columbia University Press, 2005), 8.

15. Spivak, *Outside in the Teaching Machine*, 20.

16. Salman Rushdie, *The Ground Beneath Her Feet: A Novel* (New York: Henry Hold, 1999). Salman Rushdie's novel, *The Ground Beneath Her Feet* (1999), uses the myth of Orpheus and Eurydice as the governing conceit of a story about (among a myriad of issues) the jet-setting world of globally ascendant rock musicians confronting ground-level actualities of life, love, and death, albeit from what is quite literally a parallel universe.

17. According to traditional anthropology, the native informant is "a figure who, in ethnography, can only provide data" or "can only be read, by definition, for the production of definitive descriptions" (Spivak, *Critique of Postcolonial Reason*, 49). Spivak attempts to transform this "impossible (because historically and discursively discontinuous) perspective of the native informant" into an interruptive *reader's* perspective (33, 67). The *postcolonial* native informant intervenes in the process of foreclosure by what Spivak terms plotting a history (Gayatri Spivak, "Can the Subaltern Speak?" in *Marxism and the Interpretation of Culture*, ed. Cary Nelson et al. [Urbana: University of Illinois Press, 1987], 297). A sustained *un*-reading requires tracking a contemporaneous perspective "lost" to the archive. This imagined testimony is that impossible counternarrative that provides the conditions of possibility for the difference of the present from itself. Through what Spivak terms narrative pathos, the postcolonial native informant seeks to grasp what the foreclosure of heterogeneity *means* for our lives at ground level. This ground level knowledge, which attempts to refer to the heterogeneity we *already* know to be the world, is philosophical because it is substantively historical.

18. Gayatri Spivak, *In Other Worlds: Essays in Cultural Politics* (New York & London: Routledge, 1988), 211.

19. See Spivak's discussion of how "empire messes with identity" as she criticizes the performative and, hence, virtual aspect of the postcolonial scene that embodies that "peculiar felicity of postcoloniality" where

"good and evil" become "reactive simulation." At this site/sight, "[p]
ostcolonial women and men, in many different ways, utter metropolitan
performatives on the stage of migrancy as they utter 'cultural-origin' performatives in a simultaneously shadow play; thus perhaps revealing the
constitutive theatricality of all performatives." Yet, she is called out for
giving resistance "no speaking part" (*Outside in the Teaching Machine*, 226).
I am attempting to invert the theatricality of the postcolonial performative so that postcoloniality can actually make a difference rather than
blend into the cultural landscape of neocolonial first world migrancy.

20. Spivak's fleshing out of the possibility for non-Eurocentric ecological
justice finds one of its most poignant articulations in her essay "Righting
Wrongs."

21. Rajeswari Sunder Rajan and You-me Park, "Postcolonial Feminism/
Postcolonialism and Feminism," in *A Companion to Postcolonial Studies*, ed.
H. Schwartz et al. (Malden: Blackwell, 2000), 66.

22. Asha Varadharajan and Ania Loomba have made these criticisms of
Spivak.

23. Shetty and Bellamy, "Postcolonialism's Archive Fever," 25.

24. Shetty and Bellamy state, "Spivak turns first to the *Dharmasastra*, a multi-
ply authored series of documents, dating from about the seventh to the
second centuries BCE, whose codification of Hindu law and custom
were, legally speaking, by far the most important of the post-Vedic smriti
tradition, or 'that which is remembered'" ("Postcolonialism's Archive
Fever," 36). However, the *Dharmasastra*'s "authority in codifying Hindu
law and custom derived from at least two (if not three) prior texts: the
Dharma Sutras, sectarian manuals for proper conduct written in short
aphorisms derived from the earlier ritualistic Vedic literature of the *Brahmanas*, which was concerned mostly with sacrifice and its symbolism.
These latter texts began to be orally composed and transmitted around
900 BCE, a process continuing for several centuries. . . . The *Brahmanas*
themselves were appendages of the *Vedas*, the most archaic of the religious texts of antiquity. The *Rg-Veda*, in turn the oldest of the *Vedas* and
historically considered the first and most important of the *sruti* literature
(or 'that which is heard') is a collection of hymns that were so sacred they
were rarely if ever written down until the 1780's" (36–40).

25. Shetty and Bellamy, "Postcolonialism's Archive Fever," 26, 28.

26. Ibid. 27.

27. Ibid., "Postcolonialism's Archive Fever," 28.

28. Ibid., "Postcolonialism's Archive Fever," 28.

29. Ibid., "Postcolonialism's Archive Fever," 30.
30. Spivak, *Critique of Postcolonial Reason*, 292.
31. Shetty and Bellamy, "Postcolonialism's Archive Fever," 30, 29.
32. Ibid., "Postcolonialism's Archive Fever," 30 note 5.
33. Ibid., "Postcolonialism's Archive Fever," 32. See Spivak's discussion of persuasion in her section on Hegel and the *Shrimadbhagavadgita* in *Critique of Postcolonial Reason* (37–58). The Lord Krishna in the guise of Arjuna's friend and charioteer persuades Arjuna to kill his kin by revealing himself as Law since seeing is believing. In other words, Arjuna does not kill his kin because (by Law) they are *already* dead.
34. Ibid., "Postcolonialism's Archive Fever," 34, 35.
35. Ibid., "Postcolonialism's Archive Fever," 35.
36. Spivak, "Can the Subaltern Speak?" 297. Shetty and Bellamy also cite this phrase ("Postcolonialism's Archive Fever," 35).
37. Shetty and Bellamy are citing Derrida ("Postcolonialism's Archive Fever," 36).
38. Shetty and Bellamy, "Postcolonialism's Archive Fever," 36.
39. Spivak, "Can the Subaltern Speak?," 303. Shetty and Bellamy also cite this phrase ("Postcolonialism's Archive Fever," 32).
40. Spivak, *Critique of Postcolonial Reason*, 270, 310, emphasis added.
41. Shetty and Bellamy, "Postcolonialism's Archive Fever," 38.
42. Ibid., 39, emphasis added.
43. Spivak discusses the supposed difference between "gender and development" and "women in development" and refers to Derrida's argument that the copula is a supplement. In terms of "gender and development," the copula "may mean that the relationship between men and women is patriarchal until rationalized." Earlier, she emphasizes that women in development are women who are already gendered females in the process of development. That is, development is not related to gender; they are gendered already and now they are being developed. Gender and development refers to gender as an obstacle to development: local norms of gendering hinder development (*Critique of Postcolonial Reason*, 291 notes 142, 200).
44. Ibid., 42.
45. Ibid., 43.
46. Ibid., 42.
47. Ibid., 42.
48. Ibid., 43. See their extensive discussion of the displacement of the agency of the female on three registers: she can only act out the husband's

knowledge of the insubstantiality of the self; her husband's funeral pyre is the "piety of place" and not her own sacred place, that is, proper place; and her "self" can only be killed where her husband is burning (37–38).

49. Spivak, *Critique of Postcolonial Reason*, 295.
50. Shetty and Bellamy, "Postcolonialism's Archive Fever," 43 note 15.
51. Spivak, *Critique of Postcolonial Reason*, 309.
52. Shetty and Bellamy, "Postcolonialism's Archive Fever," 44.
53. Ibid., 44.
54. Ibid., 45.
55. Ibid., 46.
56. Ibid., 45.
57. Ibid., 33 note 8.
58. Ibid., 46.
59. In her discussion of *The Mahabharata*, Spivak examines how the God Krishna indulges Arjuna's horror at killing his kin and persuades him by revealing Himself, "as containing the universe" (*Critique of Postcolonial Reason*, 55). Friendship as obligation/indulgence enables the construction-through-persuasion of the Hindu-Aryan myth such that killing becomes the metonym of action as such: there is no killing; I (Krishna) am killing, you (Arjuna) are not. It is written. Bhubaneswari's suicide, however, writes her lack of persuasion and is perfectly timed, that is, it "grasp[s] life and ground-level history," unlike Arjuna who killed for Law/Time/History, thereby "subordinat[ing] history as timing to law as the graph of time" (38, 50–56). See also note 7.
60. Shetty and Bellamy, "Postcolonialism's Archive Fever," 47.
61. Spivak, *Critique of Postcolonial Reason*, 307 (emphases added).
62. The Goddess Durga preserves the moral order and combats evil forces. She is adorned with weapons, such as a trident, mace, sword, arrow, and disc. Each weapon enables her to fight distinct enemies.
63. Spivak, *Critique of Postcolonial Reason*, 307.
64. Ibid., 308–309.
65. Gayatri Spivak, "Gayatri Spivak on the Politics of the Subaltern," Interview with Howard Winant, *Socialist Review* 20, no. 3 (1990): 95 (first emphasis added). Shetty and Bellamy also cite this phrase ("Postcolonialism's Archive Fever," 47).
66. Spivak, *Outside in the Teaching Machine*, 214.
67. Spivak refers to this metaphysical (I would argue) possibility as "thinking the undetermined wholly-other," that is, of thinking the "great, pure, unlivable, inappropriable outside" (*Outside in the Teaching Machine*, 99).

68. Saidiya Hartman, an African-American descendant of slaves from Ghana, emphasizes that the "breach of the Atlantic could not be remedied by a name and that the routes traveled by strangers were as close to a *mother country* as I would come" (*Lose Your Mother: A Journey Along the Atlantic Slave Route* [New York: Farrar, Straus, and Giroux, 2007], 9). Rather than "lopping off the past" as an "extra appendage," she asks if the "impossibility of recovering the stories of the enslaved" made "history tantamount to mourning" (15–16). Indeed, "how does one write a story about an encounter with nothing?" (16). History, "how the secular world attends to the dead" could not be settled by the "sheer will to forget" (18). Even though debates rage if "twelve million or sixty million had been sentenced to death to meet the demands of the transatlantic commerce in bodies," it is unfathomable that "all this death had been incidental to the acquisition of profit and to the rise of capitalism . . . Unlike the concentration camp, the gulag, and the killing field, which had as their intended end the extermination of a population, the Atlantic trade created millions of corpses, but as a corollary to the making of commodities" (31). This recollection assured her that the "self-forgetfulness of belonging would never be mine" (46). She wished to "resurrect the dead," and not give the "repentant" the life support system of "a new life" (54). This resurrection became the place where "*going back to* and *moving toward* coincide" (96), because it is "only when you *lose your mother* that she becomes a myth" (98). She chose her "past," and determined to "return to my native land," a return only possible for those "disbelieving in the promise and refusing to make the pledge because they have "no choice but to avow the loss that inaugurates one's existence. It is to be bound to other promises. It is to lose your mother, always" (100).

69. As Spivak emphasizes, the subaltern's foreclosed native informancy of her actions, by "inhabiting us" prevents us from "claim[ing] the credit for our proper name" (*Critique of Postcolonial Reason*, 111).

70. Judith Butler, *Undoing Gender* (New York: Routledge, 2004), 126.

71. See Spivak's discussion of this term in *Imaginary Maps*, when she speaks to the ethos of Mahasweta Devi's fiction.

72. Spivak, *Outside in the Teaching Machine*, 20. Spivak begins her critique of postcolonial reason with a contrast between "sustainability" and the "practical philosophy of living in the rhythm of the eco-biome"— the former calculated, appropriative, and Eurocentric and the latter (I would argue) almost metaphysical in its miring movement. She cites how UNESCO's document, titled *Encyclopedia of Life Support Systems*, "'defines'

the Aboriginal period of human history as the 'timescale of the *far past* . . . associated with *inactive* approaches in which there is no concern for environmental degradation and sustainability.' It was of course as impossible for the Aboriginal to think sustainability as it was for Aristotle to 'decipher . . . the secret expression of value,' because of 'the historical limitation inherent in the society in which [they] lived.' Yet, the practical philosophy of living in the rhythm of the ecobiome must now be dismissed as 'no concern'" (*Critique of Postcolonial Reason*, ix). E. O. Wilson notes, however, that the "humanization of Earth proceeds in many other ways. Most of the land-dwelling megafauna, comprising animals weighing ten kilograms or more, have been hunted down to extinction on the land. Wildlife on the plains and forests of the world today bear little resemblance to the majestic parade of giant mammals and birds driven to extinction by expert Paleolithic hunters. A large minority of those surviving today are on the endangered list. Twelve thousand years ago the wildlife of the American plains was richer than that of Africa today. Overall, humanity has altered this planet as profoundly as our considerable powers permit" (*The Creation*, 16–17).

73. Bhubaneswari perhaps leaves behind (her) blood because the woman's body/the good wife's body/the body-that-is-burning, as written-in into the archive, feels no pain.

74. Gayatri Spivak, *Imaginary Maps*, trans. Gayatri Spivak (Calcutta: Thema, 2001), 202.

75. These were the words spoken by Nanna Nungala Fejo, an Aboriginal woman stolen from her mother when she was four years old, to Kevin Rudd, Prime Minister of Australia. Kevin Rudd asked her what lesson he should convey to the nation regarding the brutal history of forced separation of "half-caste" children from their mothers as a means of eradicating all Aboriginal peoples of Australia. In his "Sorry Speech," that opened the forty-second Parliament of Australia with a formal apology to the stolen generations, Prime Minister Rudd stated: "She thought for a few moments then said that what I should say today was that all mothers are important." For the full text of the speech see: "Kevin Rudd's Sorry Speech," *Sydney Morning Herald*, February 13, 2008: http://www.smh.com.au/articles/2008/02/13/1202760379056.html.

FIVE

SHAME AND SELF-REVISION IN ASIAN AMERICAN ASSIMILATION

David Haekwon Kim

This essay offers a political phenomenology of some of the underlying structures of Asian American identity practices. Specifically, I focus on anti-Asian stigmatization and some of the self-evaluative emotions and self-making strategies with which Asian Americans respond in forming or maintaining their identities. I begin by situating Asian American experiences within the wider political framework. U.S. society is configured by a kind of orientalist liberalism in which Asian Americans are marked by a distinctive form of racism and xenophobia, while at the same time their civic-cultural practices have been characterized as benignly assimilative and hailed as a model for other racial minorities. In contrast to much public discourse as well as some of the assimilation literature in the social sciences, I examine the problematic racialization of various kinds of self-consciousness among Asian Americans, particularly the self-regard of those who try to deracialize themselves in order to assimilate into the mainstream. To better understand the values and worldly engagements involved here, I consider emotion and self-evaluative emotion, and particularly the lived experience of shame, self-contempt, and the affective validation frameworks they presuppose. I then unite the discussion of political context and of emotive experience to give an account of various kinds of Asian American responses to anti-Asian stigmata and the conditions that give rise to them. Though I believe my account pertains to many kinds of Asian American, and even non-Asian American, identity practices, I recognize that some identity practices lie outside of the discussion that follows.

If this chapter is plausible, it may contribute to three kinds of projects. First, it may add another voice to the chorus that critiques the use of Asian American assimilation practices as a sign of democratic progress or of a postracial America. Second, in philosophy, there is so little discussion about Asian American lived experience and politics, so the essay may shed a little light, at least in philosophy, on some aspects of Asian American civic and racial conditions. Finally, the essay may add to efforts that show how affectivity and politics can be deeply linked, and thus how philosophy of emotion and political philosophy can be mutually illuminating. Relatedly, unlike some sectors of political philosophy, affectivity is never excluded from phenomenological analyses of racial experience and identity. Nevertheless, more can be done to show how affectivity can be productively foregrounded, and I hope to have offered a reasonable account in this vein.

The Politics of Assimilation: Preliminary Thoughts

Assimilation is remarkably complex. So, at the start, four context-setting ideas are briefly discussed. The aim here is primarily to clarify the general approach I take to the matter and delimit the scope of inquiry.

First, following the primary meanings of the term *assimilate*, there are two very general ways of thinking about assimilation, and they need integration. According to one way, the framing idea is of an entity or collective absorbing an external element. Successful absorption requires the incorporated element to be rendered, if it is not already, sufficiently compatible with the absorbing entity. Thus, the absorbed element is placed under modifying or reconstituting pressures. In the opposite direction, the focus is on the same relation going in the other direction: to assimilate is for an exterior element to modify or convert itself into something compatible with the absorbing entity. For our purposes, the first way of talking is essentially sociological and about polity maintenance, and we might call the process in question "incorporative assimilation." Specifically, this sense of assimilation will be understood to focus primarily on racial groups and secondarily the members that compose them, and its concern is the extent to which racial groups have been incorporated into or marginalized from the societal mainstream. The second sense, then, is essentially about an agent's self-formation and thus the agent's identity, values, abilities, and projects, and we might call this process "identity assimilation."

Clearly, the latter does not transpire in a vacuum. We must understand the former, in particular the polity's incorporation-facilitating pressures and conditions of exclusion, to adequately understand the latter, an agent's aspirations and strategies for identity-formation. In understanding incorporative assimilation, profoundly significant are power, ideology, coercion, and hegemony. For the state and authoritative groups demand, covertly and openly, various kinds of norm valuation and norm compliance from the populace at large, and they have the soft and hard power to make good on these demands. But it is also true that an understanding of incorporative assimilation requires at some point an account of agent structures and their contingent and varied patterns of instantiation. We cannot in rote fashion read an agent's identity off of an understanding of the macrostructures of incorporative assimilation. At some point, moral or political psychological capacities and practices at the heart of a theory of identity assimilation must be also be invoked.[1]

Second, since the main concern here is with experiences of racial conditions, a merely cross-cultural analysis of assimilation is inadequate. In making sense of the civic struggles of, say, Puerto Rican or Chinese Americans, it would be largely unhelpful to think through the experience of Swedish immigration to the United States, except perhaps as a foil for the former. Political subordination must be at the center of our analysis. Much of the hype, controversy, and sometimes agony over race and assimilation would be difficult to grasp were it not for the distinctive concern over an extensive history of oppression against people of color. And in the last couple of decades, the empirical and theoretical work on the history, structure, and legacy of White supremacy as a political system in the U.S. has become rich, wide, and variegated.[2] While I think many acknowledge the presence of political White supremacy, even if some balk at this particular naming of the system, the acknowledgment sometimes does not get incorporated deeply enough into relevant theoretical structures. As a general point, I think culture is politicized and politics enculturated. In the case at hand, I conceptualize the transmission of language, folkways, lifestyles, group affiliation, and other cultural elements relevant to assimilation as entangled with processes of (White supremacist) racial stratification. I have already noted that an account of identity assimilation must be integrated with an account of incorporative assimilation and, specifically, that attention should be paid to the compatibility-rendering pressures of incorporative assimilation placed on an agent's efforts to form an identity. If we combine this idea with the considerations just given, then not only an asocial but an apolitical instance of identity assimilation would be exceptional. Consequently, an apolitical *account* of identity assimilation would be deficient. As I shall argue later in this essay, Asian American assimilation dynamics must be understood in the context of anti-Asian racism and xenophobia as well as correlatively conditional forms of polity incorporation.

Third, Asian American cultural retention and mainstream assimilation are conceptualized here in a broad fashion and without losing sight of political hierarchy. I am uncertain if there is any kind of Asian culture that unifies the many ethnicities that fall under that continental rubric. But since the Asian American Movement of the 1960s and 1970s, various regions of the United States have tried to develop an Asian American culture through some combination of political solidarity, ethical connection, and a broad range of aesthetic efforts. I believe the kind of culture in question here is one that aspires to make resonant some *common* structures within the American experience, broadly and sociopolitically conceived, had by a significant proportion of a significant number of the various ethnicities represented under the heading of "Asia."[3] As described in the short autobiographies of Asian American Movement activists compiled in *Asian Americans: The Movement and the Moment* and the compelling memoir by Helen Zia in *Asian American Dreams*, an Asian American social entity has been formed since the 1960s and a corresponding Asian American culture has been in formation since then.[4] In reality, this culture is aspirational in good part, but it is far more than nothing.[5] In any case, more typically, Asian American culture is understood *disjunctively*, where we simply gather the cultures of the various ethnicities that comprise Asian America and understand any of these cultures as both ethnic and Asian American. Sometimes, this is marked by pluralization, as when we speak of Asian American *cultures*. In this essay, cultural retention makes reference to either sense of Asian American culture—the historicized common culture and the disjunctively gathered ethnic cultures—since all of these have been politically subordinated in the United States.

Mainstream culture has clearly become more multicultural since the 1960s.[6] Much of this multiculturalism seems superficial since it has a strongly consumerist configuration or can be characterized as a kind of "feel good" boutique nicety.[7] But given the agency and ingenuity of minority groups as well as some contemporary liberal accommodationist efforts, the mainstream also involves some less superficial forms of multiculturalism. Importantly, whether superficially multicutural or not, the mainstream seems to be largely, even if imperfectly, White-configured. Here I refer not just to a privileged heterogeneous set of White folkways and affiliations, but also to the political phenomenon of White polity legitimation processes. Regarding the latter, what forms of multiculturalism emerge in the mainstream will often have the sanction of the White polity generally or its elite members, though this warranting power is eroding with the demographic transformations that are making many parts of the United States a minority majority. I think that the prevalence of sushi restaurants, martial arts studios, Zen references, and the like, which is by no means bad in itself, is perfectly compatible with and can obscure substantial anti-Asian racism and xenophobia. In fact, as I shall argue later, it is precisely this sort of problematic inclusion—conditional acceptance that conceals or mystifies subordination—that characterizes the accommodation of Asian Americans themselves in the mainstream.

Fourth, since choice is understood in terms of the options involved and the difficulty of their selection, we need to consider, even if only briefly, the nature of the alternatives to assimilation to better understand the decision to assimilate. As noted above, the topic of racial assimilation requires attention to the political organization of social life, its compatibility-rendering forces, and how these forces shape and influence an assimilation choice. So what set of options exists alongside assimilation in a racially stratified society like ours? Typically, assimilation is conceived of as rejecting, abandoning, or substituting one's home or native cultural ways and affiliations for generally White mainstream cultural ways and affiliations.[8] The alternative commonly discussed is refusal to assimilate.[9] Importantly, we can clarify other real options between complete substitution and total refusal, even if these two poles are understood to be imperfectly instantiated ideal-types.

One is biculturalism by means of what is sometimes called "additive acculturation," which, as the name suggests, is the process of acquiring new cultural ways without losing an original cultural capacity.[10] Many children of immigrants learn to "flip a switch" as context demands, moving, with varying degrees of ease, between ethnic culture and mainstream culture. Potentially, this could produce the feeling that one has some sort of cultural schizophrenia. At any rate, some instances of biculturalism may be a genuine alternative to assimilation, but I think the culture-switching capability by itself, even if culturally impressive and socially valuable, does not necessarily yield a politically significant alternative to assimilation. Crucial here is whether in important mainstream contexts, perhaps especially in public life or the civic sphere (as opposed to the privacy of one's home), nonmainstream cultural forms can be systematically enacted and found acceptable by the mainstream.

If a bicultural person typically or always acts in a mainstream manner in mainstream contexts, then the person is assimilated in the ways that count, politically speaking. The biculturalism is largely dichotomous in this respect. However, if a bicultural person, with some frequency and perhaps in a somewhat systematic way, enacted nonmainstream cultural forms in certain types of important mainstream contexts, then a politically significant alternative to assimilation (and its refusal) may exist in such a nondichotomous or crossover form of biculturalism.

Another is hybrid culturalism. At a trivial level, a Korean American might eat salad and spaghetti with chopsticks, and at a more serious level, he or she may in public spheres complexly blend Korean Confucian forms of deference, expressed through specifically Korean forms of body comportment, with American forms of self-assertion. This Korean American may also be bilingual and enjoy being able to switch between languages and thus particularly enjoy the company of similarly bilingual people. Perhaps hybrid culturalism is simply a more systematically integrated type of crossover biculturalism, or maybe crossover biculturalism is a species of hybrid culturalism, where the hybridity has been thinned out significantly. Either way, they offer further options beyond the dilemma of to-assimilate-or-not-to-assimilate. In fact, many seem to choose them as life paths.

In light of these considerations, when a home or neighborhood environment supports (or insists on) a nonmainstream culture, one can with relative ease (or with felt necessity) express oneself in terms of the nonmainstream culture at least in the home or neighborhood environment. Moving against this subject-forming undertow would require active resistance. Therefore, a decision to mostly or completely reject one's native or home culture when both biculturalism and hybrid culturalism are realistic options requires commitment, a principled narrowness, an unwillingness to compromise in the direction of duality or hybridity. Importantly, such a decision and correlated commitment to assimilate should be differentiated from cases in which biculturalism and hybridity are not real options. For example, a Korean adoptee in Minnesota, whose parents are White, simply would not have the right sorts of support, if any at all, to develop Korean cultural capacities. Not dissimilar would be the Filipino American child of, say, fifth- or sixth-generation Filipino Americans, who have themselves lost nearly every connection to Filipino or Filipino American cultures. In these types of cases, it is biculturalism or hybrid culturalism that would require commitment.

I turn now to a fuller account of the political context of identity assimilation.

Incorporative Assimilation and Liberal Orientalism

Crucial to the popular discourse of incorporative assimilation is a set of indices that gives substance to the idea of minority group incorporation. Nearly every index is understood to be configured by a standard set by Whites or Euro-Americans. They typically include: intermarriage with Whites; residential integration with Whites; achieving a socioeconomic status comparable to Whites (i.e., middle-class status), attaining a level of education comparable to Whites, English language acquisition, and the declining significance of racial or ethnic self-identification, which is to say self-deracialization. Within the scholarly discourse of incorporative assimilation, there seem to be two general approaches, the so-called straight-line model and the segmented model, and they are not always neatly separable. In the classic conception, the straight-line model, all or most racial or ethnic groups should and will eventually assimilate to mainstream Whiteness, according to most or all of the measures noted in the popular discourse, and many have added that just as Eastern and Southern Europeans so assimilated in the early twentieth century, Asians, especially East Asians, will follow suit in the twenty-first century, and so presumably will other non-White groups, eventually.[11]

The widely accepted critique of the straight-line model is that it ignores the strength and pervasiveness of racism and the size and impact of its effects. Also, whether or not racism is the cause, some subgroups significantly retain ethnic cultural affiliations. So, a rival model that more fully accommodates this critique, sometimes called the "segmented assimilation model," contends that only some groups, particularly European ones, follow the single-track trajectory of the classic conception, whereas non-White groups, in virtue of racism and cultural retention, follow different paths—for example, relative incorporation into the mainstream without loss of racial/ethnic identity or, more soberly, indefinite continuation in an underclass.[12]

I think it is not always clear that the segmented model is truly an advance on its theoretical predecessor. Some versions seem to harbor many of the problematic mainstream norms and ideals of the straight-line model and differentiate themselves from the straight-line model only by an empirically based cautionary note about predicting how far or how soon non-White groups will enter the mainstream. In any case, any assimilation account that takes racism seriously as social stratification, not just as individual prejudice, will have made some advance on the straight-line model.

Perhaps one indication of such political sobriety is how the account handles the notorious Model Minority Myth. This is the ideology that Asians as

a group have earned a kind of near-Whiteness in virtue of achieving many
of the social and economic standards typically attained by Whites, and that
they serve, therefore, as a model for other non-Whites and vindication of
the reality of American democracy. Almost the entirety of what is called
"Asian American Studies" rails against this ideology. Very briefly, this myth
is criticized for being insulting to other non-White groups, ignoring systemic
racism against other non-White groups, ignoring almost entirely many significant subgroups within Asian America that continue to suffer socioeco-
nomically, ignoring the working poor within valorized subgroups of Asian
America, leading people away from remedial, preventative, or compensatory
measures toward the aforementioned groups or subgroups, and subtly (or
not) valorizing Whites as the essential normative ideal.[13] I will not belabor
the point, but let me just quickly note that its problems can be summed up
this way: the Model Minority Myth is too inaccurate to be a truth and too
harmful to be an error; rather, it is a tool of social stratification or political
domination. In fact, it may be one of the greatest of the most recent inven-
tions of White supremacy as a political system.[14] The model minority myth
offers the polity a way to maintain racial hierarchy by partially incorporating
Asians while deftly normatively containing them in ways that make them
seem unthreatening. But don't take my word for it. Consider the outlook
of William McGurn, who was a long-time conservative writer for the *Wall
Street Journal* and the *National Review*, and a speechwriter for former president
George W. Bush. He marks out a distinctively anti-Black pathway for what we
might call the "Americanization" of Asian Americans:

> Precisely because Asian Americans are making it in their adoptive
> land, they hold the potential not only to add to Republican rolls
> but to define a bona-fide American language of civil rights. Today
> we have only one language of civil rights, and it is inextricably
> linked to government intervention, from racial quotas to set-aside
> government contracts. It is also an exclusively black-establishment
> language, where America's myriad other minorities are relegated to
> second-class citizenship.[15]

One of the upshots of the Model Minority Myth is the spread of public
and even scholarly opinion that Asian Americans "have made it" and that
they are "honorary Whites," which is to say that they constitute a model
for incorporative assimilation. Against this view, various Asian American-
ist scholars have argued not simply that Asian Americans continue to be

victimized by classic forms of racism, but that they are subjected to a distinctive type of racism that prevents them from being extensively incorporated into the mainstream and that they cannot truly be "honorary Whites." Specifically, many have argued that Asians in America have and continue to be conceived in terms of a distinctly xenophobic racism and that their political fate is as tenuous as U.S-Asia relations, which we know have been troubled by U.S. imperialism, anti-Asian immigration legislation, catastrophic wars across the twentieth century, and now tense relations with the Koreas, China, and most conspicuously with South Asian peoples that are rendered suspect by our recent wars in Iraq and Afghanistan and the so-called War on Terror.[16] In political scientist Claire Jean Kim's account, the extensive history of anti-Asian racism is configured largely by what she calls "civic ostracism."[17] In a similar vein, legal theorist Neil Gotanda contends that a critical legal history demonstrates that Asians in America are especially vulnerable to what he calls "citizenship nullification."[18] And legal theorist David Cole and political philosopher Falguni Sheth argue that the current incarceration and disappearings of South Asian Americans and Muslims in the United States is normatively continuous with the notorious incarceration of Japanese Americans during World War II.[19] From a diverse array of fields, then, we find over and over again that Asian Americans have been rendered rightless or distinctly vulnerable in ways that are profoundly linked to how they are racialized as inferior and how they have been deemed to be a *xenos*, cultural alien, or civic outsider. And yet, as noted, the model minority myth is an important emergent discourse. The combination, then, of civic exclusion and racism, on the one hand, and the model minority myth, on the other hand, has led sociologist Mia Tuan to describe Asian Americans as trapped by the double bind of being an "honorary White" and a "forever foreigner."[20] Or, as sociologist Edward Park and political scientist John Park suggest, Asian Americans have been longtime "probationary Americans."[21]

In spite of these works and the phenomena they point to, many scholars continue to speak favorably about the so-called Whitening of Asian Americans. Nadia Kim, one of the important sociologists working to critique the new versions of the straight-line model and some versions of the segmented model, voices critical concern this way:

> I ... question the methodologies that racial assimilation theses employ
> to forecast the racial future of the United States. ... most predictive
> studies do not empirically interview or systematically observe Asian
> Americans (or Latinos) in the United States to capture if and how

"race" might matter; nor do they draw on the many qualitative/his-
torical studies that have already done so. . . . Additionally, predictive
studies do not draw on data from representative surveys which tap
Asian Americans' experiences with racial bias and discrimination,
especially pertaining to global inequalities, immigration and social
citizenship.[22]

I could not agree more. And if, as Nadia Kim contends, race *matters* for
Asian Americans and we must tap Asian American *experiences*, then we do well
to consider the politics of self-evaluative emotions. For without our feelings,
nothing matters. Without our feelings, our experiences fail to engage. And
we find that Whiteness matters in a variety of problematic ways for Asian
Americans, who are so often glibly or perfunctorily presented as models of
incorporative assimilation and thereby cited as a reason to hail the progress
of American democracy. Before turning to this, I offer some general considerations on emotion and self-evaluative emotion.

Emotion, Self-Evaluative Emotion, and Phenomenology

In the last couple of decades, philosophy of emotion has become an active
and productive area of research. A general consensus in this subfield is that
emotion, and affectivity more generally, is not a brute sensation, like an itch
or tickle, and that it pervades virtually every aspect of human life and plays
a variety of positive and important roles.[23] Here I follow the lead of Michael
Stocker, Peter Goldie, and like-minded philosophers.

   In Stocker's view, what is important about emotion or affectivity is not
simply that they are needed for reason and for disclosing or understanding
the world, but also that they richly and necessarily color and constitute life
itself. Emotion or affectivity can be variously ends or goods, essential constituents, or added perfections of activities or relations, as when, respectively,
one has fun in playing, cares in a relationship, or takes pride in finishing a
book long in the making.[24] Living a life, then, is being widely and variously
emotionally engaged in activities and relations, and living well is being so
engaged in the right ways.

   Any plausible theory of the nature of emotion will construct an explanatory niche that is sensitive to these realities or, simply, to human reality. However, many such theories end up filling the niche with an account that reduces
emotion to belief or judgment or sometimes to desire. Such cognitivist or

conative accounts divest emotion of affect or feeling, which is the heart of emotion. This is because beliefs and judgments can be held without feeling, as when one believes or judges that weaving through highway traffic at ninety miles per hour is dangerous but is too distracted to feel fear. And desires too can be had without affectivity as when one desires to help many in need, and even does so out of that desire, but all the while is too exhausted to feel care. As Stocker contends, emotion may well be characterized as a *mode* of belief, judgment, or desire, when these are held in a feelingful manner. Thus, emotion cannot be reduced to any one or complex of these.[25] Stocker, and Goldie as well, contend that whatever else emotion may be, our lived experience shows that it is fundamentally a feelingful form of intentionality or an affective mode of awareness. And on Stocker's account, this intentionality must be understood not merely as an informing or disclosive state but as a participatory capacity, one that enables and constitutes activities and meaningful relations. Emotion is living intentionality.

In characterizing feeling or affectivity, Stocker notes that we come to a base-level phenomenon that can be triangulated by notions like care, interest, and concern. When I feel fear—actually *feel* fear—I do not merely, or perhaps at all, judge that something is threatening or dangerous, which I can do perfectly well in a very intellectual or ratiocinative way without any sense of charge or valence. Rather, I experience concern about or interest in this thing as threatening: I am *enlivened* to the danger; the threat *matters* to me. Thus, no care or interest, no affectivity or feeling. And without affectivity, we have no emotion. Moreover, since care or interest ushers us into the relevant aspects of the world, or since care or interest is how things matter to us, it follows that without such, the relevant kinds of mattering would be lost to us.

Peter Goldie contends that one of the features of emotion's intentionality is that it is a *feeling toward* some relevant feature of the world. In the end, I do not think this phrase, which suggests outward projection, describes our phenomenology adequately. Our experience is better described in terms of disclosures or presentings.[26] But it does usefully highlight the transcendental feature of intentionality while making essential reference to feelings. In his account, then, fear is a feeling toward danger; contempt a feeling toward inferiority or lowliness; and shame a feeling toward one's dishonored state or failure to realize an ideal. I think the importance of this general idea cannot be overstated. Something matters or has import in a dangerous way, offensive way, or an intriguing way precisely because of the types of feeling found in fear, resentment, or curiosity. If there was no feeling, nothing would matter to us. We could aptly be conceptualized strictly in terms of beliefs and desires, and arguably we would no longer be considering real human beings. In fact, if we divested human beings of feeling and thus of emotion, we would in the same act be divesting the world of the offensive, the exhilarating, the threatening, the lowly, the repulsive, the intriguing, the adorable, and all the other attributes that exist in virtue of their mattering to us or being important to us. Feeling and worldly import are facets of the same structure.[27] And this is why feelings are almost never "merely" feelings and, as we shall see, why consideration of them is so important for political philosophy.

I think it is important to emphasize, whether or not Goldie or Stocker would agree, that the feeling involved in feeling toward is a feeling *of* the body. Here I do not mean the feeling involved in a bodily sensation, like a pounding heart or a constricting throat, though that can be a part of the feeling in question.[28] I mean, rather, a feeling had or possessed by the body and specifically the living phenomenal body.

One of the significant contributions of Merleau-Ponty is a way of understanding how the body is not a sophisticated mechanism that the mind skillfully uses, but rather a sentient, sensitive, living, animate entity and absolutely essential to understanding our kind of being in the world. In a famous passage about a subject's two hands touching each other, Merleau-Ponty notes that we do not have the experience of touching and the experience of being touched side by side, completely separate from each other, as when one sees an object next to another object. Rather, a distinctive ambiguity descends on the experiences in question because we can and do alternate between feeling one's hand and one's other hand being felt. And so, throughout, we have the enactments of an animate entity, not the manipulations of a mere mechanism.[29] Also, he gives remarkable articulation to the idea that perception is always perception from a particular bodily point of view or angle of emanation or postural stance and that with finesse and nuance, the motor functions of our body are in constant coordination with perception enabling us to strengthen our "grip on the world," as when we, *without reflection or effort*, focus our eyes, tilt our heads, sit up, stand, or walk around an object to enable, maintain, or improve perception. Indeed, as phenomenologists often point out, the body is our opening onto the world, and correlatively our sense of possibilities in the world is embodied. Importantly, this living body can have this animated responsiveness and dynamic attunement at a tacit or preconscious level, and this preconscious responsivenss is *crucial* to our explicitly reflective activities.[30]

In the account of emotion discussed above, I noted how Stocker and Goldie insist on the affective intentionality of emotion and thus concern or interest in salient elements of the world. If we accommodate the insights of Merleau-Ponty, then this link between the subject's concern and the world's imports is mediated through the living phenomenal body. Part of the sentience or animation of the phenomenal body is sensory perception intimately linked to motor intentionality in such a way that we can effectively intelligently engage with the world, but feeling what is significant in the world is also part of this condition. And these aspects of the phenomenal body come together in a variety of ways. One of the most obvious is when perception and body comportment is guided by affective awareness of special features of the world. For example, a tourist afraid of theft may visually scan the faces or movements of an encroaching crowd for potential thieves or constantly feel for the presence of a wallet or the tautness of a purse strap.

If we return to some of Goldie's language, we might say that emotions are feelings toward only because they are *feelings of* the phenomenal body, by which again I mean a feeling had by the lived body, not a sensation of the body. Thus, "feeling toward" is shorthand for "feeling-of-thus-feeling-toward." Ultimately, the focus of emotion is worldly imports, and the phenomenal body is often transparent or backgrounded in the experience. So it might also be said that emotion is a feeling *through* the body *to* what matters in the world. Shifting away from Goldie's projective language to classic phenomenological locutions, emotions are feelingful disclosures or presentings of what matters to us. But they are more than this. Returning to the earlier discussion, emotions in their myriad forms and occurrences are world-constituting in addition to being world-disclosing. In having emotion, we deeply participate in the world.[31]

In light of this brief account of emotion, I offer now a few words on self-evaluative emotions. The classic trinity is shame, guilt, and pride. Sometimes, embarrassment is included. But I think it is clear that if we look at our actual emotional lives, we find that the spectrum of self-evaluative emotion is much more expansive. Many of our paradigmatically other-directed feelings can be rendered reflexive, in both interesting and mundane ways. One can experience self-respect, self-love, self-hate, self-disgust, self-contempt, and self-directed forms of adoration, disappointment, anger, rage, and so on. But for my purposes, I briefly discuss shame and self-contempt.[32]

Though difficult to define, shame admits of general characterization.[33] To begin, it is commonly observed that shame involves a painful apprehension of the self or its attributes as diminished, lowered, or lessened somehow, attended often by a hiding impulse. This lowered regard can result from noting that one has failed to live up to certain cherished ideals. But this cannot be the whole story of the onset of shame, for at least three reasons. First, as is common, people can undergo shame against their considered judgment, which here may be the belief that one has fared well morally or in life at the particular time in question. The fact that one can feel shame in spite of such a belief suggests that the intrapsychic authority behind the condemning force in shame can ignore features of reality, like the fact that one has *not* failed to live up to one's ideals.[34] As psychoanalytic accounts of shame clarify, a prime candidate for the internal authority is an imago, an internalization of, typically, one's parents, which is often modified into a demanding psychic structure, sometimes of a very severe kind.[35] Second, without oneself failing, one may feel a kind of associational shame through strong identification with another person or a group that the agent deems to have failed in some respect. Third, as John Deigh and Sandra Bartky have emphasized, the sense of diminution need not even concern failure in the voluntaristic or accountability sense, whether in regard to ideals the agent explicitly sanctions or to ideals that constitute the imago.[36] For it might be a result of coming into a world in which one is in some sense a failed or diminished subject well before arriving in it, precisely like the situation faced by the racially stigmatized. When this is the case, the lowered view of the self is not the result of considerations of flawed agency but of flawed being. In the now familiar story, which has a variety of theoretical articulations, the agent internalizes demeaning images and messages in the course of learning social reality. Importantly, these images and messages do not simply float around in culture. They are politically organized, and the discussion of the prior section shows that anti-Asian messages deriving from American orientalism is a case in point. Therefore, this sort of shame is not the result of failed agency but the *inward resonance of a suppressive social order*. And, of course, these three forms of shame are not mutually exclusive.

Self-contempt, though often collapsed under the category of shame, has a different dynamic. My readings of psychic doubling in Du Bois (i.e., double consciousness) and Fanon (i.e., corporeal malediction) lead me to think that they were onto this distinction between shame and self-contempt, even if neither elaborated on it.[37] In any case, the paradigm of contempt is other-directed.[38] One feels negative affect, perhaps some sense of offense, at somebody's or something's perceived inferior nature or qualities. More than this, however, one's feeling is phenomenologically hierarchical: with varying degrees of intensity or clarity, one feels in the affective backdrop one's own superior status relative to the target whose perceived inferior qualities occasioned the negative feelings or sense of offense. Also, in typical cases, there is a desiderative element wherein the agent seeks intrapsychically and sometimes more literally and outwardly some sort of detachment from the "unworthy" or "sullying" target. This seems to indicate the basic psychological function of the emotion: status-conservation. And contempt may have this function, at least typically, within a psychic esteem economy, which is why contemptuous agents often feel some sense of pleasure or pride over their demeaned target. Given this basic function and the highly interpersonal character of contempt, the primary (though not exclusive) role of contempt in the wider social ecology would seem to be the preservation of social hierarchies. So self-contempt will be characterized by negative affect, maybe involving a sense of offense, felt toward one's own perceived inferior nature or qualities along with a sense of vertical detachment, perhaps tinged with pleasure, from one's own self. Depending on one's situation, history, and personality structures, this could be felt in a cool or hot way, experienced episodically or pervasively, mingled with pity or with anger, followed by shame or by defensive other-contempt, accompanied with chiding of oneself or with violence toward oneself, and so on and so forth. And as with shame, certain kinds of intransigent self-contempt can indicate the inward resonance of a suppressive social order, rather than accountability for failed agency.

Having briefly described shame and self-contempt, it will be useful to bring them together in a comparative frame. There are many forms of activity and passivity in emotion. In one respect, self-contempt is phenomenologically active in a way that shame is not. In shame, one realizes, concedes, acknowledges, bows before, or otherwise passively accepts within the parameters of the emotion's phenomenology the painful conception of the self as constitutive of the emotion. By contrast, in self-contempt, one judges, belittles, pokes at, mocks, sneers, or otherwise actively asserts or pushes a disparaging conception of the self on the self. So if shame centrally involves realizing, self-contempt centrally involves judging or contemning.

Another comparative point to consider, a significant one, is the kinds of intrapsychic identification and proximity involved in the two emotions. It seems clear that in shame one is intimately connected, indeed fully identified, with one's own self, which is why the ashamed agent can receive the condemning givens in a deeply personal manner. But in self-contempt, one looks down upon one's shame-able self and, hence, is distinctly detached from one's own self. The case of shame seems relatively straightforward in this respect, whereas the case of self-contempt does not. The agent-self, that is the contemning self, in the process of detaching from the object-self, that is the contemned self, disaffiliates from the main self, as it were, because that object-self is the main self, which is to say the self with whom one is ordinarily identified and with whom one ordinarily self-identifies. Therefore, who is the agent, or contemning self, who is looking down on his or her own self, or main self, in contempt? Part of the unclarity here results from the fact that the contemning self, though real in agency, is in some sense illusory from the standpoint of its identification structure. The contemning self takes on the perspective, and intrapsychically assumes the position, of the superior in the specific or general respects in which the main self is deemed inferior. But since in actuality the contemned self is the main self, the contemning self is fabricated from the materials of *an other's identity*, specific or general, accurate or distorted. The materials for this fabrication of the contemning self are gathered and framed by a process of imaginative identification. And the imaginative affiliation or projection is, of course, directed on those perceived to be relevantly superior to the disparagingly perceived main self. This attachment to, and alignment with, perceived superiority is typically a precondition for the production of self-contempt. Since the preconditional attachment and alignment can remain mostly in the phenomenological backdrop, and sometimes receive support from the social order, the source of self-contempt can remain largely hidden and the production of self-contempt relatively easy.

> As a final note, consider Sartre's provocative depiction of the assimilated Jew. Like the timid person, like the scrupulous person, the Jew is not content to act or think; he sees himself act, he sees himself think. . . . It is not the man but the *Jew* whom the Jews seek to know in themselves through introspection; and they wish to know him *in order to deny him*. . . . The Jew, because he knows he is under observation, takes the initiative and attempts to look at himself through the eyes of others. This objectivity toward himself is still another ruse of inauthenticity; while he contemplates himself with the "detachment" of another; he becomes another person, a pure witness.
>
> However, he knows that this detachment from himself will be effective only if it is ratified by others. That is why one finds in him so often the faculty of assimilation. . . . He hopes to become "a man," nothing but a man, a man like other men, by taking in all thoughts of man and acquiring a human point of view of the universe. (italics his)[39]

Sartre notes that in a certain type of Jewish person, the detachment from and negation of one's own self is not free-floating. Rather, these issue from the standpoint of the imagined, presumably superior, normal, or normative Gentile. In addition, this doubling of the self and affiliation with the Gentile is deemed to be tenuous without the social support of Gentiles, and this helps to explain some types of Jewish assimilation. What I've described above, then, can be understood as providing some of the affective dynamics of this sort of activity. A version of this phenomenon can be seen in a couple of the cases to be discussed.

Identity Assimilation, Emotions, and Strategies of Self-Making

As noted in the early sections of this essay, conceptions of identity assimilation shift the focus from large-scale group processes to an agent's self-conception, ethical life, and engagement with the world. So why is an examination of self-evaluative emotions relevant here? Generally speaking, assimilation or its alternatives is a self-evaluative project since it is a self-directed normative shaping of one's own identity. And insofar as anything matters in this project, the emotions are already involved—not just discrete emotions but a whole affective constellation. One of the most conspicuous involvements of emotion concerns the stigma of Asianness or Orientalness in a polity that continues to be stratified by race. As discussed earlier, classic forms of anti-Asian racism endure and the xenophobic or civically ostracizing forms of racism retain a deep and wide configuring structure in the U.S polity. And here it is interesting to consider John Rawls's classic statement that a people's self-respect is among the primary goods of a just society.[40] In a similar vein, recently, Martha Nussbaum has argued at length that shame should never play a role in law or public policy. The effects of shame are overly undermining when they derive from the issuances of power.[41] Although anti-Asian stigmata are not a part of public policy in any direct sense, they are nevertheless features of the public order, and presumably Nussbaum's forceful criticisms against legal shaming would apply to cultural and political shaming as well.

Among the various forms of anti-Asian stigma, at least three seem to have some real weight in our culture: (1) the aesthetic devaluation of Asian faces and bodies; (2) the derogation of alleged Asian personality traits, especially in terms of passivity, nonindividuality, or social ineptness; and (3) the derogation of alleged Asian foreignness, alienness, or being a FOB (Fresh Off the Boat). Each of these, and still others, are potentially shaming or productive of self-contempt. These are among the worldly imports that are the counterparts of Asian American shame and self-contempt. And, as noted, these emotions may be experienced as intransigent inner resonances of the social hierarchy. Consequently, one must deal or cope with a world in which one's identity is already, seemingly everywhere jeopardized.[42]

Here, my claim is not that in virtue of the stigmata, all Asians feel shame or self-contempt and still less that all Asians are characterologically shame-prone or shame-ridden. Rather, my point is that in virtue of these entrenched public stigmata and the conditions that sustain them, they all potentially experience, to use made-up words, *shameability* and *self-contemnability*, that is to say, a distinctive vulnerability to being shamed or undergoing self-contempt. Also, my concern here is not to brand all cases of assimilation. My concern is with the how and why of identity assimilation, especially when biculturalism and hybridity are options. So given the particularities of certain cases, perhaps there can be a genuinely unproblematic preference to disidentify with one's ethnic group. In addition, Korean adoptees in Minnesota, for example, may have very few opportunities to do anything other than assimilate, and no blame is laid on them. But these sorts of cases aside, there are plenty of others, the majority of them surely, where the issue of stigma and shame-ability emerge as nontrivial considerations. And so, in virtue of the capacity to be shamed or undergo self-contempt, most Asians must devise a psychic strategy to contend with or manage this sort of vulnerability in the world. Forgiveness and courage may offer analogues. Just as forgiveness is effective normative management of resentment or hatred, and courage is the effective normative management of fear, Asians Americans must develop efficacious normative structures of esteem or stigma management.

But what sorts of effects have been produced by anti-Asian stigmata in our polity? Have Asian Americans successfully produced effective anti-racist forms of managing shame and self-contempt? Since the 1960s Asian American Movement, a strong sense of group pride has been formed as a way of dealing with anti-Asian stigmata and other forms of racism. This would seem to offer one effective coping structure. Alternatively, perhaps Asian Americans could follow a path of genuine democratic deracination and thus strive to repel anti-Asian stigmata and any form of racism without any sense of racial identity. I have my doubts about this as a general course of group action at this moment in time. In any case, the assimilation studies discussed at the start of the essay do not ask these sorts of questions. They only see the satisfaction of exterior indices of mainstream incorporation.

The exception of course is the measure of declining racial self-identification. But they do not take seriously the possibility that some Asian Americans may have a declining sense of Asian self-identification in virtue of an inclining sense of White self-identification. And surely White self-identification is not deracination! Assimilation of this sort cannot be heralded as proof of "getting beyond race" or entering a "postracial America."

Consider here a recent Harvard University student honors thesis featured in a *Washington Post* article.[43] Jennifer Tsai, while a senior at Harvard, sought to examine the racial attitudes of her Asian American Harvard peers. In her thesis, she notes,

> Among blacks, 'acting white' is socially stigmatized, but Asian students who 'act white' usually occupy the more socially prestigious positions. Because 'acting Asian' is equated with acting foreign or like a nerd, 'acting white' among Asian people becomes a source of pride, and is valued as the ability to assimilate into American society. While both performances are frequently practiced, the Asian students who 'acted white' are more likely to achieve extracurricular activity status within the school, which often led to admissions into more prestigious colleges.[44]

And the reporter noted that Tsai told him, "One of the most alarming features of my research was how Asian students who went to Harvard were very aware of and often shied away from having too many Asian friends. They saw having only White friends as sort of a badge of honor."[45] Tsai also mentions that at Harvard, there is a thirty-four-member Facebook group, called Twinkies, that aims to gather people who are "yellow" on the outside and "White" on the inside.

Earlier, I mentioned shame vulnerability and the need for effective and proper ways of dealing with it. Jennifer Tsai's research illustrates two kinds of coping. First, those Asian Americans who sought to emulate whiteness and even go as far as to avoid Asian friends—they like to be the lone Asian within a White group—seem to manifest a strategy consistent with what Erving Goffman calls a "normal deviant." On his account, a normal deviant is one who accepts the normative force of the relevant stigma but seeks to be "unobtrusive" in the right sorts of ways to receive conditional acceptance by the dominant group.[46] The shame- or self-contempt-inducing vulnerability in question is a disposition, and the "Lone Asian" has through a certain type of assimilation not eliminated the disposition but reduced the number of ways in which it can be triggered. Though Goffman doesn't put it this way, the Lone Asian's strategy is a tenuous form of shame repression, not shame elimination. This strategy may also be expressive of self-contempt, given the very strong identification with Whites and the apparent disdain directed on other Asians.

Second, the so-called Twinkies at Harvard seem so unabashed about their White-valuation—recall that they actually formed a group and thus are *not* the Asian loners just discussed—that they seem to have achieved something extraordinary: White-identified *shamelessness*. They appear to have moved beyond "shameability" in virtue of a peculiarly ironic disconnection from Asianness. The former type of person, the Lone Asian, partly accepts his or her Asian identity because he or she values being and, importantly, *being seen* as an atypical or exceptional Asian who can "hang" with Whites. They value themselves as a kind of "credit to the race."[47] But the Harvard Twinkies do not seem to have the same anxieties about being accorded the status of exceptional Asian. Conspicuously, neither do they seem to care about being or being seen as so-called White-wannabes.[48] For them, Asianness is purely external, and their ability to negotiate or play with this externality makes their rationale for forming the Twinkie collective primarily instrumental. Presumably, their shared outlook offers a networking opportunity, or perhaps they can get together for comic relief. So if the Twinkie collective disbanded, these Harvard students would not grieve the loss of one of their last ties to Asianness. Nor would they worry about their unabashed White-identification.

In contrast, if completely separated from Asians, the Harvard Lone Asian would lose something very meaningful: a group that he or she inferiorizes in order to have a contrast class against which he or she shines as an exception. Returning to Sartre's discussion of the self-contemptuous Jew, the Lone Asian seems to roughly instantiate the character type Sartre delineates. But the members of the Twinkie collective seem to have "perfected" their White-identified assimilation, for they no longer have the devaluing kind of self-monitoring and need for ratification that Sartre attributes to the Lone Jew, as it were. It seems possible that some of them arrived at that condition in unproblematic ways. Perhaps they truly have an "innocent" aesthetic disinclination toward Asian or Asian American culture or identity, and this somehow has no connection to anti-Asian pressures in the wider public. But given the foregoing, for the majority of them, the completion of White-affirmation habits seems a plausible explanation. In any case, neither form of coping is deracination, and arguably neither of them is unproblematic assimilation.

To fill out the scene further, consider some of the qualitative research conducted by sociologists Rosalind Chou and Joe Feagin on the lived experience of a variety of Asian Americans.[49] In examining "the sociopsychological costs of white hostility and discrimination," Chou and Feagin summarize their findings thus:

> some respondents report having gotten openly angry about racist events, or have worked collectively to respond, but such overt responses are relatively rare. Instead, our respondents mostly seem to manage discriminatory incidents internally and individually. The personal battle with hostility and discrimination often leads to feelings of isolation, sadness, disillusionment, or hopelessness. Serious consequences flow from such emotional withdrawal, and/or suppression of memories of racial hostility and discrimination. Seeking out professional assistance appears to be relatively rare for these respondents or their families. Moreover, when a few have tried to find help, they usually have not known where to turn or have been misunderstood or rejected by those whom they contacted.[50]

Unlike the presumably privileged Harvard students, these Asian American respondents seem to be both more trapped by their "shameability" and have less material and status-related resources for dealing with anti-Asian stigmata and racism. In fact, as I read the interviews, many of the subjects were perfectly willing to talk about their "objective" problems but seemed to be unable or unwilling to discuss their shame or shame vulnerability in any real detail, which is of course consistent with the hiding or covering impulse in shame. When one is ashamed, one is typically ill at ease announcing this fact. But the largely inferred nature of their shame or "shameability" was itself revealing and important for a study concerned with the dynamics of self-evaluative emotion. In fact, it is interesting to note that Helen Block Lewis, in her classic treatment of shame, also found that in a very large number of the clinical cases out of which she produced her book, shame was rarely cited by the subjects as part of the problem for which they sought clinical help. She points out that the overall pattern in these subjects was the presence of "overt but unnamed" shame. And precisely this seems to be a recurring element in the interviews conducted by Chou and Feagin of ordinary Asian

Americans. What is more, some of the subjects indicated that they felt a certain helplessness with regard to their stigmatization and the way it oppressed them. I can think of few psychosocial phenomena that exacerbate shame more than the sense of helplessness.

As I noted earlier, I do not think that all Asians suffer from racial shame or self-contempt. Interestingly, many contend that California Asians, especially those in San Francisco and Los Angeles, have overcome anti-Asian stigmata. There is surely something to this. I now live in the San Francisco area, so I see this phenomenon in contrast to Asian Americans I knew when growing up in various parts of the Northeast and Midwest. But I have noticed that many Asian American young adults in the San Francisco area nevertheless feel distinctly uncomfortable about the stigma of being a FOB. This is not necessarily shame or self-contempt since it may be fear of the consequences of other people's benighted views about recent immigrants. But I have also found it curious that many of these same people find it difficult to make friends with recently arrived Asian immigrants and strenuously emphasize the American aspect of their being Asian Americans. In fact, I often hear of sub–Asian American student organizations—like clubs for Korean Americans or Filipino Americans—in various universities in California, struggle with the issue of relations between, for example, Korean immigrants and second- or third-generation Korean Americans or Filipino immigrants and second-, third-, or fourth-generation Pinoys/Pinays. On my campus, I have known Asian immigrants who have felt more comfortable in the International Student Association than in their respective ethnic student clubs, not because of language barriers but because of the stigma of being a FOB foisted on them by people who claim the same ethnicity. Perhaps this is all merely incidental. But if the foregoing holds, then we have just as good an explanation, if not a better one, in terms of residual struggles with the xenophobic elements of anti-Asian stigmata. Correlatively, in such communities, the modest ability to modify the relevant worldly imports is telling.

If the foregoing holds, then insofar as Asians are the focal point of celebrations of a "postracial" America, the strategy of Asian American valorization backfires to a large extent. Psychic forms of White supremacy persist with vitality, even if not universally, in the Asian American community. Arguably, healthy forms of Asian American self-identification retain their normative appeal, in contrast to complete deracination and to White-identification, because they enable Asian Americans to more effectively engage with the world they have been given. But that argument must be left for another occasion.

Notes

1. Consider, for example, the works of two widely different political philosophers, Herbert Marcuse and John Rawls. The former connects critical theory with psychoanalytic psychology—see, for example, *One Dimensional Man: Studies in the Ideology of Advanced Industrial Society*, 2nd ed. (Boston: Beacon Press, 1991). The latter connects liberal contract theory with Aristotelian moral psychology—see his *A Theory of Justice* (Cambridge, Mass.: Harvard University Press, 1971). Whether their connective work is plausible is of course another issue.

2. Political White supremacy, whether or not this title has been adopted, has been conceived as one of the major political traditions of the United States. And some go further to argue that it has been at the core of the U.S. polity. For just a sampling, consider Michael Omi and Howard Winant, *Racial Formation in the United States: From the 1960s to the 1990s*, 2nd ed. (New York: Routledge Press, 1994); Charles Mills, *The Racial Contract* (Ithaca, N.Y.: Cornell University Press, 1997); Rogers M. Smith, *Civic Ideals: Conflicting Visions of Citizenship in U.S. History* (New Haven, Conn.: Yale University Press, 1997); Gary Gerstle, *American Crucible: Race and Nation in the Twentieth Century* (Princeton, N.J.: Princeton University Press, 2001); Gary Okihiro, *The Columbia Guide to Asian American History* (New York: Columbia University Press, 2001); Evelyn Nakano Glenn, *Unequal Freedom: How Race and Gender Shaped American Citizenship and Labor* (Cambridge, Mass.: Harvard University Press, 2002); and Dylan Rodriguez, *Suspended Apocalypse: White Supremacy, Genocide, and the Filipino Condition* (Minneapolis: University of Minnesota Press, 2010).

3. There is good deal of complexity and controversy here. I offer a fuller discussion in my essay "What Is Asian American Philosophy?" *Philosophy in Multiple Voices*, ed. George Yancey (Lanham: Rowman & Littlefield, 2007). For another account, see David Palumbo-Liu, *Asian/American: Historical Crossings of a Racial Frontier* (Palo Alto, Calif.: Stanford University Press, 1999).

4. See Steven Louie and Glenn Omatsu, eds., *Asian Americans: The Movement and the Moment* (Los Angeles, Calif.: UCLA Asian American Studies Center Press, 2006); and Helen Zia, *Asian American Dreams: The Emergence of an American People* (New York: Farrar, Strauss, and Giroux, 2000).

5. It has had limits, to be sure. For example, it seems to have been paradigmatically about Chinese, Japanese, and Filipino American experiences since these were the groups most heavily represented in the

Asian American Movement. But in recent decades, Korean Americans, Vietnamese Americans, and Indian Americans have been increasingly included and, lately, other Southeast Asian Americans and Pacific Islander Americans as well. So the limits do not seem to be principled, and there seem to be efforts at expansion or inclusion. I think the great challenge for the making and maintenance of Asian American culture is the combination of two broad processes, namely resistance by an orientalist polity against meaningful and critical Asian American culture-making and sustained immigration from Asia since racial blockades were removed in 1965.

6. For some interesting documentation with regard to Asian or Asian American influences, see Jeff Yang, Dina Gan, Terry Hong, and the staff of *A. Magazine*, eds., *Eastern Standard Time: A Guide to Asian Influence on American Culture: From Astro Boy to Zen Buddhism* (New York: Metro East Publications, 1997).

7. On the notion of boutique multiculturalism, see Stanley Fish, "Boutique Multiculturalism, or Why Liberals Are Incapable of Thinking About Hate Speech," *Critical Inquiry* 23, no. 2 (Winter 1997). Thanks go to Yoko Arisaka for this reference.

8. For two sophisticated accounts of the normativity of assimilation (e.g., whether it is morally permissible for people of color to assimilate to the mainstream), see Tommie Shelby, *We Who Are Dark: The Philosophical Foundations of Black Solidarity* (Cambridge, Mass..: Harvard University Press, 2005) and Eamonn Callan, "The Ethics of Assimilation," *Ethics* 115, no. 3 (2005): 471–500. I should note here that how one characterizes real-world assimilation dynamics can make a difference for normative assessment, and my account of this differs in some respects from what we find in Callan's important essay. For example, he notes the potential relevance of state-imposed assimilationism for the moral assessment of assimilation and asserts that such a condition does not exist currently in the United States. He is right, but there can be substantial forms of polity-preserving assimilationism that are not state-imposed in any explicit way. Would these alternative forms of assimilationism make a difference for moral assessment? One way to think of this essay is to see it as offering the beginnings of a case for the existence of one such form of assimilationism.

9. In empirical psychology, there is more attention to alternatives. The work of John Berry has been particularly influential in ethnic psychology, including Asian American psychology. See John W. Berry, "Conceptual

Approaches to Acculturation," in *Acculturation: Advances in Theory, Measurement, and Applied Research*, ed. Kevin Chun, Pamela Balls-Organista, and Gerardo Marin, (American Psychological Association, 2003). I think his account is insufficiently informed by political theory and even takes as the paradigm scenario of analysis the free encounter of two people from different cultures. On his account, then, racism is primarily about discrimination, and discrimination is but an obstacle to multicultural integration. But I believe racial stratification deeply configures polity and subjectivity and thus the underlying context in which discrimination is raised as an issue. I think some of the work of Asian American psychologists reveals subtle tensions due to the use of critical history derived from Asian American studies, which powerfully articulates American Orientalism, and their inheritance of the Berry model. Obviously, adequate treatment of this matter extends beyond the confines of this essay.

10. On the idea of acculturation, see Kevin Chun, Pamela Balls-Organista, and Gerardo Marin, ed., *Acculturation: Advances in Theory, Measurement, and Applied Research*.

11. The Chicago School of Sociology was an early and influential advocate of this view. See, for example, Robert E. Park, *Old World Traits Transplanted* (New York: Harper and Brothers, 1921). For perhaps the most sophisticated resuscitation of this type of account, see Richard Alba and Victor Nee, *Remaking the American Mainstream: Assimilation and Contemporary Immigration* (Cambridge, Mass.: Harvard University Press, 2003).

12. See, for example, "Segmented Assimilation: Issues, Controversies, and Recent Research on the New Second Generation," *International Migration Review* 31, no. 4 (1997): 825–858.

13. There are many works that explain and critique this myth. Here are just a few: Edward J. W. Park and John S. W. Park, *Probationary Americans: Contemporary Immigration Policies and the Shaping of Asian American Communities* (New York: Routledge Press, 2005); Don T. Nakanishi & Tina Yamano Nishida, eds., *The Asian American Education Experience: A Source Book for Teachers and Students* (New York: Routledge, 1995); Rosalind Chou and Joe Feagin, *The Myth of the Model Minority: Asian Americans Facing Racism* (Boulder, Colo.: Paradigm Publishers, 2008); and Min Zhou and James V. Gatewood, eds., *Contemporary Asian America: A Multidisciplinary Reader* (New York: New York University Press, 2000), chs. 19–21.

14. On the notion of White supremacy as a political system, see Charles Mills, *The Racial Contract* (Ithaca, N.Y.: Cornell University Press, 1999).

15. William McGurn, "The Silent Minority," *National Review*, June 24, 1991,

128 *David Haekwon Kim*

19. Cited from Glenn Omatsu, "The 'Four Prisons' and the Movements of Liberation: Asian American Activism from the 1960s to the 1990s," in *The State of Asian America: Activism and Resistance in the 1990s*, Karin Aguilar-San Juan, ed. Boston: South End Press, 1994, 49.
16. Racism and xenophobia are clearly related, but they are separable. Asians, among others, have been classically subjected to both and in very evident ways. Some of these ideas are being worked out in Ron Sundstrom and David Kim, "Xenophobia and Racism," *Critical Philosophy of Race* (forthcoming).. Claire Jean Kim, "The Racial Triangulation of Asian Americans," in *Asian Americans and Politics*, ed. Gordon H. Chang (Palo Alto, Calif.: Stanford University Press, 2001), ch. 2.
18. Neil Gotanda, "Citizenship Nullification: The Impossibility of Asian American Politics," in *Asian Americans and Politics*, Gordon Chang, ed., ch. 3.
19. David Cole, *Enemy Aliens* (New York: New Press, 2003), and Falguni Sheth, *Toward a Political Philosophy of Race* (Albany: State University of New York Press, 2009). Sheth's account has a broader focus and a more radical assessment of race and liberal societies. It is an important contribution to political philosophical treatments of race.
20. Mia Tuan,*Forever Foreigners or Honorary Whites: The Asian Ethnic Experience Today* (Brunswick: Rutgers University Press, 1999).
21. Edward Park and John Park, *Probationary Americans*.
22. Nadia Kim, "Critical Thoughts on Asian American Assimilation in the Whitening Literature," *Social Forces* 86, no. 2 (December 2007): 562. See, as well, her excellent book, *Imperial Citizens: Koreans and Race from Seoul to L.A.* (Palo Alto, Calif.: Stanford University Press, 2008).
23. For a range of views historically presented, see Robert Solomon, ed., *What Is an Emotion? Classic and Contemporary Readings*, 2nd ed. (New York: Oxford University Press, 2002). And for book-length treatments, it is interesting to compare the different approaches and emphases of such fine work as, Michael Stocker with Elizabeth Hegeman, *Valuing Emotion* (New York: Cambridge University Press, 1996); Sue Campbell, *Interpreting the Personal: Expression and the Formation of Feelings* (Ithaca, N.Y.: Cornell University Press, 1998); Martha Nussbaum, *Upheavals of Thought: The Intelligence of Emotion* (New York: Cambridge University Press, 2003); Jesse Prinz, *Gut Reactions: A Perceptual Theory of Emotion* (New York: Oxford University Press, 2004); and Matthew Ratcliffe, *Feelings of Being: Phenomenology, Psychiatry, and the Sense of Reality* (New York: Oxford University Press, 2008).

24. See Stocker, *Valuing Emotions*, esp. chs. 5–6.

25. Stocker, *Valuing Emotions*, ch. 1.

26. Interestingly, a similar concern can be raised with the phenomenologist, Charles Taylor, in his essay, "Self-Interpreting Animals," where he characterizes emotion not only as an affective mode of awareness, which seems fine, but also in terms of import *ascriptions*. I would have thought that a phenomenologist would have talked in terms of import disclosures or disclosings. This essay is chapter 2 of his *Human Agency and Language: Philosophical Papers 1* (New York: Cambridge University Press, 1985).

27. See Charles Taylor, "Self-Interpreting Animals," for another take on this idea.

28. On Stocker's account, feelings often involve bodily feelings in the sense of felt sensations of the body, as in the obvious case of fear churning in the stomach or anger heating one's collar. But, contrary to a position like William James's, Stocker contends that not all feelings are bodily in this way. Some of the subtler passions, like hope or curiosity, or instances of them, are felt more in the soul, as it were. Though emotion typically involves bodily feeling in the sense of recruiting bodily sensations, such sensations are not necessary for emotion. So he is only committed to the notion that the feelings or affectivity at the core of emotion are *psychic feelings*. Stocker's case for emotions as psychic, not bodily, feelings is phenomenological. Goldie adds to this account. He argues that the world-directed intentionality crucial to emotion can only be discerned in psychic feelings, not bodily feelings. See Peter Goldie, *The Emotions: A Philosophical Exploration* (New York: Oxford University Press, 2000), 58.

29. Maurice Merleau-Ponty, *Phenomenology of Perception*, trans. Colin Smith (New York: Routledge, 1989), 92–3. For valuable discussion of this, see M. C. Dillon, *Merleau-Ponty's Ontology*, 2nd ed. (Evanston, Ill.: Northwestern University Press, 1997), ch. 8.

30. On this foundational topic, I have found helpful: M. C. Dillon, *Merleau-Ponty's Ontology*, 2nd ed.; Shaun Gallagher, *How the Body Shapes the Mind* (New York: Oxford University Press, 2006); and Hubert Dreyfus, "Intelligence Without Representation—Merleau-Ponty's Critique of Mental Representation: The Relevance of Phenomenology to Scientific Explanation," *Phenomenology and the Cognitive Sciences* 1, no. 4 (2002): 367–383.

31. I think it is not a stretch to read some of Stocker's work as running parallel to Heidegger's. As Matthew Ratcliffe has argued in *Feelings of Being*, ch. 2, an emended Heideggerian account of mood can help us understand

that there is a type of feeling, which he calls "existential feeling," that is not an in-world experience but forms a basic way of relating to the world itself, giving us a fundamental sense of the world's reality or our belong-ingness within it. Some aspects of Stocker's work resonate with this idea. But apart from the deliverance of the world as a totality, other elements of Stocker's work can be understood as positing feelings as the myriad forms of meaning that saturate the world immanently. Heidegger's total-ity and Stocker's myriad—are they the same?

32. In this subsection, I draw heavily from my earlier essay "Self-Contempt and Color-Blind Liberalism in *The Accidental Asian* in *The Boundaries of Affect: Ethnicity and Emotion*, E. Ann Kaplan and Susan Schekel, ed. (Stony Brook: Stony Brook University and The Humanities Institute at Stony Brook, 2007), 39–70.

33. On the topic of shame and self-evaluative emotions, I have learned from many. See Helen Block Lewis, *Shame and Guilt in Neurosis* (New York: International Universities Press, 1971); Gabrielle Taylor, *Pride, Shame, and Guilt: Emotions of Self-Assessment* (Oxford: Oxford University Press, 1985); Andrew Morrison, *Shame: The Underside of Narcissism* (Hillsdale, N.J.: Analytic Press, 1989); Sandra Bartky, *Femininity and Domination* (New York: Routledge, 1990), ch. 6; Bernard Williams, *Shame and Necessity* (Berkeley: University of California Press, 1993); Eve Kosofsky Sedgwick and Adam Frank, eds., *Shame and Its Sisters: A Silvan Tomkins Reader* (Dur-ham, N.C.: Duke University Press, 1995), ch. 6; John Deigh, *The Sources of Moral Agency: Essays in Moral Psychology and Freudian Theory* (New York: Cambridge University Press, 1996), ch. 11; Richard Wollheim, *On the Emotions* (New Haven, Conn.: Yale University Press, 1999), ch. 3; Martha Nussbaum, *Hiding from Humanity: Shame and Disgust in the Law* (Princeton, N.J.: Princeton University Press, 2004); Daniel Haggerty, "White Shame: Responsibility and Moral Emotions," *Philosophy Today* 53 (2009); and esp., Michael Stocker with Elizabeth Hegeman, *Valuing Emotion* (New York: Cambridge University Press, 1996), chs. 8–9.

34. For a particularly deep account of this and related matters of shame, see Michael Stocker with Elizabeth Hegeman, *Valuing Emotions*, 217–229.

35. Helen Block Lewis, *Shame and Guilt in Neurosis*.

36. For very helpful discussion here, see Sandra Lee Bartky, *Femininity and Domination*, ch. 6; John Deigh, *The Sources of Moral Agency*, ch. 11; and Martha Nussbaum, *Hiding from Humanity*, chs. 4–7.

37. The work of Sylvan Tomkins does elaborate on the distinction between shame and self-contempt. A discussion of it is beyond the confines of

this essay. See Eve Kosofsky Sedgwick and Adam Frank, eds., *Shame and Its Sisters: A Silvan Tomkins Reader.*

38. The brief characterization of other-directed contempt in this essay draws from some of what I still take to be plausible in an earlier account of mine: "Contempt and Ordinary Inequality," in *Racism and Philosophy*, ed., Susan Babbitt and Sue Campbell (Ithaca, N.Y.: Cornell University Press, 1999). For a recent and developed philosophical account of other-directed contempt, one that differs in some important respects from the one I give, see Michele Mason, "Contempt as a Moral Attitude," *Ethics* 113:2 (2003), 234–272.

39. Jean-Paul Sartre, *Anti-Semite and Jew* (New York: Schocken Books, 1948), 96–98.

40. John Rawls, *Theory of Justice.*

41. Martha Nussbaum, *Hiding from Humanity: Disgust, Shame, and the Law* (Princeton, N.J.: Princeton University Press, 2004).

42. In bringing a phenomenological analysis to Asian American identity concerns, I take inspiration from Linda Martin Alcoff's *Visible Identities: Race, Gender, and the Self* (New York: Oxford University Press, 2006) and Emily S. Lee, "The Meaning of Visible Differences of the Body," *American Philosophical Association Newsletter on the Status of Asian/Asian Americans* 2, no. 2 (Spring 2003): 34–37, and "A Phenomenology for Homi Bhabha's Postcolonial Metropolitan Subject," *The Southern Journal of Philosophy* v. xlvi, no. 4 (Winter 2008): 537–557.

43. Jay Matthews, "Asian American Students and School Stereotypes," *Washington Post*, January 8, 2008. I accessed it online at: http://www.washingtonpost.com/wp-dyn/content/article/2008/01/08/AR2008 010802038_pf.html.

44. Cited in Jay Matthews, "Asian American Students and School Stereotypes."

45. Ibid.

46. Erving Goffman, *Stigma: Notes on the Management of Spoiled Identity* (New York: Simon & Shuster, 1963), ch. 4.

47. I discuss this in greater detail in "Self-Contempt and Color-Blind Liberalism in *The Accidental Asian*." Eric Liu, the author of *The Accidental Asian* (New York: Random House, 1998), at least when he was younger, seems to have shared the outlook of the Harvard "Lone Asian" who values being an atypical Asian.

48. Indeed, the accountability structure of self-hatred discourse, even if flawed, seems to have no hold on them at all.

49. Rosalind Chou and Joe Feagin, *The Myth of the Model Minority: Asian*

Americans Facing Racism (Boulder, Colo.: Paradigm Publishers, 2008). For insightful discussion about the variety of Asian American experiences of racism and coping with racism, I thank Jonathan Leung, my commentator for an earlier oral address of this essay. In addition, I would like to thank various members of the audience at CSU Fullerton for their very helpful comments, including Craig Ihara, Emily S. Lee, and JeeLoo Liu.

50. Rosalind Chou and Joe Feagin, *The Myth of the Model Minority: Asian Americans Facing Racism* (Boulder, Colo.: Paradigm Publishers, 2008), 101.

SIX

A PHENOMENOLOGY OF HESITATION

Interrupting Racializing Habits of Seeing

ALIA AL-SAJI

This chapter provides a phenomenological account of racializing vision, with the aim not only of understanding its intransigent and closed logic but of sketching the avenues and practices needed for its interruption.[1] To begin, three examples can help frame the concerns lying behind my phenomenological reflections on racism; albeit anecdotal, and though this chapter will deal with racializing perception at a more general level, these examples clarify the stakes involved. The examples are not meant to be exhaustive of experiences of racism or of the antiracist responses open to us, but they are meant to remind us of the difficulties involved in thinking how racism (especially at the level of perception, affect, and prereflective experience) operates and can be overcome.[2]

1. In the context of the public debate surrounding the Muslim headscarf or "veil" in France, a debate that led to the passage of the 2004 law banning conspicuous religious signs in public schools (and that continues today with the face veil, or niqab, as its object), a frenzy of media and news coverage about girls wearing headscarves in schools occurred in France. In one such news story on a public television channel, just prior to the passage of the law, a common though baffling reaction was documented (baffling at the time, at least to me). A Muslim girl attending

secondary school had attempted to circumvent the interdiction on
the headscarf imposed in her school (at the time decisions regarding headscarves were made on a case-by-case basis and, hence,
left up to school administrations). Instead of a hijab covering
the head and neck, she wore a high-necked sweater and wrapped
her hair in a bandana or scarf tied at the back of the neck. This
achieved a certain level of cover while in the classroom; when
the girl left the gates of the school, she would put on her headscarf over her bandana and go back to life as usual. Though this
"compromise" was accepted by the school for a time, tensions
were palpable in the news piece. As the girl entered her classroom (in high-neck and bandana), the teacher responsible for the
class reacted with immediate and visceral repulsion; she could not
(physically and emotionally) tolerate the presence of the girl in
her classroom, expressing violently and vocally her desire for the
girl to leave.[3] What was clear was that the teacher *saw* the girl as
willfully incarnating religious dogmatism and gender oppression;
her reaction was not that of worked-through argument or judgment, but of prereflective perception and affect.[4]

2. In her essay, "You Mixed? Racial Identity Without Racial Biology," Sally Haslanger describes how living with her adopted African American children, and in a "mixed" family, has altered her
own body sense and image.[5] More than being simply a question
of comfort zones, this transformation takes place at the level of
perception, affective openness and sense of community with
African Americans. Importantly, it is an alteration that disrupts
racializing habits and aesthetics, and that changes her perception
of, and response to, other bodies as well as her own. It reconfigures her bodily attachment to, and physical presence among,
others. Such transformation is not limited to interactions with
her children; rather Haslanger finds that her bodily, affective, and
social map has been redrawn.[6] She notes how this has made her
sensitive to the implicit racism of some social spaces, in a bodily
and affective (and not simply reflective) way, since "[r]acism is no
longer just something I find offensive and morally objectionable;
I experience it as a personal harm."[7]

3. A personal example. When I first met my partner in 1996, he was
an elementary school teacher working in a socially disadvantaged
school in the south of France (a school with a visible proportion

of students of North African descent). The debate around heads-carves in schools was already very much alive in France, and at that time and for several years after, I would attempt to convince him, through all the arguments and analyses at my disposal, that the widespread reaction to veiling in France was misconceived. As a good public servant and citizen, he was committed to the principle of *laïcité* (the French version of secularism) in the pub-lic school system. What this meant, for him and for many other friends and colleagues in France, was that veiling could not have a place in schools. As someone whose immediate family includes both women who wear the hijab and unveiled women, and where veiled women have attained a high level of educational and pro-fessional achievement (as engineers and lawyers), I saw the French reaction to veiling as eliding the reality and multiplicity of Muslim women's experiences. My arguments, however, did not seem to work on my partner, so we left it at that. Several years later, hav-ing moved to Montreal, the question of veiling arose again in the context of the debate that led up to the 2004 French law. In the meantime, my mother and grandmother (who both wear the hijab) had been very much a part of our everyday lives. At this juncture, it became apparent that my partner was not only critical of the proposed law but had revised his reaction so thoroughly that his previous attitude seemed alien to him. Instead of owing to my persuasive abilities, it was the transformed affective tissue of collective living that seems to have shifted my partner's per-ceptions. Women wearing the hijab, and the modalities of inter-action that such veiling dictated, were now, to him, part of inter-subjective life. New habits of seeing had emerged: veiling was no longer perceived as a homogeneous object (hiding subjects from view); rather, differentiations in ways of veiling and interacting were seen as adumbrations of individuated and concrete subjects who commanded singular and contextual responses.

In what follows, I propose to explore the question of racializing vision and the possibilities for its critical interruption by drawing on the phenom-enologies of Frantz Fanon, Maurice Merleau-Ponty and Iris Marion Young and on Henri Bergson's philosophy of time. My account also proceeds in conversation with contemporary race theorists such as Linda Martín Alcoff and Shannon Sullivan. I should note that although Merleau-Ponty's work lacks a systematic consideration of "race," I find his phenomenology to offer a nuanced framework for thinking racializing perception.[8] This stems from Merleau-Ponty's attention to the ambivalence and contextualism of visual relations, a nuanced approach he shares with Fanon. Vision is neither inherently harmonious nor necessarily objectifying and hostile. It can become the location for violent and objectifying misrepresentation, but also for critical attunement and affective openness.[9] Vision, then, contains the ground for both objectification and its critique, for racialization and for antiracist interventions into social practice. My aim in this chapter is to disclose both these possibilities. While sections 1 and 2 uncover the phenomenological structures of racializing vision and affect, section 3 explores the power of hesitation to open such structures to transformation and critique. Hesitation, I claim, is a necessary condition for critical and ethical seeing, although hesitation by itself is not a sufficient response. To understand this, I distinguish generative from oppressive forms of hesitation in section 4, and I show in section 5 how hesitation is in need of enduring relations with others and of the critical work of memory in order to become productive. In the second half of the chapter, I thus present a phenomenology of hesitation as a means for interrupting the racializing habits of seeing and affect, described in the first half. In the course of these phenomenological studies, I will revisit the above examples.

1. A Phenomenology of Racializing Vision

In *Black Skin, White Masks*, Frantz Fanon shows how racialization is not only a process by which the identities of self and other are constituted (an othering process à la Jean-Paul Sartre); it is a socially pathological othering with important structural features.[10] This othering involves a projective mechanism (or intentionality) by which what is undesirable in the self is projected onto the other; the result is a negative mirroring whereby the other is constituted as that which this self is not, or does not take itself to be.[11] "Black" is hence oppositionally constructed as that which "white" identity disavows. Through this racialization, difference no longer appears to be relational or fluid; difference is made into opposition and hierarchy, so that identities appear to be mutually exclusive and in-themselves terms. What allows this hierarchy to be seen as a feature of the world, and racializing operations to remain hidden from view, is the way in which race is perceived as belonging to visible features of the body (such as skin color). Racialization, hence, relies on the naturalization of projected and oppositional difference to the perceived body.

Moreover, racialization not only structures the ways in which bodies are represented and perceived, it describes the ways in which colonialism and White supremacy divide bodies politically, economically, spatially, and socially in order to exploit and dominate them.[12] Racialization is, then, the historical and social process by which races are constructed, seen and, when interiorized or epidermalized, lived. The power of Fanon's account of racism is twofold, in my view, for he is interested both in the *naturalization* of race, its constitution in relation to visible bodily markers that come to unconsciously stand in for race, and in its *rationalization*, the way in which racism takes itself to originate as a mere reaction to the racialized other. He shows that it is of the essence of racism to forget the histories and operations of power, which constitute it, and to scapegoat or blame its victims. What Fanon reveals in his account of racialization is that the construction of race in the White imaginary has more to do with white domination and demarcations of "whiteness" than with the concrete racialized others that are its ostensible objects. In other words, there is a ignorance to racism that is not merely accidental, but that sustains its operations—a forgetting which actively hides racializing mechanisms and misconstrues its objects.

A primary way in which racialization takes hold in lived experience, while remaining unconscious and invisible, is by means of perception. As critical race theorists have shown, racializing perception operates by projecting race as a property of the visible body, naturalizing racial categories to bodily features such as skin color, facial attributes, bodily styles, and in cultural racism, bodily practices and clothing.[13] In this way, "race" becomes perceived as a natural category and not a social, cultural, and historical construct. The seeming naturalness of perceived "race"-categories works to justify the very racist logic that produced them. That the racialization of bodies and the rationalization of racism are intimately tied to their naturalization in visual perception opens a site of phenomenological questioning; for it is important to ask not only what in the structure of vision allows it to become racializing, but also how racializing vision operates, what is distinctive about it.[14] More generally, is the objectification of others in racist and sexist perception simply the elaboration of a universal tendency within vision (as one may be tempted to conclude from the Sartrean theory of the gaze, for instance); or is there a distinctive phenomenological structure to these ways of seeing?[15] In my view, it is by interrogating the recalcitrance and rigidity of racializing vision, at the same time as its contextualism and contingency, that the means for criticizing and transforming this vision can come to view.[16] Such a race-critical and feminist interrogation can find resources in Merleau-Ponty's phenomenology, as Linda Martín Alcoff has shown.[17] Significantly, within a Merleau-Pontian frame, the visual naturalization of "race" can be understood to be made possible by the intentional structure of vision and its reliance on habit, but not to be necessitated by them.

For Merleau-Ponty, vision is not a mere neutral recording of the visible. As the *Phenomenology of Perception* shows, we learn to see.[18] This means that vision not only *makes* visible, it does so *differentially* according to sedimented habits of seeing—according to the tacit ways our bodies relate to and move in the world, allowing certain aspects of that world to be foregrounded. Such habits of seeing owe to a social, cultural, and historical field—a visual field structured in such ways as to motivate, without fully determining, certain forms of perception, certain meaning-making schemas.[19] Through sedimentation and habituation, the constitutive operations of vision remain tacit or unconscious; its intentionality works in us without our reflective awareness. It is the perceived object that is seen, as figure against ground, while the habits of visual perception remain themselves invisible. As Alcoff notes, we see *through* our habits; we do not see them.[20] Invisible is the gaze (or seeing body) in its constitutive and dynamic relation to the object, as well as the historical horizon and spatial ground against which that object is adumbrated. Indeed, the object appears *visible in itself*, while the relational and perspectival conditions of that visibility are elided.

Though vision is generally habitual, not all vision is objectifying or, more specifically, racializing (i.e., vision is not inevitably racist, but contextually and historically so).[21] I would claim that racializing vision builds on the intentionality and habituality of vision in general, on the self-reflexive erasure of vision before the visibility of its object. *But racializing vision is both more and less than this.* Although I agree with Alcoff that racializing vision is, like all vision, habitual, I believe that a further dimension structures racializing vision and explains its closure.[22] In other words, it is important to ask not only how racialization takes hold as perceptual habit, but also how that habit differs, in its intransigence and dehumanization, from the improvisational fluidity and responsivity of habit more generally. I believe this can be traced by asking after the structure of racializing vision as *more and less* than vision in general. Racializing vision is *less* in that the affectivity and receptivity of vision are circumscribed—the openness of vision to other ways of being, which may destabilize or shatter its perceptual schemas, delimited. The dynamic ability of vision to change is partially closed down. Racialized bodies are not only seen as naturally inferior, they *cannot be seen otherwise*. In its overdetermination, racializing vision is also *more*. The mechanism of othering, which undergirds this vision, sustains itself by means of the very perceptions, representations, and affects it produces.[23] Hence, witness the homogeneity and persistence of this vision. In a narcissistic and self-justifying move, racializing habits of seeing inscribe their cause in the perceived body, positing themselves as the objective or natural reaction to that body. In this way, these habits rationalize racism. Although the *inability* to see otherwise is a limitation that belongs to racializing vision (and not to the bodies seen), this limitation is naturalized to those bodies, so that they are taken to correspond to that and *only* that which this vision sees.

Racializing vision thus wears "blinders" (to borrow an expression from Bergson).[24] It is a representational and objectifying way of seeing. This inability to see otherwise—what I call the "I cannot" of racialization—should be understood to belong to social-cultural horizons, historically tied to modernity and colonial expansion in the West and motivated by imaginary and epistemic investments in representation and the metaphysics of subject-object.[25] But the logic of racialization dictates its own self-forgetting; the horizon, to which the construction of "race" owes, is elided by the visual naturalization of "race."[26] To see "race" as belonging to certain bodies is to overlook the social, historical, economic dimensions that contextualize "race." Here, I would claim that there is a kind of "I cannot" that structures racializing vision and that is not in contradiction with its "I can."[27] This "I cannot" institutes, circumscribes and indeed makes possible the objectifying teleology of the racializing "I can": I can see bodies as raced only because I cannot see them otherwise. Had it been possible to see *more* than raced object-bodies (to be affectively open to the difference and becoming of lived bodies), or to see *less* than naturalized bodies (to be aware of the social-historical structures of domination that institute my own vision), then it is not "race" as such that I would see.[28] "Race"-perception operates through a double exclusion or invisibility. In seeing bodies as "raced," their and my dependency on social positionality cannot be seen. Bodies are recognized in neither their relationality, nor their plasticity and lived-ness, but as "biologically" inborn or culturally invariant types composed of inherent traits. At the same time, the very mechanism by which racialization hierarchically stratifies and congeals the visual field is disavowed.[29] In this sense, ideals of postracial color-blindness do not overcome but rather repeat and confirm such racist disavowal.

By means of this double exclusion, racializing vision circumscribes and configures what is seen, so that the realm of visual objectivity is narrower than the historicity and social structure on which it relies. More importantly, it is not only structures of oppression that are invisible, but the affective and lived subjectivities that undergo their effects, and which are more than those effects. What I want to claim is closed down in racializing perception is the *receptivity* of vision: its ability to be affected, to be touched, by that which lies beyond or beneath its habitual objectifying schemas. It is the openness to unanticipated (and not immediately cognizable) difference—an affective openness that usually grounds the dynamic and improvisatory character of perceptual habits—that the "I cannot" of racializing vision aims to limit.[30]

2. Racializing Affect

The affective closure of racializing perception requires further scrutiny, for, at the same time, this perception is often deeply visceral (as we saw in the first example of this chapter). Indeed, racialization proceeds not only through unconscious perceptual habits, but also through habituated and socialized affects that inextricably color and configure perception. Though affect is pre-intentional, on the phenomenological account, it can provide the motivating and material support for the projective intentionality of racializing perception, and, hence, is implicated in naturalizing its reactive directionality. Affect and perception form two sides of the same phenomenon, linking that which is seen as racialized to its immediately felt effects on the racializing body.[31] This immediacy is crucial for the naturalization that sustains racializing habits.

To see this we must return to the first example and examine more closely the teacher's repulsion in response to her Muslim student. While this repulsion appears to have been caused by the Muslim girl's attire (or the hint of a headscarf that her attire recalls), it is the teacher's repulsion that casts this student's body and her clothing as "intolerable." The girl's presence is at once seen and felt to be intolerable (to the teacher); and this works to justify, indeed naturalize, the racist reaction of repulsion itself.[32] The mechanism of othering by which racializing perception inscribes its cause in the racialized body proceeds here at the prereflective level. The teacher's perception thus appears immediate, the more so because it is colored by affect. And it is this very immediacy that seems to justify the teacher's response. Since the racist reaction of intolerance takes the form of a quasi-automatic, bodily, and affective reaction to the appearance of the girl's body, this reaction can be read as itself a "natural" reaction to the way things are (rather than as a culturally, socially, and historically constituted comportment). The nonreflective level at which perception and affect operate function to hide the ways in which these operations are mediated and constituted by a history and culture of racism, effectively naturalizing what is seen and felt. It is in this sense that (moral) responsibility for cultural racism is blamed on its victims. The source of culturally racist hostility is taken to lie in the "irrational" and "intolerable" practices of cultural others (here Muslim girls who veil), exculpating both racist bodies and the racist social body that enables and circulates such affect.[33]

Affect does not here break out of the circle of the "I cannot see otherwise"; indeed, it guards this circle and contributes to its closure. "I cannot feel otherwise" serves to both naturalize the intolerability of the other and exculpate the teacher, and the social body of which she is a part, from responsibility for her response. What is "otherwise" is not only occluded from vision, but also from feeling, imagination, and understanding; that a veiled Muslim female *subjectivity* or *agency* may exist, which cannot be reduced to the false consciousness of gender oppression, is not only invisible but affectively inaccessible and unimaginable. The affect of repulsion marks the limits of tolerance and polices the intolerable, simultaneously defining it. In this dichotomization, the complexity of lived subjectivities is elided. While, in this example, the tolerable may be defined by secularized Muslim women and the intolerable by oppressed veiled women, the possibility of real Muslim women's lives that do not fit into this schema remains a blind spot.[34] Rather than engaging in the affective work of responding to those lives, repulsion blocks that response, effectively congealing the porosity and fluidity of the affective sphere. Ethical unresponsiveness to the other (the perceptual and affective "I cannot") is hence masked and justified by an affective hyperreaction that, at once sustains racialization and blocks the difficult work of responsivity by taking its place.

This phenomenon can be described, following Fanon, as "affective ankylosis."[35] "Affective ankylosis" conveys, at once, the rigidity, immobility, and numbing that characterize racializing affects; it explains the recalcitrance of these affects. The *rigidity* of racializing affect can be witnessed in its temporality, for this affect is not only frozen in its response but repetitive in its form. This is not simply to say that racializing affect repeats the schemas of the past acontextually in future settings. It is to say that the past is here congealed as schema and is, as such, overdetermined and fixed in its sense; this is the past as "historico-racial schema," the past constructed as myth, stereotype, distorted and isolated remnant.[36] Corresponding to this overdetermination of the past, there is a predetermination of the future. The future is not the open setting where newness can be created; its possibilities are projected and mapped in advance based on the ossified schemas of the past. It is in this vein that Fanon describes affective ankylosis as an "inability to liquidate the past," for, instead of being worked-through and remembered, this past is repeated in the present and closes down the future.[37] By only being receptive to that which is determined in advance, such rigidity enacts, in a temporal register, the negative mirroring characteristic of racialization.

The rigidity of racializing affect can be seen not only in the closed temporality it projects onto the bodies it racializes (and which it takes to belong to the "closed" nature of those bodies themselves), but also in its own temporal *immobility*. There is a lack of fluidity or becoming to racializing affect, a totalizing sense of completeness or absorption that means it does not hesitate in its course and does not become otherwise. Not only is receptivity to that which does not already figure on its racialized perceptual map foreclosed, this affect does not search beyond that foreclosure and does not open onto other affective responses or modes of response. In this sense, racializing affect short-circuits the work of responsivity and self-critical engagement that comes with sustained coexistence with others. This highlights the *numbing* of receptivity that paradoxically accompanies the strong affects of racialization—as if these affects serve as blinders. This numbness is twofold, for it affects both the self—in its lack of critical self-awareness and its active forgetting of the structures of oppression and privilege on which it relies—and the relation to others, eliding nuance, modulation, and adaptive effort in responding to singular others and divergent situations. Not only is the receptivity and responsiveness of the affective sphere curtailed, the creative and critical potential of affect to hesitate, which I will discuss below, is blocked.

The recalcitrant invisibility that structures racializing vision and affect—the "I cannot see or feel otherwise"—means that antiracist practice needs to be more than a discursive or cognitive intervention (though this discursive level is also required).[38] Precisely because of the role of perceptual habit and affect in naturalizing racism, it is within perception and affectivity that I believe critical antiracist practice must find its tools. Here, the inner weakness (or potential) of habits of seeing to become aware of their own affective limitations and conditions, to recall their historicity and social horizonality, must be mined. Drawing on Bergson's account of habit, I find this critical potential in the form of hesitation.

3. Hesitation and Affect

Hesitation defines the structure of time for Bergson, the ontological interval wherein time makes a difference, wherein it acts in experience. The difference that time makes is felt as delay: "time is what hinders everything from being given at once. It retards, or rather it is [delay]."[39] This implies, as in Gilles Deleuze's formula, that the whole is not given, that there is no completion or closure for an enduring reality.[40] That all is not given means that what is must be understood as tendency and becoming rather than thing; this is important not only for how we see objects and bodies, but for what it means to see, feel, and think. If experience itself is tendency, to use Bergson's term, then its temporal structure is that of indetermination, becoming, and potential change. Tendency connotes not simply movement, but "nascent change of direction."[41] For to hesitate is to feel one's way tentatively and receptively; time is "tâtonnement," says Bergson, that is, a search without finality or teleology, an experimentation that does not dictate the future it will find.[42] Such a search does not take the form of linear progression; it forks and diverges continually, so that the futures it encounters were not those initially anticipated, being irreducible to the repetition of the past. But neither is the past a self-same or congealed idea, on this account. Though the past as a virtual whole pushes on each present, actualizing itself there, this past is dynamically reconfigured through the passage of events. The past is not the accumulation of events in a container, but the continuous immanent transformation of sense and force that is tendency.[43] Newness, in other words, arises not only from the openness to the future but from the way the past is remembered in hesitation; memory and invention are here intertwined. Hesitation does not only delay, it also opens onto elaboration and becoming otherwise. Since all is not given, what happens in the interval is becoming.

Phenomenologically, affect plays a vital role in the bodily experience of temporal hesitation. In *Matter and Memory*, Bergson notes that affect is felt when the body hesitates in the course of habitual action.[44] The causal sequence of excitation and response is interrupted and hesitation takes its place. Here, hesitation is felt as bodily affect—so that we might speak of affective hesitation or of hesitating affect. This affect not only takes the place of, and hence delays, habitual action; it also prefigures the delayed habit, making it visible as an anticipated future among others in the world. Through affect the body waits before acting; it has the time not only to perceive, but also to remember. In this sense, to feel is to no longer repeat the past automatically, but to imagine and remember it.[45] Affective hesitation can thus make felt the historicity, contingency, and sedimentation of habitual actions and perceptions, as well as their plasticity. Moreover, if we understand affect as tendency, then affect is not a completed reality or atomistic thing, but a process always open to further elaboration, forking, and becoming. Such affect opens up routes for feeling, seeing, and acting differently.

Although the teacher's affective reaction described in the first example of this chapter would seem to belie Bergson's account of affective hesitation, I believe that Bergson's theory allows us to distinguish the ankylosis of affect in racializing perception from the critical potential of affect in hesitation. Bergson's account makes visible, by contrast, that which is missing, distorted or *ankylosed* in racializing affect. While Bergson is not concerned with racialization but with the general objectifying effects of socialization, his account points to the *necessary condition* by which affect becomes receptive and responsive, namely hesitation. Though hesitation is not sufficient in my account—it must rely on a context that motivates it and a sustained working-through that holds it open—it represents a necessary step. In presenting this Bergsonian diagnosis, I do not mean to propose hesitation as an isolated or willful remedy to racializing habit. My purpose, rather, is to show what is phenomenologically needed for perception and affect to become responsive, and the ontological ground of this possibility in the structure of temporality and affective life. It is in this sense that the phenomenology of hesitation I am offering can be read as a corrective—potentially critical and ethical—to the reifying structures of racializing perception and affect described above.

Though it may be tempting to align racializing and responsive affects with so-called positive and negative emotions, such a categorization not only overlooks the way in which emotions can serve different functions (e.g., anger can be hostility or the beginning of critique), it also mistakes the nature of the difference between the affects in question. At stake in the distinction between racializing and responsive affects are, I believe, different ways of relating to the interval of hesitation, and thus to temporality. This structural and temporal difference also means that affects that are closed may, through various strategies and circumstances, become responsive, and that those that are responsive must be guarded against closure.

Returning to the example of the teacher, it would seem that she felt, but did not hesitate. Indeed, the interval of the present was saturated with an affect so seemingly immediate and deeply absorbing that there was no time for anything else. The totalizing sense of completeness that characterizes racializing affect means that, for it, *all is given* (in contrast to the incompleteness of Bergsonian hesitation). First, that *all is given* means that racializing affect projects and narcissistically perpetuates itself in all contexts and times, expecting to encounter confirmations of itself there. This recalls Shannon Sullivan's description of habits of white privilege as "ontologically expansive."[46] Second, I would add that the *all which is given* has been circumscribed in advance according to racializing schemas, so that we must understand this "expansiveness" to be based on a structural closure, an "I cannot see or feel otherwise." And, third, to take *all to be given* is to short-circuit hesitation. Racializing affect thus attempts to overdetermine what happens in the temporal interval, constructing it as closed horizon. This not only truncates the ability of affect to become otherwise, it numbs both self-awareness and receptivity.

In contrast, as we saw in Bergson's account, affect does not simply take place in the interval of hesitation, as if interposed from without; this affect embodies hesitation and, hence, opens the interval from within. It would be more accurate to say, along with Deleuze, that this affect happens in the interval but does not fill it.[47] In this sense, affect can hold open the interval of hesitation, leaving the space, the time, for more to come. Since *all is not given* for this affect, it can become otherwise—opening onto other affective tendencies and perceptions, but also recalling divergent memories and becoming imagination, action, language, and thinking. In other words, by hesitating, affective becoming has the potential to destabilize itself and transform, to become self-aware and respond. Here, affect is tendency rather than thing. The interval of hesitation—of indetermination and nonteleological searching—structures not only the evolution or winding course of affect itself, but its relations to others and the world. This interval of indetermination, with all its creative potential, is not yet critique, however. To see how affect can become critically responsive, let us return to Bergson's account of affect in *Matter and Memory*.

Affect constitutes a singular and positive phenomenon for Bergson.[48] Though affection is different in kind from perception, according to Bergson, they are inextricably linked. Bergson notes that there is no perception without affection, since the body is not a mathematical point in space, but flesh exposed to the world.[49] But while perception designates the body's relation to and virtual action on its situation, affection enacts a "useless" self-relation or self-perception—the body's effort on itself in response to that situation.[50] Three elements are worth noting. First, affect follows from and expresses the vulnerability of the body, its exposure to what is other. It marks the passivity of the living material body. But for the body to feel itself affected, to undergo affect, its passivity cannot be mere inertia or indifference. Affect arises not in opposition to activity, but could be described, in paradoxical terms, as the activity of bodily passivity itself. This is because, second, affect defines a peculiar kind of effort. It is an effort in which the body works on itself in response to the world.[51] Affect is hence a situated response to the context in which the body finds itself, but it is not a response that acts on that situation directly. Rather, affect is an effort to stave off habitual reaction by prefiguring it as bodily feeling; the body acts on itself and affectively works through, instead of enacting, a reaction. The peculiar activity (and passivity) of affect lies in this effort to delay, to hesitate. In this way, the structure of affect undermines several dichotomous schemas: it lies at the hinge of passivity-activity, but also inside-outside, or more accurately, self-affection and hetero-affection.[52]

Third, in Bergson's words, affect is "*un effort impuissant*" [a powerless effort].[53] Though affect is ineffective from the point of view of the teleology of action, a teleology in which hesitation figures only as failure and lack, this very powerlessness of affect is also generative. As an interruption of habitual reaction, affect allows the time both for a situation to be undergone and affectively registered and for marginal self-awareness, searching, and recollection to take place. Since affect responds to its context by working on itself, it holds together receptivity to that context and bodily awareness of its habituated (albeit delayed) response. The importance of affective hesitation for critical and antiracist vision can be located at this juncture. Bergson's account shows that affect is not only the openness onto an outside, but also the lived-through and self-aware undergoing of that alterity.[54] The lived-through bodily awareness of affect can allow the historical, social, and habitual frame that structures my positionality and embodiment to be glimpsed on the horizon of experience. Indeed, there are two ways in which racializing habit can become visible in hesitation. *Marginally and affectively*, the delayed objectification is prefigured but not explicitly seen. The seeming coincidence between habits of seeing and the visible is decentered, revealing the ways in which vision is already ahead of itself, constituting the seen according to habitual schemas. At the same time, *memorially*, affect can be cast in the role of a witness, connecting to a kind of "memory of the present."[55] This affective receptivity to, registering and memory of, the present has the function of an "involuntary witness" (to use a phrase from Deleuze).[56] As witness, affect both becomes a memory of habit and an occasion to remember; it makes time for receptivity and responding differently. When we note, in addition, that affectivity can be openness to that which does not count as representation, the critical and responsive potential of affective hesitation comes to view. For it is precisely the receptivity to what registers *otherwise* than in the logic of objectification that is excluded in racializing perception and affect. Hesitation thus points not only to this unrecognized affective field, but also reveals the blinders through which the visibility of this field is circumscribed.

What I believe is important, from the perspective of critical and antiracist practice, is attention to the ways in which affect can become responsive. And what I find in reading Bergson is a call for perception and affect to slow down. Racializing perception proceeds at a velocity such that we cannot see it happening, faster than the speed of thought.[57] This contributes to its apparent immediacy and its naturalizing effect. Hesitation is a deceleration that opens up the affective infrastructure of perception, in order both to make it responsive to what it has been unable to see and to make aware its contextual and constructed features. It may be objected that locating antiracist work on the level of affect overlooks the way in which affect is the source of what is recalcitrant and irrational in racism; so that the solution must lie at a level amenable to rational change, in cognitive work at the level of belief. The first example above might be read in this way. But if racializing affect is not deconstructed from within, its violence remains and will be displaced into other processes of othering and onto other racialized bodies. To deconstruct racializing affect is to interrupt the totalizing sense of completeness, the "ontological expansiveness" by which all is felt to be given. In this way, the naturalized immediacy, repetitive overdetermination, and reactive directionality, which this affect sustains, would be destabilized. It is hesitation that I believe offers the possibility of this interruption. It does so not by eliminating affect but by modulating and transforming its temporality. This reconfigures affect in at least five ways.

First, to hesitate is to slow down, making the temporal interval that affect occupies, and which racializing affect tried to fill up and overdetermine, felt. This puts the immediacy and automaticity of affect into question; phenomenologically speaking, it can be said that hesitation puts the immediacy of affect in brackets, while allowing affective experience to continue. This means (1) that racializing affect can be denaturalized, so that its immediacy no longer stands in for its "naturalness" and self-evidence; (2) that the mediations—the social-historical horizon, positionalities, and attachments—that constitute this affect can be revealed, allowing further mediations and interventions to take place; and (3) that the reification of affect, as instantaneous thing, can give way to an experience of affect as tendency and process.

This brings us, second, to an important consequence of hesitation as slowing down; for in modulating its temporality, affective experience continues but with a different quality or intensity. I want to claim that this modulation both discloses structures of affectivity, which had been elided and distorted in racializing affect, and allows affect to resume its flow. In this vein, third, the *ambiguity* of affect is revealed. Affect, as we have seen, is an encounter of self and other, where the body works on itself in response to what is other. It represents the intersection of self-affection and hetero-affection, an encounter mediated by forces of sociality and historicity, by structures of domination and privilege, which themselves remain invisible. Though preintentional and prereflective, this encounter is neither immediate nor unaware; it includes a lived-through bodily awareness.[58] Racializing affect reduces this ambiguity to ambivalence (to use a distinction from Merleau-Ponty).[59] That which is felt in affect is projected onto the other as cause, hiding both self-involvement and structural conditions. This means that the ambiguity of affect is reduced to, and naturalized as, a univocal and reactive directionality, which takes the place of any effort at critical awareness or receptivity. Denaturalizing affect involves, then, not only the suspension of its immediacy, but also changing its directionality; for the naturalized causality that affect enforces needs to turn back onto the feeling, perceiving, social subject as its source.

Fourth, as ambiguous and multiple, affect resumes its course as *tendency*; it is unfrozen, able to become otherwise and to respond differently. Rather than being determined in its reactions by a racialized perceptual field mapped in advance, affectivity becomes a tentative search that is receptive to that which is not already given on this map. This is because, fifth, to hesitate is to delay and to make affect wait. The incompleteness, both of affect and of that to which affect responds, is here felt. To wait is to testify that time makes a difference for experience, that all is not given in the present. To wait, without projection, is not only to be open to a futurity that escapes prediction, but also to a past that can be dynamically transformed through the passage of events, and that grounds the creative potential of events. This breaks with the closure of the past and the predetermination of the future found in racialization. More so, it permits mediation and antiracist work at the level of memory and the past to make a difference for future attachments, for the ways in which we see and feel according to others.

The critical power of hesitation is linked to memory. Affect, as I noted above, functions as a witness to situated bodily response. This links affect to a memory of the present and to memory more generally; affect is both an occasion to remember and an event that reconfigures the network of memories of the past, my own past in its relations to the memories of others. In my view, there are several ways in which memory can serve a critical function with respect to racializing habits of seeing and feeling. On the one hand, memory is already a destabilization of habit; it replaces the performance of habit. On the other hand, it is the memory of habituation; it serves to contextualize and historicize our habits. In so doing, memory can connect habit to its temporal ground. This temporality is more than any given habit; it is the ontological duration that makes habit possible, despite its crystallization. Indeed, since temporal becoming is interval and hesitation, since each repetition is never quite the same, the possibility of interruption is inscribed within the same temporality that habit relies on to establish closure. Duration at once structures and fractures habits of seeing. As we have seen, this dimension explains not only how affectivity is closed down and ankylosed in racializing vision; it also makes possible, though difficult, the resumption of responsive affectivity and openness in experiences of waiting and wonder. In this context, a supplementary function of memory can be discerned, for memories are not atomistic entities but networks of relations, wherein the critical reconfiguration and destabilization of one sector of the past recasts the whole. For affectivity to be opened up in the present, the past should also be worked-through; memories of other pasts need to find voice, interrupting the ankylosed and dominant stories that are repeated there.

But can racializing habit be undermined simply by hesitating? My argument is not that hesitation is sufficient to overcome racializing habit, but rather that the necessary role of hesitation should be taken into account when considering antiracist strategies for overcoming such habit. Hesitation is both the ontological ground that makes possible transformations in habit, and the phenomenological opening that can be utilized and supplemented for such change to take place. Neither does this mean that hesitation can be willfully enacted, nor that it can form a self-contained experience. Phenomenologically, hesitation happens *within* a context wherein it interposes an opening; this opening must yet be *taken up* for new possibility to be created. What this suggests is that critical and antiracist practice include indirect strategies for fostering hesitation; this involves the creation of situations and attachments that bring hesitation about, as well as attention to ways of holding hesitation open and allowing it to become productive. Albeit uncertain in its effects and partial in its reach (like most strategies), the work of critical memory is one such route.

In *Revealing Whiteness*, Shannon Sullivan presents another route: to disrupt habits of white privilege indirectly through change in one's environment (understood broadly as social, geographical, aesthetic, or political environments). Sullivan notes that a changed environment—in particular one that undermines white solipsism—can help produce new habits of living.[60] She cautions, however, that environmental change can also reinforce the ontological expansiveness of white habits, offering new spaces for their appropriation. That habits are reinforced rather than disrupted relies, I think, on another dimension missing from Sullivan's account, namely, on the lack of affective hesitation. As Sullivan rightly points out, white privileged bodies expect to feel "at home" in all spaces, including those that they colonize. This implies, on my reading, that environmental change can only be effective if it is able to create a certain tension or discomfort, a fracture, at the level of habits of white privilege—what I have called hesitation. Hesitation is certainly not sufficient to overcome racializing habits, but the discomfort it performs, if fostered and made productive, is a crucial step. Sullivan notes that discomfort can lead to fearful or angry attempts at its eradication, reinforcing the expectations of white privileged bodies to comfortably inhabit and possess all spaces.[61] The response to hesitation can thus be a defensive reaction of intensified closure—the avoidance of hesitation through ankylosed affect. In this vein, Sullivan's proposal that white privileged subjects need to accept discomfort as fitting is suggestive.[62] To allow discomfort is to make the time within experience for hesitation to occur; this suspends for an interval the reflexes of white privilege that project comfort, seamlessness, and expansiveness in all contexts.

But can the discomfort of environmental change suspend these habits for more than an interval? Environmental change, in my account, should not only induce hesitation but sustain it. If focused only on changing the present environment, it risks missing the weight of the past.[63] For the inertia of racializing habit is supported by past attachments that remain alive in the present, just as others are actively forgotten. Unless working-through the past recasts this network of relations, so that hitherto unrecognized attachments and debts to others can be felt, change will be difficult to sustain. (Recalling Fanon, I would note that the hold of the historico-racial schema on experience and its predetermination of the future have to be broken.)[64] Environmental change and critical memory go together in my account. As we will see in section 5, this requires an enduring commitment to living with others, so that affective attachments can shift and relationality mutate in both present experience and memory.

4. Hesitation and Bodily "I Can"

My appeal to hesitation as a means (albeit partial) for interrupting racializing and objectifying habits of seeing may appear problematic.[65] For hesitation is an ambiguous phenomenon. Though hesitation may make habit visible and allow its reconfiguration, the experience of hesitation also seems to undermine agency—one's sense of oneself as an "I can"—and to install a passivity at the heart of the activity of the embodied subject. More troubling, hesitation tracks social positionality. On the one hand, those in positions of privilege hesitate the least; indeed, the projective sense of ease and mastery of one's surroundings, presumed by the "ontological expansiveness" of white privilege, seem to foreclose hesitation.[66] On the other hand, hesitancy in bodily movement and action tends to characterize the lived experience of systematic oppression. This is the case for the internalized (or "epidermalized") experience of antiblack racism, as Fanon describes it, an experience in which the racialized body is felt to be "amputated" or "distorted," paralyzed through the fragmenting effects of reification.[67] Hesitation is also typical of "feminine" bodily comportment in our culture, as Iris Marion Young has shown. It is by rereading Young's landmark essay that the phenomenology of hesitation I offer can be further nuanced.

In "Throwing Like a Girl," Young provides a compelling account of the inhibited and contradictory modalities of women's movements in our culture. Young shows how women perceive two sets of (im)possibilities with respect to the same intentional goal: an "I cannot"—socially constituted as "feminine" yet experienced by women as self-referred—is superposed on an imaginary and generalized, human, "I can."[68] These contradictory projections result in a lived tension within one's body in the context of teleological action; one feels oneself, anonymously and generally, called on to act, yet at once feels one's concretely feminine body to be incapable of such action.[69] Young's analysis of the sources of this specifically feminine "I cannot" points to the role of habituation. Such habituation is both privative (enforced by lack of practice) and "positive," so that, Young argues, in growing up *as a girl* one learns a style of acting that is hesitant, fragile, and constantly self-referred—one learns to move through the world *like a girl.*[70] But habituation arises within a social horizon that motivates particular habits and that habit reinforces and actualizes in turn. Hence the root of "feminine" hesitancy is located, for Young, in the societal patriarchal gaze that systematically positions "feminine" bodies as mere objects, and in response to which women come to live their bodies on such terms.[71]

To take seriously, following Young, the inhibiting effects of social objectification on women's agency means understanding the hesitancy of "feminine" embodiment as more than the tentative suspension of habit. This hesitancy has to be conceived not as the indeterminacy within habit, but as the *overdetermination* of "feminine" body schemas and habits. This overdetermination can be linked to the exclusionary logic of objectifying, sexist and racist, vision that "cannot see otherwise than objects"—that cannot see beyond or beneath its objectifying constructions.[72] In particular, the objectifying patriarchal gaze operates a certain exclusion with respect to "feminine" bodies, which it defines as mere bodies, objects rather than subjects.[73] It is by feeling oneself seen in this way—and living this exclusionary logic whether in complicity or resistance—that "feminine" embodiment becomes instituted and felt as tension and alienation. In contrast to Young, however, I would argue that this tension is produced not only from the "I cannot" that my body takes up as "feminine" body, but also from the imaginary "I can" that is, at the same time, adopted as the norm of bodies in general. The contradictory "feminine" bodily modality that holds together "I can" and "I cannot" with respect to the same goal owes, I think, to the paradox of a social order that presupposes the general seamlessness and expansiveness of *the* lived body, while excluding certain categories of bodies (gendered and/or racialized) as those that "cannot." It is in their social reference, as Gail Weiss has argued, and not in any inherent ambivalence within women's bodies, that the key to the hesitancy described by Young can be found.[74]

Questioning Young's, and Merleau-Ponty's, model of the "I can" reveals the possibility of another hesitation, one that has been covered over by the idealized seamlessness of the phenomenological "I can." I think it is important to distinguish two kinds of hesitation—with different structural roots and bodily experiences—hesitations that call for different phenomenological accounts. For there is a hesitation that corresponds to the *indeterminacy* within habit; it makes one susceptible to be affected by that which cannot be captured in the logic of objectification (as in Bergson's account). This hesitation is not an internalized effect of objectifying vision. It stems, rather, from the structure of temporality that sustains habit while remaining invisible. To experience this hesitation is to be open to the virtual multiplication of other ways of seeing, feeling, and acting—alternative routes to that of objectifying vision, routes that could lead to affective responsivity and critical awareness. Significantly, such hesitation does not come about through the contradictory superimposition of "I can" and "I cannot"; it is not reducible to this binary and exclusionary logic. But neither does this mean the proliferation of optimal and unobstructed "I can[s]." Rather, this hesitation expresses the constitutive passivity *within* each "I can," its affective and temporal infrastructure.[75] Here, the phenomenological model of the "I can" needs to be revised, as in Merleau-Ponty's later work, in order to imagine activity that is not opposed to passivity, agency that is also powerlessness, and vision that acknowledges its blind spots.[76]

Recognizing this structural hesitation within habit allows us to reread the imaginary and general "I can" in opposition to which the feminine "I cannot" is posited in Young's "Throwing Like a Girl." What is finally overlooked by Young is the way in which this normative "I can"—posited as human but in fact correlated to white, male bodies—itself relies on a certain "I cannot see otherwise" that excludes other ways of seeing and acting.[77] By means of this exclusion, the teleology of objectifying—racializing and sexist—vision can be constituted as "efficient," "seamless," and "expansive." This teleology is based not only on a strict delimitation of affective receptivity with respect to certain others, but also on actively forgetting this very delimitation and the structures of power and privilege that it reflects. Thus the dependence of the normative "I can" on closure to, and domination of, others remains itself invisible. Here, the self-directed bodily effort to delay and open up response—that effort which is affective hesitation—not only interrupts the seamless and projective execution of objectifying habit; it also makes felt and destabilizes its blinders. The bodily "self-reference" or self-awareness of hesitation is therefore not always a limitation, a negativity that distracts from the action at hand. Hesitation allows an interval wherein vision can become self-critical—questioning the structures of habituation and socialization that it takes for granted and yet cannot see. Hesitation can be expanded into an effort of openness and responsivity toward an affective field which is unrecognized by the objectifying gaze. In this sense, hesitation would be a remedy for the ignorance and arrogance—to use Marilyn Frye's term—of racializing and sexist vision.[78]

But what of the *othered subjects* who already hesitate? Having internalized or "epidermalized" the "I cannot" of objectifying vision into one's body schema, this "I cannot" leads not only to a split sense of bodily self (between a subject who can and an object who cannot), but also to a form of hesitation that can be paralyzing. It is reasonable to object that presenting hesitation as a solution, albeit partial, to racializing habit ignores the difficulty experienced by racialized and gendered subjects in breaking with their overdetermined cycle of hesitation. Though I take this objection seriously, I think it poses an artificial dilemma—a choice between unwavering seamless habit, on the one hand, and paralyzing hesitation, on the other. First, to clarify, not all habit is objectifying, or more precisely *reifying* and *othering*, as sexist and racializing habits are. I propose hesitation as an intervention into the latter. But this does not mean that nonobjectifying habits of everyday life are unhesitating

and seamless; in being receptive to their situation, in searching and impro-
vising their response, such habits already include a minimum of hesitation.
Embodied in the very temporal unfolding of habit—in its adaptive modulation and prereflective improvisation—hesitation is unreflectively lived without being felt as a disruption. That hesitation is felt to disrupt objectifying
habits has to do with the desired seamlessness and intransigence of those
habits themselves.

Second, the seamlessness of objectifying habit is based on a structural
closure that suppresses affective and ethical responsivity. As long as such habit
is held as the ideal, escaping hesitation will involve closure to, and exclusion
of, *some* other. The dilemma, by which unwavering action is the only remedy
to paralyzing hesitation, elides other ways of *acting hesitantly* in which habit is
not unhearing and hesitation not immobilizing. Although forms of reverse
objectification may be useful as intermediate *reactional* strategies against the
objectifying social gaze, I believe that the cycle of paralyzing hesitation can
only be broken through a critical and responsive form of hesitation.

This is because, third, both paralyzing hesitation and objectifying habit
rely on the same deterministic logic, as two sides of othering and reification
(with clearly incomparable effects). Both instantiate the closed temporality
by which racializing and sexist schemas overdetermine the sense of the past
and map the possibilities of the future in advance. Thus, the two forms of
hesitation I have been describing can be distinguished not only ontologically
in their temporal structure, but also phenomenologically in their relations to
futurity. Since it stems from the overdetermination of interiorized schema
and habit, paralyzing hesitation tends to be predictable and determinate in
its effects; the othered subject expects failure in advance. She sees her future
possibilities as circumscribed by her present incapacity. In contrast, responsive hesitation inserts indeterminacy into habit; it loosens the net of internalized determinism and stereotype, the hold of the "I cannot" on the othered
subject. In so doing, the racialized and/or gendered mapping of possibilities
that the "I cannot" delineates is glimpsed on the margins of experience;
other responses to this map then become possible (and anger, critique, separation, and violence are all creative responses when they arise in this interval).
Whereas the first kind of hesitation delimits possibility based on present
actuality, the second *creates possibilities* that have been hitherto foreclosed and
which can transform actuality. This is to say that for responsive hesitation the
future is unpredictable and open; it is yet to be created.

Finally, this does not mean that the immobility of the first hesitation can
be directly or easily unfrozen, by willing new possibilities into existence for

instance; I cannot willfully begin throwing better, to recall Young's example. But through an effort that mediates and redirects the way it is lived, this immobility can be made productive. Instead of being caught in a cycle of hesitation and self-blame, hesitation can be reflected onto the social reference that gave rise to it, creating the possibility of critical awareness. In other words, the first hesitation can be the occasion for the second.[79] And though I cannot throw better, I can act differently, thinking, writing, and engaging in activism as motivated by experiences of oppression and othering. Such action should not be understood as tangential, for in addressing the structures of power and domination that ground habit, it is arguably more direct. I see this route exemplified in the work of both Young and Fanon, where paralyzing hesitation is mined and becomes philosophy and action. This is possible, I have argued, because another form of hesitation arises, a hesitation that makes us think on the way to, and within, action; this hesitation can make us *actional* and no longer merely *reactional* (to use Fanon's terms), so that "having taken thought, [one] prepares to act."[80]

5. A Phenomenology of Critical-Ethical Vision

Can this critical and affective hesitation be the opening to an ethical and antiracist vision—a vision that does not exclude but, to use a phrase from Merleau-Ponty, *sees with* or *according to* others?[81] The notion of lateral passivity that Merleau-Ponty develops in his lecture course on "Le problème de la passivité" shows both how every vision is already an institution—how there is a socially, historically, and habitually sedimented normative structure or level according to which we see—and how institutions of seeing may resist or be open to transformation.[82] The motivations for the intransigence or the plasticity of vision are difficult to decipher. Merleau-Ponty speaks, on occasion, of the "adversity" of events that are unassimilable to the "normal" organization of the field and that cannot be made sense of through the given level.[83] These are events for which we cannot account from within our instituted system of meaning—events that reveal, if we are open to them, the fractures in the coherence of the visual field. There are two ways of responding to such events: by maintaining the normative organization of the field and refusing to see them, or by receptively allowing an event to insinuate itself into our vision as the dimension according to which the visual field is restructured—thus changing how we see:[84]

Passivity [operates] in the assimilation or the resumption or the *Nachvollzug*. According to what? Not according to the sense given with the event. We can be crafty, maintain the operation of the old practical schema, repress. But although there is no sense given, there are events whose historical inscription we can prevent only by refusing to see them, events that are unassimilable for our system, that refuse our *Sinngebung*. The choice to maintain [the *Sinngebung*] would then be pathological. Thus, the sense is never simply given to us, but it does not always allow itself to be constructed. When it does not allow itself to be constructed without division of the self from the self, our truth falls outside of us. [. . .] There is passivity right there in activity. It is because such direction was given as "oblique" in the old level that by setting [myself] up in it as "normal" I modify the sense of all the rest and establish a new level. [. . .] [And there is] activity right there in passivity. Outside certain limit cases where the event is not assimilable, I could always maintain my old level through regression.[85]

The transformation of the visual field is thus not one of radical discontinuity for Merleau-Ponty, for the new level was "obliquely" or tangentially implicated in the old.[86] This would seem to limit the novelty and difference that can be recognized within the visual field. It seems to imply a conservatism of the visual field, whereby possibilities for seeing differently are delimited in advance by the very norms that refuse the radically new. On this reading, the unassimilable difference of an event would bar it from becoming the dimension according to which we see; that is, we could not come to see such events on their own terms. As unassimilable affects they remain unconscious (at the risk of psychic and visual disruption). Though this is one reading to which Merleau-Ponty's text lends itself, another direction is also suggested. While it is always possible, according to Merleau-Ponty, to maintain habitual ways of seeing, this insistence in response to unassimilable events (and the corresponding exclusion of other ways of seeing) could itself be read as pathological. Here it becomes important to distinguish two possible senses of lateral passivity—two ways in which we *see with* or *according to* others, structures, and attachments.

First, there is a sense in which we can say, with Merleau-Ponty, that we always *already* see with others. These others form the invisibles that have been laterally implicated in my field of vision. Since it only sees according to its racialized schemas (it "cannot" see otherwise), racializing vision elides this lateral passivity and dependence on others. I believe that this forgetfulness should be understood to be double: (1) What is forgotten is my dependence on social-historical structures and social others who have accompanied the development of my vision; this invisible "weight of the past" institutes a particular way of seeing as normative for me.[87] (2) There is the exclusion of the nonfamiliar and "alien" other, the racialized other, whose difference may be represented as exotic or threatening, but whose abjection plays a constitutive role in how I come to see. This second forgetting corresponds to the structural elision of other ways of seeing and being that do not "make sense" within my instituted level. I want to claim that, while the first form of forgetting institutes the level according to which I see based on the *appropriation* of the flesh of others to whom my attachment is rendered invisible,[88] the second forgetting means that even *excluded* others are "obliquely" and structurally inscribed within the field of vision, as its "constitutive outside" (to use Judith Butler's term). The "unassimilability" of the other cannot be understood to mean absolute difference or separation in this case, as if others were new lands to be discovered. Rather, those defined as "alien" are already presupposed and appropriated within the workings of vision, even as they are relegated to its "unassimilable" and unrecognized margins.

Racializing vision is thus reductive of lateral difference as relationality: by rendering familiar, and indifferent, the social horizon on which I depend and, by positing as absolute and alien, differences in opposition to which my identity becomes defined. In this way, difference is either subsumed to a homogeneous identity or projected as racialized opposition. These two attitudes toward otherness are interconnected: the self-certitude and naturalization of racializing vision requires that its roots in social-historical ways of seeing remain invisible; and it is this self-forgetfulness of partiality and contingency that refuses to recognize other ways of seeing and being, foreclosed as "unassimilable."

Second, there is an important sense in which to *see with* others must be an attentive effort—an effort that I have argued in this paper begins in hesitation. In this light, the first sense of seeing with others is revealed to be ignorance of others; it is a willful gaze that takes itself to be a self-sufficient, unhesitating, and seamless "I can see," ranging over the visible by disregarding its affective roots in sociality and historicity. The insistence on maintaining the normative schema of racializing vision, in response to an affective complexity that cannot be reduced to that level, would thus be "pathological."[89] Witness the affective ankylosis of racializing vision in the first example of this essay.

But, while Merleau-Ponty's lectures on "Le problème de la passivité" speak of the disruption that comes to vision from unassimilable events, it is clear that such events are not sufficient in themselves to generate critical awareness and change. Here, we may ask what role hesitation plays in connection with unassimilable others or events. Their relation can be understood not as linear causality but as a relation of motivation (in the phenomenological sense), in which unassimilability calls for hesitation and hesitation is an affective recognition of unassimilability. For Merleau-Ponty, unassimilable events are those whose sense "does not allow itself to be constructed without division of the self from the self." Unassimilable events pose an impediment for the perceiving self; they are experienced as "adversity," as tension and, we may say, discomfort.[90] What hesitation registers and allows us to feel is this *unassimilability* of an event; this is not the event in its singularity and detail, but in its resistance to our perceptual and conceptual schemas, as a "truth [that] falls outside us" and that reflects our failure to incorporate it.[91] Hesitation registers this very tension and, hence, recognizes the forgetfulness of normative vision, the exclusion and abjection on which it relies. This does not mean, of course, that the unassimilable will be acknowledged on its own terms, or acted on; only that its difference has been affectively received. A perceptual and affective response is, then, called for. Though the unassimilable event may yet be ignored, or reduced to an aberration according to the old level, these responses should be understood as the suppression of hesitation. As Merleau-Ponty notes, it is always possible to refuse to see events deemed unassimilable, to abide in a kind of affective and ethical closure toward others and the world. This refusal, I would claim, emerges from the pathological rigidity that is a feature of racializing vision and affect, the "I cannot see or feel otherwise" that structures them.

More difficult and less frequent, when hesitation is held open, the normative level according to which one sees can itself be transformed in response to unassimilable events. Perceptual and affective maps shift; one comes to see according to attachments that reflect hitherto repressed events and excluded others, so that it may become possible, with time, to see and act differently. But while this interrupts old racializing schemas, it does not necessarily prevent the return of racialization under new guise and the transmutation of othering into new forms of exclusion.[92] To interrupt the affective closure and rigidity of racialization itself, transformation cannot only be forward-looking but must be based in the critical memory that hesitation enables. In hesitating, the old level according to which one sees is destabilized and denaturalized. This level comes into focus for the first time in memory. As normative levels shift, the old level comes to be remembered in its social-historical contingency and affective limitation; its exclusion of that which now appears "normal" is recollected, an exclusion that was unconscious in the present, since it defined the operation of the perceptual field. This memory is hence self-critical; more so, it can be the source of vigilance with regards to habits of seeing. Not only can the memory of the old level produce affect in the present through feeling answerable for the past, holding hesitation open a little longer,[93] but this memory can motivate a different way of living the present. Here, the present is imagined as that which *will have been*; it is imagined in what it will reveal for a future critical and recollective regard, whether mine or another's. The present is lived in watchfulness and with responsibility to the future. In these ways, hesitation allows us to feel the weight and answerability of the past; it makes visible—indirectly, affectively, and laterally—the processes of habituation, socialization, and exclusion involved in the institution of the level according to which we see.

Finally, to see with others requires, as my second and third examples show, that one take up the task of living-with. Such sustained effort, in difficulty and in joy, can reconfigure and rehabituate one's body to see differently. But how? In both Haslanger's and my own example, a shift can be witnessed at the level of attachments to others. Both transracial adoption and extended family life bring subjects together in bodily and affective intimacy, creating attachments that are neither necessarily willed nor consciously formed. These situations make familiar what may have been alien; those others, on whom racializing vision relies but whom it excludes and reifies, come to have affective presence. This presence polarizes the affective field changing its configuration and relief, so that zones of tension and comfort shift; this motivates affective hesitation. Returning to Merleau-Ponty's account of unassimilable events, can we see affective attachments as playing the role of such events? To focus on my third example, Muslim female *subjectivity*, which is formed through veiling and not oppressed by it, is unassimilable, even unimaginable, from the perspective of the secular French racial map. For such subjects to become familiar, to register in their concrete specificity and subjectivity, is for one's affective map to shift, even while one's perceptual and conceptual schemas may not yet have changed. In my account, this affective shift can be felt as hesitation. As noted, hesitation is not sufficient and it can be closed down in a defensive ankylosis of affect. But hesitation, when held open, can also lead to a more thoroughgoing shift in racial maps and a more binding reconfiguration of the network of attachments; thus, hesitation can go all the way up and transform perception and thinking.

In this vein, I think that making hesitation productive requires that living-with, in whatever form it takes, be an enduring process. Both Haslanger's and my own example suggest this. Though isolated events and punctual efforts may provoke hesitation, such hesitation can be difficult to sustain and may revert to a defensive reaction once the event has passed. It is, in my view, the seemingly minor and incessant experiences of everyday living that may be able to hold hesitation open, since such events insinuate their way into one's prereflective life and cannot be easily isolated or dismissed. This is because what is required is a shift at the level of passivity, an intervention into the workings of unreflective, even unconscious, perception and affect. Specifically, what is at stake is a reconfiguration of relationality and "lateral passivity," a shift in the dimensions and attachments *according to which* we perceive, act, and think. As my example with my partner shows, attempting to change perception at the level of perceptual *acts*, by means of persuasion and argument, misses the unreflective and unconscious habituality of perception; more so, it misses the ways in which perceptual and cognitive acts rely on, and are already structured by, socially instituted attachments (that include some and exclude others). We see *according to* these affective attachments, and hence do not see them; they function as normative level, as unconscious and "neutral" ground, selectively demarcating and configuring what is seen. Only by altering this frame, making it at once marginally visible, can perceptions and acts themselves be susceptible to change. Though my partner listened to and engaged with my arguments when I tried to convince him that veiling should not be banned from French schools, our perceptual maps so differed that ours was ultimately "*un dialogue de sourds*." The racializing map, which subtends secular French space, means that veiling is overdetermined as a *conspicuous* sign incompatible with that space, not only because it is religious (crosses, after all, are allowed), but because it is seen as invariantly oppressive to women. This racializing perception maps in advance the positions that veiled Muslim women can occupy, as victims or pawns of their religion; what is unassimilable in this racializing schema, what cannot be recognized, is the agency and subjectivity of concrete Muslim women who veil. Living with Muslim women who wear the hijab, and forming attachments with them, puts this map under strain in ways that arguments could not; this was, for my partner, an enduring "environmental change" (to use Sullivan's term) that served to interrupt habitual perception.[94]

That an effort of living with others is needed points to the ways in which *time makes a difference* for how we see and feel. As I have argued, it is not merely environmental change that is needed, but an environmental change that sustains hesitation and allows critical memory.[95] For affective hesitation is the opening that permits attachments and events to register, to be retained and sedimented, shifting the level according to which we perceive. To see *according to* others is not to see through their eyes or to assimilate them to my vision; it is to find the perceptual field to have been reoriented by others. Here, the other is not an object in the perceptual field, but a magnetizing center, or counterweight, whose very style of being, way of seeing, and memory inflect that field. To see *with others* is hence to find one's perceptual and affective map to be redrawn through the force of attachments to others.[96] Such a shift not only reorients the present but is accompanied by a working-through of the past. We have seen how memory can serve as critique of the old level and vigilance with respect to the new. More so, critical memory can be an opening onto a *shared* and *intersubjective* past. Structured through privilege and domination, this past was shared without recognition or justice, so that it remained ignorant of the intersubjectivity on which it relied. To remember this past differently, and intersubjectively, is for other memories to be heard. These memories reconfigure the past, making what was familiar and taken for granted appear alien. Once his perceptual field had shifted, the racializing map of secular space began to appear alien to my partner, even though his attachments to that space remained in play (for they constituted his past and belonging). Such critical permutation does not mean that the past is left behind; to the contrary, this past in its very reorientation is felt as one's shared past and actualized in the present. But this actualization does not simply reproduce old racializing maps and attachments; it skews those maps by navigating them differently. To borrow a useful distinction from Haslanger, one may navigate *around* white privilege rather than *toward* it, and in so doing reconfigure one's racial map; as Sullivan notes, one may use white privilege against itself.[97]

What is at stake is a transformation of habitual living through intimacy, affectivity, and coexistence to become critical and ethical. It will be noted that in both Haslanger's example and in my own, the space for relearning ways of seeing and for transformative affect was the intimate space of the home or the extended family. Neither do I mean to restrict hesitation and transformative affect to these contexts, nor do I intend to romanticize the home as the abode of social change. Living-with can take many forms: in activism and in friendship, in the shared spaces of work and school as well as home, enduring experiences of coexistence take place.[98] Moreover, I do not mean to portray the coexistence that motivates hesitation as necessarily harmonious, or its affective quality as primarily joyful; we learn much from the tension and resistance of others, from their efforts to push back, when we are able to see them on their own terms. Hence, my description of coexistence is not meant as an argument for forced integration, which generally occurs on the terms of the dominant social group, neither is it meant to impose on racialized others the presence of the well-intentioned and privileged; coexistence includes allowing racialized groups the space of separation, on their own terms.[99]

What I am suggesting, rather, is that in a present where experiences of coexistence already take place (both in social spaces and within structures of the self)—and given the non reflective and contradictory attachments by which we live—hesitation and attentiveness within these experiences is called for.[100] The examples I have given are meant to show how transformative affect and perception are possible, not to prescribe the means by which they must come about. Although the means will differ, what I believe I have shown is that antiracist transformations need to occur at the affective, perceptual, and bodily level, the prereflective level of habit, and not merely at the reflective level of cognition or belief. In this context, I have attempted to show the value for ethical and antiracist experience of what is normally seen as a negative to be avoided: hesitation. Racism aims at, manages, and takes place through lived bodies; it is through embodied practices that it can be critically resisted and interrupted.[101]

Notes

1. This paper was written during time spent at the Camargo Foundation in Cassis, France and at the Institute of Advanced Study at Durham University, UK. The paper was also made possible by support from the Social Sciences and Humanities Research Council of Canada.

2. I am using the term *affect* in a broad phenomenological sense, that follows Husserlian and Merleau-Pontian usage (in particular, Husserl's *Analyses Concerning Passive and Active Synthesis: Lectures on Transcendental Logic*, trans. Anthony J. Steinbock [Dordrecht: Kluwer Academic Publishers, 2001]). In this usage, the realm of affectivity is wider than what can be called *emotion*, since emotion is an intentional, sense-giving relation (to an object) that is built on affect, whereas affect is the preintentional tendency or force (attraction, repulsion, pain, pleasure, etc.) that can motivate and support this intentional turning toward an object.

3. The affective investments witnessed in many reactions to veiling in France have caused one commentator to speak of "political hysteria."

See Emmanuel Terray, "L'hystérie politique," in *Le foulard islamique en questions,* ed. Charlotte Nordmann (Paris: Éditions Amsterdam, 2004), 103–117.

4. For a philosophical analysis of the public debate on the veil in France, see my essay "The Racialization of Muslim Veils: A Philosophical Analysis," *Philosophy and Social Criticism* 36, no. 8 (October 2010): 875–902.

5. Sally Haslanger, "You Mixed? Racial Identity Without Racial Biology," in *Adoption Matters: Philosophical and Feminist Essays* (Ithaca, N.Y. and London: Cornell University Press, 2005), 265–289.

6. Ibid., 279–280.

7. Ibid., 282.

8. Several thinkers have used Merleau-Ponty's phenomenology to think racializing perception and racialized embodiment and space, notably: Linda Martín Alcoff, Gail Weiss, and Cynthia Willett. See also the critique of the elision of race in Merleau-Ponty's phenomenology by Helen Fielding, "White Logic and the Constancy of Color," in *Feminist Interpretations of Maurice Merleau-Ponty,* ed. Dorothea Olkowski and Gail Weiss (University Park, Pa.: The Pennsylvania State University Press, 2006).

9. This dual account of vision is most clearly presented in "Eye and Mind," where Merleau-Ponty distinguishes between "profane," objectifying vision (which sees only what can be made object) and the painter's vision (which is attuned to the invisible infrastructure of visibility). See Maurice Merleau-Ponty, "Eye and Mind," trans. Carleton Dallery, in *The Primacy of Perception and Other Essays on Phenomenological Psychology, the Philosophy of Art, History and Politics* (Evanston: Northwestern University Press, 1964), 159–160; and Merleau-Ponty, *L'Œil et l'Esprit* (Paris: Éditions Gallimard, 1964), 9–12.

10. Frantz Fanon, *Black Skin, White Masks,* trans. Charles Lam Markmann (New York: Grove Press, 1967).

11. Ibid., 190–191. Such undesirability is, of course, itself constituted in the collective unconscious for Fanon.

12. What Ladelle McWhorter calls biopolitical racism (in *Racism and Sexual Oppression in Anglo-America: A Genealogy* [Bloomington: Indiana University Press, 2009]) and what Falguni Sheth has called the technologies of race (*Toward a Political Philosophy of Race* [Albany: State University of New York Press, 2009]).

13. Although it may seem strange to speak of the *naturalization* of race to cultural practices, this accurately describes the way in which particular features (e.g., backwardness, gender oppression, closure) come to be seen,

in cultural racism, as part of the nature of certain cultures and of the bodies that belong to those cultures.

14. This is neither to imply that other senses are immune to racism, nor to forget the imaginary and discursive dimensions that are also clearly implicated in racialization.

15. This echoes Kelly Oliver's concern in *Witnessing: Beyond Recognition* (Minneapolis: University of Minnesota Press, 2001). My response will be that, though racializing seeing relies on the intentional and habitual structures of vision, it also includes a distinctive structural limitation.

16. In noting the recalcitrance and rigidity of racism, I do not mean to imply that the stereotypes and contents projected by racism have remained the same over time. Indeed, racism adapts to make use of the tools available in different historical epochs (e.g., biological sciences, cultural preconceptions, gender norms, etc.), *even while it maintains its othering structure*. It is this projective othering mechanism, which manages and divides people, that I see as recalcitrant. It is also for this reason that I think critical memory and vigilance are needed to overcome racism (section 5). For a genealogy of Anglo-American racism that shows its historical fluidity, yet persistence, see McWhorter's *Racism and Sexual Oppression in Anglo-America*. In this vein, following Robert Bernasconi's recent work, it might be better to understand racism as drawing borders rather than defining essences. (Robert Bernasconi's "Crossed Lines in the Racialization Process: Race as a Border Concept," *Research in Phenomenology* 42 [2012]: 206–228, came to my attention too late to be incorporated into this section.)

17. Linda Martín Alcoff, *Visible Identities: Race, Gender, and the Self* (Oxford: Oxford University Press, 2006), 187–188.

18. Maurice Merleau-Ponty, *Phenomenology of Perception*, trans. Donald A. Landes (London: Routledge, 2012), 154–155; *Phénoménologie de la perception* (Paris: Éditions Gallimard, 1945), 190.

19. In this sense, the visual field of colonialism can be understood to motivate the othering of the "native," and that of Western phallocentrism the production of Western, white femininity as object of desire of the male gaze.

20. Alcoff, *Visible Identities*, 188.

21. As Fanon has noted, racism and colonialism are pathological for both colonized and colonizer. See *Black Skin, White Masks*, 11. Fanon does not understand racist vision as inevitable, but presents the possibility of disalienation through revolutionary engagement and the production of a "new humanism."

22. See Alcoff, *Visible Identities*, 188.
23. For an account of racializing affect, see section 2.
24. *"Des œillères."* See Henri Bergson, *The Creative Mind: An Introduction to Metaphysics,* trans. Mabelle L. Andison (New York: Carol Publishing Group, 1992), 139; *La pensée et le mouvant* (Paris: Presses Universitaires de France, 1938), 151–152.
25. See David Theo Goldberg, *Racist Culture: Philosophy and the Politics of Meaning* (Oxford: Blackwell Publishers, 1993), 3–8, and Alcoff, *Visible Identities,* 179–181.
26. Though all institutions involve forgetting for Merleau-Ponty, a productive forgetting that belongs to the process of sedimentation (*Signes* [Paris: Librairie Gallimard, 1960], 74), I want to claim that racialization involves an ignorance that is more limiting. This is the exclusion contained in the "I cannot" analyzed here.
27. See the discussion of Iris Marion Young's "Throwing Like a Girl" below.
28. This is not to deny that *racial identity* may be configured, lived, and perceived in different ways. It is helpful to distinguish here between "race" as constructed through racism and racial identity as lived. The perception of the latter includes, in my account, an awareness of its historical constitution and lived multiplicity.
29. The function that the "I cannot" of racism performs is hence structural rather than simply definitional. Racism involves an attempt at policing borders—a mechanism of othering or projective exclusion—in the face of complex and messy lived realities that exceed those borders (to draw on Bernasconi's proposition that race be thought as a "border concept" in "Crossed Lines in the Racialization Process," 226–227).
30. My account of racializing habits has resonances with Shannon Sullivan's rich description of white privilege as "ontological expansiveness." But the unobstructed and expansive "I can" of white privilege, which sees itself as entitled to all spaces and that does not hesitate to occupy them, is based, in my view, on a necessary limitation. While I agree with Sullivan that repressive forgetting plays a role in maintaining habits of white privilege, I believe that the recalcitrance of these habits also owes to an internal and structural flaw, an "I cannot" that limits their receptivity and ability to hesitate and change. See Shannon Sullivan, *Revealing Whiteness: The Unconscious Habits of Racial Privilege* (Bloomington: Indiana University Press, 2006), 8, 10.
31. That affect and perception go together recalls Merleau-Ponty's account of operative intentionality as dialogue of body and world (in *Phenomenology*

of Perception)—perception being an intentional response to the call of the world in a prior affective moment. This dialogue is distorted in racialization, but it is not suspended. In other words, racialization is not simply projective, but constitutes its own affects, *as if* it were reacting to the world.

32. See Etienne Balibar, "Is There a 'Neo-Racism'?" in *Race, Nation, Class: Ambiguous Identities* (London: Verso, 1991), 22, 26. Hence the backward belief that it is the ostensible visibility of bodily practices, such as veiling, that "causes" racist reactions in Western society.

33. Such affect can be conceived as circulating collectively, almost as if by contagion. See Terray, "L'hystérie politique," 117, and Kelly Oliver, *The Colonization of Psychic Space: A Psychoanalytic Social Theory of Oppression* (Minneapolis: University of Minnesota Press, 2004).

34. To say that secularized Muslim women are "tolerated" is still to mark them as marginal, as Wendy Brown's account of tolerance shows. See *Regulating Aversion: Tolerance in the Age of Identity and Empire* (Princeton, N.J.: Princeton University Press, 2006), 14.

35. Fanon, *Black Skin, White Masks*, 122. See also Oliver, *The Colonization of Psychic Space*, 50.

36. Fanon, *Black Skin, White Masks*, 111.

37. Ibid., 121–122. Merleau-Ponty refers to this as "perceptual rigidity," citing the psychologist Else Frenkel-Brunswik's work on "psychological rigidity." Although his brief account includes "racist opinions" under phenomena of psychological and perceptual rigidity, he does not go beyond the psychological in this essay. (See "The Child's Relations with Others" in *The Primacy of Perception*, 105, 107.)

38. I share Shannon Sullivan's skepticism regarding the ability of conscious argumentation and intellectualized change to disrupt unconscious habits of white privilege. Sullivan proposes indirect strategies, in particular changing one's environment, as potentially more effective. But I would note that, in order to motivate and then be responsive to environmental change, hesitation and critical awareness are needed (a point with which I think Sullivan might agree). (*Revealing Whiteness*, 1, 9–11, 159–165).

39. Bergson, *The Creative Mind*, 93; *La pensée et le mouvant*, 102. Translation corrected.

40. Gilles Deleuze, *Le bergsonisme* (Paris: Presses Universitaires de France, 1966), 108.

41. Bergson, *The Creative Mind*, 188; *La pensée et le mouvant*, 211.

42. Bergson, *The Creative Mind*, 93; *La pensée et le mouvant*, 101.

43. Bergson, *L'évolution créatrice* (Paris: Presses Universitaires de France, 1907), 4–7.

44. Henri Bergson, *Matière et mémoire: Essai sur la relation du corps à l'esprit* (Paris: Presses Universitaires de France, 1896), 11–12. I have called the account I am presenting a "phenomenology" of hesitation. This is justified insofar as it is mainly the first chapter of *Matière et mémoire* that is concerned.

45. Ibid., 251.

46. Sullivan, *Revealing Whiteness*, 10.

47. "Affection is what occupies the interval, what occupies it without filling it in or filling it up." Gilles Deleuze, *Cinema 1: The movement-image*, trans. Hugh Tomlinson and Barbara Habberjam (Minneapolis: University of Minnesota Press, 1986), 65.

48. Describing the phenomenon of pain, Bergson says: "Il y a dans la douleur quelque chose de positif et d'actif, qu'on explique mal en disant, avec certains philosophes, qu'elle consiste dans une représentation confuse" *(Matière et mémoire*, 55.) This quotation shows how Bergson blurs the lines between positive and negative affects. It also evokes the complex question of the role of pain in subject formation and diminution.

49. Ibid., 57 and 59.

50. Ibid., 56 and 58.

51. Ibid., 58.

52. Bergson notes that bodily affectivity is the limit at which hetero-affection and self-affection, outside and inside coincide (Ibid., 57–58). In this regard, we find important phenomenological resemblances, but also ontological differences, between Bergson and Husserl's *Analyses Concerning Passive and Active Synthesis*, avenues I do not have space to develop here.

53. *Matière et mémoire*, 56.

54. To speak of lived-through self-awareness recalls Husserl's prereflective self-consciousness, which accompanies all our experiences. Though there are resemblances here, the ontological commitments differ. Bergsonian self-awareness is bodily effort, hesitation, and the occasion for remembering.

55. "Memory of the present" is Bergson's term for the redundant memory that accompanies the present and remains unconscious. I have argued that this "memory of the present" is a memory of the world and of what is not directly grasped in perception, a memory that is colored by affect. See my essay "The Memory of Another Past: Bergson, Deleuze

and a New Theory of Time," Continental Philosophy Review 37 (2004): 203–239.

56. Gilles Deleuze, *Cinema 2: The Time-Image*, trans. Hugh Tomlinson and Robert Galeta (Minneapolis: University of Minnesota Press, 1989), 52.

57. I wish to thank Ed Casey for pointing out to me this implication of my essay.

58. Two senses of immediacy need to be distinguished here: the immediacy of an experience that does not involve reflection, and the immediacy of an encounter that gives the other directly.

59. Merleau-Ponty, "The Child's Relations with Others," 103. Ambiguity can accept a multiplicity of perspectives, whereas ambivalence hides contradictions and imposes a univocal perspective. In the same article, Merleau-Ponty links emotional ambivalence to psychological and perceptual rigidity.

60. Sullivan, *Revealing Whiteness*, 9-–10.

61. Ibid., 149.

62. Ibid., 164–165.

63. Sullivan takes this into account. See in particular her argument for reparations in chapter 5 of *Revealing Whiteness*.

64. Fanon, *Black Skin, White Masks*, 226. Fanon sometimes seems to claim that the past should be left behind altogether. I think his account is more nuanced, for it is white history and reactional attempts to recuperate it in "Negritude" that he rejects; the past as a nondeterministic whole is to be recaptured but for the sake of creating a different future.

65. Earlier, shorter versions of the following sections appeared in my essay, "A Phenomenology of Critical-Ethical Vision: Merleau-Ponty, Bergson, and the Question of Seeing Differently," in *Chiasmi International: Publication trilingue autour de la pensée de Merleau-Ponty* 11 (2009): 375–398. What follows is a substantially revised and expanded analysis.

66. Recalling Sullivan's term, *Revealing Whiteness*, 10.

67. Fanon, *Black Skin, White Masks*, 11, 112–113.

68. Iris Marion Young, *On Female Body Experience* (Oxford: Oxford University Press, 2005), 34.

69. Ibid., 37.

70. Ibid., 43–44.

71. Ibid., 44–45. This is not to imply that women's responses to the patriarchal gaze are homogeneous, but that, whether complicit, resistant, or subversive, by being socially positioned as "feminine," one finds oneself

already having to work within a field defined by this gaze and, hence, already hesitating, even as one seeks to overcome that hesitation.

72. I am drawing a parallel between the logic of racism and that of sexism, insofar as they are objectifying schemas. I do not mean this to imply a seamless analogy between these structures of domination.

73. Ibid., 44.

74. I agree here with Gail Weiss's critical reformulation of Young's account to highlight the "socially referred" character of bodily existence (Weiss) rather than its "self-reference" (Young). *Body Images: Embodiment as Intercorporeality* (New York and London: Routledge, 1999), 46–48.

75. The "I can" is always accompanied by a certain "I cannot" that serves to circumscribe and set limits to the field of my possible actions in the world. But, as Young points out, "I can" and "I cannot" are in this case only juxtaposed; it is their superimposition that gives rise to the contradictory modalities of "feminine" bodily existence (*On Female Body Experience,* 37). The passivity within the "I can" that I wish to point to here is more than the external limitation of a juxtaposed "I cannot."

76. For Merleau-Ponty's attempts to overcome the activity-passivity dichotomy, see *Institution and Passivity: Course Notes from the Collège de France (1954–1955),* trans. Leonard Lawlor and Heath Massey (Evanston: Northwestern University Press, 2010), 192; *L'Institution, La Passivité, Notes de cours au Collège de France, 1954–1955* (Paris: Éditions Belin, 2003), 250. Also see Leonard Lawlor's critique of Merleau-Ponty's "I can" in *The Implications of Immanence: Toward a New Concept of Life* (New York: Fordham University Press, 2006), 85–86.

77. Young offers her own critique of this tendency to treat the masculine as neutral measure, in "Throwing like a Girl: Twenty Years Later," in *Body and Flesh: A Philosophical Reader,* ed. Donn Welton (Oxford: Blackwell Publishers, 1998), 286–290.

78. I am drawing on Marilyn Frye's term "arrogant vision" from *The Politics of Reality: Essays in Feminist Theory* (Freedom, Calif.: The Crossing Press, 1983), 52–83. In other words, such hesitation would be a critical corrective to the exclusionary logic—the "I cannot see otherwise"—of objectifying, racializing and sexist vision.

79. One may conclude that the othered subject who hesitates in the first sense has privileged epistemic and affective access to the second form of hesitation. This may well be the case, though I think the connection is neither direct nor guaranteed. This owes to the tension that this subject

feels, and that leads to her paralyzing hesitation, for this tension reflects the way in which the schemas of racialization and sexism, even when internalized, do not quite fit. This is an experience of prereflective bodily awareness—a conflict at the affective and perceptual level between one's subjectivity and one's social positionality—that is much more than discomfort and that can be unbearable, leading to revolt and critique.

80. Fanon, *Black Skin, White Masks*, 222.

81. Merleau-Ponty, "Eye and Mind," 164; *L'Œil et l'Esprit*, 23.

82. The description of "lateral passivity" occurs in the context of a discussion of how an organization of the visual field, that had been *the* level according to which we saw, comes to be reorganized: "Passivity [is] not frontal, toward another *I,* but congenital to the *I,* insofar as something which happens to it, i.e., sparks redistribution of its landscape, of its cathexes, of the dimensions of its being in the world; i.e., [introduced] into a certain level, and [affected] in accordance with it [by] certain values and significations, [it] ends up by upsetting the level (Wertheimer's experiment) and reorganizing it" (Merleau-Ponty, *Institution and Passivity*, 191; *L'Institution, La Passivité*, 249–250, translation corrected). The reference here is to an experiment by M. Wertheimer, *Experimentelle Studien über das Sehen von Bewegung, Ztschr.* f. Ps. 1912, cited in Merleau-Ponty's *Phenomenology of Perception*, 259–260, *Phénoménologie de la perception*, 296–297.

83. Merleau-Ponty, *Institution and Passivity*, 192, *L'Institution, La Passivité*, 250.

84. For more on Merleau-Ponty's notion of "dimension," see Renaud Barbaras, *The Being of the Phenomenon: Merleau-Ponty's Ontology*, trans. Ted Toadvine and Leonard Lawlor (Bloomington: Indiana University Press, 2004), 174ff.

85. Merleau-Ponty, *Institution and Passivity*, 191–2, *L'Institution, La Passivité*, 250, translation corrected. There exists an ambiguity in Merleau-Ponty's text: "Le choix de la maintenir sera alors pathologique." Here "la" can refer to "*Sinngebung*" or to "historical inscription" in the previous sentence, but cannot, because of gender, refer to "our system." The term that makes most (grammatical and interpretative) sense is "*Sinngebung*."

86. "The new level would be nothing definite without what preceded it, without my history" (Merleau-Ponty, *Institution and Passivity*, 192; *L'Institution, La Passivité*, 250).

87. Merleau-Ponty, *Institution and Passivity*, 192; *L'Institution, La Passivité*, 251.

88. This is an "arrogating" vision, to use Marilyn Frye's term (*The Politics of Reality*, 69). As Maria Lugones points out, such vision grafts the flesh

of the other to myself, instrumentalizing the other and refusing to see her within her own "worlds" ("Playfulness, 'World'-Traveling, and Loving Perception," in *Women, Knowledge and Reality: Explorations in Feminist Philosophy,* ed. Ann Garry and Marilyn Pearsall [London and New York: Routledge, 1996], 420–424).

89. This can be related to the way in which racializing perception, and racism and colonialism more generally, are pathological according to Fanon. See *Black Skin, White Masks,* 10–11, 192.

90. Merleau-Ponty, *Institution and Passivity,* 192; *L'Institution, La Passivité,* 250.

91. I use the term *unassimilable* here following Merleau-Ponty. But what I am describing should not be conflated with the *intolerable* of ankylosed affect discussed in section 2. Whereas the *intolerable* was already defined by racialization, the unassimilable is that which cannot fit within racializing schemas and hence poses a difficulty for the racializing imaginary. This recalls what Falguni Sheth calls "the unruly" (*Toward a Political Philosophy of Race* [Albany: State University of New York, 2009]).

92. I am thinking of the ways in which racism recasts itself as cultural racism, once biological theories of race have been discredited. I am also thinking of the way in which color-blindness allows systemic and implicit forms of racism to continue.

93. This can include regret, guilt, and remorse, but also shared pain and anger through love, and hope for changing the future. As I believe I have shown, it is not the kind of affect, negative or positive, but its structure and responsivity that matter in my account.

94. Even if my partner had been convinced by my arguments, a willful and momentary decision would not have been sufficient to sustain lasting change. Here, I agree with Shannon Sullivan that willful and self-reflective attempts to change oneself and one's habits are unlikely to be successful (*Revealing Whiteness,* 9). This is not only because we do not have such direct and transparent access to ourselves, as phenomenologists have tirelessly discovered, but also because such attempts are instantaneous and sporadic efforts which, moreover, precisely reinforce the sense of mastery and control of oneself that excludes hesitation.

95. Haslanger is cautious to point out that not all transracial parenting will involve a transformation in racial maps (racial schemas and bodily habits of navigating social space). Where parents' white norms and habits do not shift, this will have the damaging consequence of casting their Black children as racialized others ("You Mixed?" 287–288). In other words, though experiences like transracial adoption can enact "environmental

change" and force tacit racial maps into consciousness (284), more is required to put those racial maps into question and critically reconfigure the way in which they are navigated.

96. See Haslanger, "You Mixed?" 283–285. Also see bell hooks, *Black Looks: Race and representation* (Boston: South End Press, 1992), 177, where she gives the example of white people who shift locations and begin to see the world differently.

97. Haslanger, "You Mixed?" 284; Sullivan, *Revealing Whiteness*, 161–162.

98. For instance, Haslanger speculates that "close inter-racial friendships and love relationships" may lead to similar disruptions in racializing habits as the ones she describes in transracial parenting ("You Mixed?" 278).

99. See Sullivan, *Revealing Whiteness*, 176–177.

100. This is to evoke a multiplicity within the self, in terms of identity and attachment.

101. This is, I believe, the import of the last line of Fanon's *Black Skin, White Masks*: "O my body, make of me always a man who questions!" (232).

SEVEN

HOMETACTICS

Self-Mapping, Belonging, and the Home Question

Mariana Ortega

Home is a name, a word, it is a strong one; stronger than magician ever spoke, or spirit ever answered to, in the strongest conjuration.

—Charles Dickens

A whole history remains to be written of spaces—which would at the same time be the history of Powers—from the great strategies of geopolitics to the little tactics of the habitat.

—Michel Foucault

There is nowhere you can go and only be with people who are like you. It's over. Give it up.

—Bernice Johnson Reagon

To start, I have to make a confession: this is an exercise of self-mapping, an attempt to deal with a certain nostalgia, a painful fixation on loss and a desire to return to a place called home, a persistent desire that keeps returning, like the snow of February in Cleveland, the city I sometimes call home. In self-mapping, one locates oneself in life and space and recognizes locations imbued with histories, power relations, cultural and economic forces, and personal dreams and imagination. Home, says bell hooks, is "the safe place . . . the place where the me of me mattered."[1] Quoting Michael Seidel, Caren Kaplan says that home is the exile's "belated romance with a past, through memory heightened by distance."[2] I am that exile who unwittingly falls for this romance yet is perfectly aware of its traps.[3] Perhaps it is exile that brings forth the will to belong in a more insistent and gripping way—I

173

am not sure. This essay is my way of writing my way home by leaving it, by stripping it away of its magic and its strong conjuration.

In one of its multiple appearances, the notion of home can emphasize the personal, the affective, such as "home is where the heart is," where I can feel comfortable and safe, where I can scratch my itches, where I can be who I am. Home is, as Dickens reminds us, a truly magical word, offering a most needed relief from the world of the weird, the unsafe, the *unheimlich*. Yet, as personal as this notion is, Chandra Mohanty reminds us that it is also a profoundly political question. She asks, "What is home? The place I was born? Where I grew up? Where my parents live? Where I live and work as an adult? Where I locate my community, my people? Who are my "people"?[4] Answers to these questions are complex and call forth a nexus of histories and experiences, playful and painful, chosen and inherited. Home is where the personal sometimes unexpectedly, sometimes inextricably meets the political. The home question can thus carry us from the confines of our own skin to the open space of a world inhabited by others like and unlike me. The notion of home carries us to a politics of location.

My aim here is to discuss this notion of home in connection to the notions of belonging and location. Importantly, I carry out this discussion of home, location, and belonging in light of the experience of what I call multiplicitous selves—selves that occupy multiple positionalities in terms of culture, race, sexual orientation, class, and so on. In part I, I discuss how the notion of home may be connected to a politics of location, which reaffirms so-called authentic identities and serves to exalt those identities by negating those who are deemed as not belonging. Home may become the "barred room" that Bernice Johnson Reagon warned us about in her now famous speech on coalitional politics.[5] Moreover, in this section I illustrate some of difficulties that arise when considering the meaning of belonging given the multiplicity of the self. We will see that given this multiplicity we cannot adhere to a notion of belonging that privileges so-called authentic or primary characteristics of identity.

Informed by Michel de Certeau's analysis of tactics, I conclude by introducing the notion of hometactics, practices that allow for a sense of familiarity with and a particular sense of "belonging" to a place, space, group, or "world" while avoiding the restrictive, exclusive elements that a notion of belonging may carry with it. Ultimately, while I look at the connection between the notion of home and location, it is not my aim to work out a politics of location here so that we can use it in order to form coalitions across multiple oppressions. I am deeply interested in a productive, nonexcluding, relational politics of location and coalitional work. Yet, what I reveal here is another part of the story of home, location, and belonging, the small yet important everyday practices of multiplicitous selves as they negotiate their multiple and complex identities and attempt to get a sense of connection to those worlds, what we may call micropractices of lived experience.

Part I: Belonging, Location, and Multiplicitous Selfhood

Following Aimee Carrillo Rowe, I see the notion of belonging as a point of departure for understanding, naming, and imagining location.[6] In other words, the notion of belonging is intimately tied to a politics of location, location here meaning not just spatial but also social location.[7] Carrillo Rowe asks that a feminist politics of location theorize the conditions for the possibility of belonging rather than assume an individual subject already belonging to a location.[8] While Carrillo Rowe ultimately moves away from a politics of location to what she terms a "politics of relation," in which locations are formed by a series of affective and political ties with others, her insistence that we understand conditions for the possibility of belonging is key to an analysis of the relationship between home, belonging, and location.

A politics of location that merely assumes individual subjects as already belonging to a location is indeed problematic as belonging is quickly interpreted by way of specific identity markers. Rather than understanding the complex ways in which an individual is said to belong to a social location— the ways personal identity markers as well as relational aspects are linked and negotiated—such a politics of location may quickly turn into a "home" for some members but also a "barred room" for those who are deemed not to belong. In other words, when belonging is a matter of satisfying particular conditions of identity, which in turn become homogenizing conditions, home serves to block out those who are not like us or whom we deem are not like us. Our bodies, our selves, are thus blocked from the entrance of that special room that is home for some but not others, the barred room that Bernice Johnson Reagon warns us about.

As Mohanty notes, Johnson Reagon's concern lies with the problematic spaces created by oppositional political movements that provide a "nurturing space" for a while but ultimately only provide the illusion of community and a freezing of difference.[9] Johnson Reagon is concerned with the idea some have that a coalition should be as safe as a home when in reality it is not safe or comfortable. The barred room of those who believe in narrow identity politics and who are seduced by overly nationalistic tendencies may serve as a nurturing space but not for long. Questions arise as to why I don't belong in that room, or why doesn't he or she belong? Why have others been let in and not me? Don't I satisfy the conditions of belonging? Am I not one of you? And soon enough the walls of that room become too thick. That nurturing space reminiscent of the mythic, safe home is transformed into an illusive community in the attempt to reify our difference as Latinos, as Asians, as African Americans, as lesbians, and so forth.[10] Yet, as Johnson Reagon says, "the room don't feel like the room nomore [*sic*]. And it ain't home no more."[11]

According to Johnson Reagon, community doesn't mean those that are or look like me. Spaces that have been created to reify certain characteristics can be modified when we take into consideration the heterogeneity within our group. I will then have to open the doors for others to get in or for me to get out of my zone of comfort. In the same way, we all have to leave the safety of the home at some point so as to not hide from the rest of the world and others in that world . . . not to speak of those for whom home has never been safe or comfortable and have known better.

In order to problematize further the notion of home as connected to a particular kind of belonging, what we may call "authentic belonging," I would like to bring to light some specific experiences by selves that I call multiplicitous selves. A multiplicitous self is a self capable of occupying multiple positionalities in terms of gender, race, sex, sexual orientation, physical ability, class, and so on, and thus capable of occupying a liminal space or a space of in-betweenness. One specific description of multiplicitous selfhood is that of the border crosser "new mestiza" provided by Gloria Anzaldúa.[12] While Anzaldúa's account of the new mestiza emphasizes issues connected to the north-south border and the lived experience of Chicanas, in my view an account of multiplicitous selfhood can consider various other positionalities, such as race, sex, bodily ability, economics, class, and so forth in other contexts.

In this paper I highlight my own experience as a multiplicitous self due to my exile and relocation to the United States. In my view, there is a sense in which all of us are multiplicitous selves but there is a crucial difference between those whose experience is one of being mostly at ease in the world and those whose experience is marginalized, oppressed, or alienated in some way and have to constantly engage in what María Lugones calls world-traveling.[13] So, it is key to note that multiplicity is more at issue for some selves than others, depending on the different ways in which their positionalities are perceived or negotiated given specific social, economic, and cultural contexts as well as power relations. For example, consider the way in which power relations and other economic, social, and cultural issues related to the north-south border affect the new mestiza self and lead her to feel the contradictory aspects of herself and the sense of being at the limen. Consider the way in which such power relations and social and cultural issues affect a newly arrived immigrant to this country who does not speak the language and who is marginalized as opposed to the way in which these factors affect the life of someone who is part of the mainstream and who finds herself feeling comfortable in her world.

Multiplicitous selves are constantly negotiating their multiple social locations. They are also constantly involved in world-traveling. For example, I, as a Nicaraguan-born, bilingual, lesbian, academic Latina living in the United States, have constantly to negotiate the multiple aspects of myself and have to travel to the different worlds associated with my various positionalities. And I, as a multiplicitous self, also find myself asking the home question—a home question that comes in terms of geography—is Managua, Nicaragua really my home, or is it Los Angeles, or Cleveland? And also in terms of associations with others—do I belong with U.S. Latinos, Chicanos, Latin American exiles, or women of color?

The home question is particularly difficult for the multiplicitous self whose life and context are such that she has to continually worldtravel, and thus the home question becomes a question of *homes*. Reflection on such a question paradoxically shatters any illusion of there being a definite place of belonging, while it also shatters the very multiplicity of our selves by way of a feeling and a questioning—that feeling of wanting to come home and that question of whether there is a home (or even homes) for me—as if there were a will to belong, as Nietzsche claims there is a will to truth that inspires us to many a venture.[14] It cannot be denied that even for those multiplicitous selves who are border crossers and world-travelers, the home question is still a question. Perhaps it is even a more painful question precisely because that home seems harder to find. Yet, despite the determination of this will to belong that may provide a feeling of security and comfort, we cannot avoid recognizing the limits and pitfalls of such security, namely the reification of certain identity categories as opposed to others, and thus the expulsion of those who do not fit a version of authentic belonging.

Recall María Lugones's early essay "Hispaneando y Lesbiando: On Sarah Hoagland's Lesbian Ethics," in which Lugones replies to the call of lesbian separatism. In this essay, Lugones describes the contradictory nature of her lived experience as she asserts her identity as both a Latina and a lesbian in the context of Nuevomejicano culture. While she finds it empowering to participate in keeping the Nuevomejicano culture alive by being part of its community, she realizes that she cannot be openly lesbian there, and thus she feels that her self is lacking in that environment. As she says, "These communities do not recognize us as fully their own if lesbian. The culture is heterosexualist. It does not recognize the possibility of women loving women unmediated by male domination."[15] Yet, Lugones still cannot follow Sarah Hoagland's advice to render the homophobic culture meaningless and agree to lesbian separatism, as this would entail becoming an "obsolete being" or assimilating into another culture that disregards the needs of lesbians who are not white. Lugones concludes that

> such a lesbian must, for her own survival and flourishing, acknowledge herself as needing more than "one world." Her ability to inhabit both a world where radical criticism of her culture is meaningful and to inhabit the world of her culture constitute part of the possibility of her future as a creative being.[16]

Lugones then inhabits both the Latina and the lesbian "worlds." In each world she is lacking, but, as a border-dweller, she is not completely caught in either world. Inspired by Anzaldúa, she continues to have the perspective of the crossroads or the borderlands, a position that allows her a critical edge from which to interpret the multiple worlds she inhabits. She asserts her Latina and lesbian identities without accepting the homophobia present in the context of Nuevomejicano culture and the ethnocentrism present in the Anglo lesbian community.

Like Lugones, I have also found myself wanting to belong in the Latino community, and yet being hurt as I experienced the Latino community's homophobia as well as alienation in the Anglo lesbian community. My positionality as lesbian and as Latina cannot be easily reconciled. In many cases these two identities appear as mutually exclusive. There is no acceptance within the Latino community, unless I hide an important aspect of myself or I confine myself to a smaller Latino community, that of Latina lesbians, yet another barred room. As Lugones so aptly puts it, "Pluralism also requires the transformation of those 'home' cultures so that lesbians can be rid of 'homo-phobia' in Anzaldúa's sense: 'the fear of going home.'"[17]

And yet, like Anzaldúa and Lugones, I still want to be part of the Latino community. This example as well as countless others (think of Anzaldúa's own example about the difficulties in being Chicana and American, Chicana, and lesbian; Du Bois's example of being an African American and an American; Lorde's example of being lesbian and African American) illustrate why it is that the experience of the multiplicitous self may be complicated and fraught with painful moments of what Anzaldúa describes as "intimate terrorism." It also illustrates the need that even the multiplicitous self has of belonging and the drawbacks that such a need generates. While many agree with Anzaldúa's claim that the ambiguities and contradictions of the self of the borderlands lead in fact to creative ventures and critical resistance, others question what this multiplicitous self can do besides be tormented by the contradictions and ambiguities brought about by her multiplicity. What can we do except feel the cactus needles embedded in our skin?

In *Wealth of Selves, Multiple Identities, Mestiza Consciousness and the Subject of Politics*, Edwina Barvosa tackles critics of what she calls the multiple self and attempts to show that it is in fact this multiple self with its ambiguities and contradictions that can become an agent capable of political critique and social transformation.[18] Barvosa's strategy is to explain the ways in which a multiple, socially constructed self constitutes a cohesive whole that is capable of shifting its social identities in different contexts and is capable of using ambiguity and contradiction to form a critical stance capable to be deployed for political activism. While Barvosa provides an interdisciplinary, complex explanation of the multiple systems at work in the multiple self, I would like to concentrate on the way she explains Lugones's experience of being a Latina and a lesbian described above.

According to Barvosa, Lugones integrates her mutually exclusive identities as a result of a conscious "self-integrative life project," rather than the usual rank-ordering of identities as some philosophers suggest multiple selves should do. A self-integrative life project is one in which "self-chosen endorsements are loosely interwoven into broad self-guiding projects that serve as the basis for integrating the self."[19] For Barvosa, it is precisely the experience of contradiction, ambiguity, and ambivalence that play an important role in the project of self-integration. Thus, she sees Lugones as being able to integrate her different identities of Latina and lesbian due to the fact that she has a life-project of antiracism, antiethnocentrism, and antiheterosexism. According to Barvosa, because of this life project Lugones remains highly identified as a Latina and a lesbian while she simultaneously uses different identity markers at different times to claim a group identity ("selective identification/differential self-presentation"), for example, not including the issue of her sexuality in the Latino context. Thus, Lugones's own ambivalence about belonging to the Latino group, given its homophobia, represents a strategy to hold her multiple identities together.[20] Through having a life project Lugones, according to Barvosa, can form intersections between her mutually exclusive identities and can claim a space in both communities.

While I see the value of Barvosa's appeal to a strategic self-integrating life project and, in fact, it is something that may be helpful as multiplicitous selves carry on with their lives, it should not be understood as the preferred practice guiding multiplicitous selves as they negotiate their multiple positionalities. Despite the advantages associated with practicing the kind of strategic self-integrating life-project, not all multiplicitous selves have such a project or desire it. Many may prefer to give up the illusion of integration and be willing to live with the ambiguities and contradictions that their multiplicitous selfhood entails. Moreover, given Lugones's own characterization of her experience as well as the experience of world-traveling in general, it is unclear that she would call for an integration of her multiplicitous self. Yet, Barvosa's explanation of a multiple self's negotiation of its various and sometimes mutually exclusive identities by way of a self-integrating life-project is illustrative of the complexity of the notion of belonging. What we learn from examples such as Lugones's and from Barvosa's attempt to deal with the contradictions inherent in multiplicitous selfhood is that given the complexity of the selves as well as the complexity of spaces of belonging (in terms of its members as well as criteria for membership), there is no sense in which one can be said to *fully* belong. There are only different senses of belonging depending on which markers of identity are chosen. Full membership and belonging, the safe, comfortable home is indeed an imaginary space in need of demystification.

In both its personal as well as political instantiations, "home" can easily become a space of exclusion despite its many possibilities of providing nurture and inclusiveness. The childhood home not only may awaken our sense of comfort and love, if there was love and comfort within its walls, but also the sense of insecurity and bitterness at being merely a child that does not know better and a sense of alienation from the outside world. The political "home," the space to nurture our identities, not only affirms us and empowers us as group members but can also deny entrance to others not deemed as belonging unless they silence themselves. When thinking of the case of Lugones strategically choosing different identity markers in different situations, I see how despite being able to claim both identities as Latina and lesbian, when she joins the Nuevomejicano communities, she has to follow their rules/practices/norms and is making herself vulnerable to them. She embeds herself within a regularized location, and silence about her sexual identity is her main option if she is going to participate and build community in such a location. Clearly, reconsiderations, reframings, remappings of the notions of home, of location, of belonging are necessary.

Part II: Hometactics

As we have seen, despite the problems associated with the notions of home, belonging, and location, there is no denying the power that the notion of home has in producing sentiments of safety, comfort, and belonging. But there is no forgetting its mythical, "unreal" qualities. The reality of the notion of home is often quite different from our imagined home, both in its personal and political instantiations. I wonder though, whether we can go beyond the myth of home and move toward a decentered praxis of home-making and belonging, one that gives up the possibility of full belonging and allows for the possibility of not longing to be on one side or site of belonging.[21]

Here I would like to introduce such a praxis as "hometactics."[22] Importantly, I am not suggesting that we should give up all notions of belonging connected to a politics of location, as in Mohanty's work or to a politics of relation as in Carrillo Rowe's work, or that we should give up all attempts at projects of self-integration as in Barvosa's account. There is room and necessity for larger political projects of cobelonging, as well as moments when it might be necessary to integrate certain aspects of our multiplicitous selves. Yet, I would like to add another layer to our attempt to understand home, location, and belonging, a layer that is often overlooked as we emphasize the grander project of forging a politics of location capable of generating resistance to oppression or projects that emphasize unity or integration. This layer is that of the lived experience of selves who are being-in-worlds and being-between-worlds and that find themselves constantly negotiating their multiple identities in light of both ambiguities and contradictions, but also in light of what I have referred to here as a will to belong. Thus, my introduction of the notion of hometactics is an uncovering of what multiplicitous selves are already practicing in their everydayness, a disclosure of that which is already happening in our lived experience.

As opposed to strategies, which de Certeau sees as bound up with regulations or set ways (norms/practices/laws) upheld by a dominant order, de Certeau sees a tactic as "a calculated action determined by the absence of a proper locus" and as the "art of the weak."[23] Tactics are creative, inventive, combining different elements of a system (or a set of strategies) "blow by blow" and cannot be easily traced or mapped. In terms of their relation to specific spaces, unlike strategies that impose and place limits on spaces, tactics divert spaces. According to de Certeau, tactics utilize time in a clever way, produce alternative opportunities, and introduce play into the foundations of power.[24] In short, tactics are temporal interventions aimed at producing favorable situations but not necessarily at abolishing a system of power.

De Certeau's classic example of practicing tactics is walking in the city (he also considers reading, storytelling, and cooking)—the different ways in which we improvise when we walk—walking in the city without a set map, getting a sense of the city despite its largeness and foreignness (the pedestrian reading the city but also writing it through his or her walking). For example, de Certeau discusses the example of a migrant of North African descent now living in Paris and walking this city's streets—the way he dwells in his housing development and uses the environment that he now has with plurality and creativity, and thus, "by an art of being in between, he draws unexpected results from his situation."[25] According to de Certeau, he develops modes of use or "re-use" as he acculturates in his new environment.

Although I realize the difference of the context within which de Certeau introduces the distinction between strategies and tactics, an analysis of capitalist modes of production and consumption, it is possible to apply it to the context of an examination of the notion of belonging in light of the experience of multiplicitous selfhood. As we shall see below, Maria Lugones has already engaged de Certeau's distinction to analyze the possibility of resistance on the part of those who are marginalized, although my discussion and hers have some significant differences. Hometactics share some of the characteristics described by de Certeau above, but not all. For example, while I doubt de Certeau would want to circumscribe tactics in this manner, I see hometactics as a decentered praxis, which is at the same time capable of having a general aim or result. The aim of hometactics can be understood as the production of a sense of familiarity in the midst of an environment or world in which one cannot fully belong, due to one's multiple positionalities. Such a sense of familiarity, is of course, not to be associated with the problematic idea of belonging that leads to barred rooms generally associated with so-called authentic markers of identity. And while hometactics can be said to have this general aim, no specific set-formulation of what these practices look like is possible, since one of the main features of tactics is precisely their unmapability and their working "blow by blow" and thus taking advantages of opportunities as they present themselves.

In "Tactical Strategies of the Streetwalker/Estrategias Tácticas de la Callejera," Lugones problematizes de Certeau's dichotomous distinction between tactics and strategies.[26] Lugones believes that de Certeau's view cannot offer the possibility of theorizing resistance from the point of view of the oppressed and from what she terms a concrete body-to-body engagement, because the strategist is not able to understand the logic of the tactical and the tactical is seen as "haphazard, happenstance, disjointed intrusions on dominant sense, a troubled sort of passivity."[27] Lugones thus proposes "tactical strategies" in order to disrupt the dichotomy between strategy and tactic and in order to offer a position in which a liberatory project is not guided by a mastermind or strategist. Instead, the liberatory project is intersubjective and based on concrete, embodied subjects at the street level (tactical strategists, "street-walkers," or "active subjects"), who perform acts that go beyond merely "making do."[28] As Lugones states, "As we move from tactics to tactical strategies we move from ephemeral contestatory negotiations of sense to more sustained engagements."[29]

For Lugones, such sustained engagement is connected to the practice of "hanging out" which allows the tactical strategist to develop a sense of the spatial context so as to see new possibilities in it. This sense of the spatial context available to the street-walker or tactical strategist, is, according to Lugones, neither the "nowhere" of de Certeau's tactitian nor the "proper" space of the strategist. It is constituted by hangouts that are fluid spaces that allow for multivocal sense and critical interventions against structures of domination.[30] In effect then, while problematizing de Certeau's distinction between strategies and practices, Lugones provides a "spatial politics."[31]

Lugones's emphasis on spatiality is one aspect of her analysis that I find particularly important and helpful. I agree that de Certeau's analysis misses the significance of spatiality as it is connected to tactics. While de Certeau's own characterization of tactics, as opposed to strategies, prioritizes the importance of time to that of place, in my view it is possible to understand tactics as giving meaning to both time and space without necessarily reifying them. De Certeau notes,

> Tactics are procedures that gain validity in relation to the pertinence they lend to time—to the circumstances which the precise instant of an intervention transforms into a favorable situation, to the rapidity of the movements that change the organization of a space, to the relations among successive moments in an action, to the possible intersections of durations and heterogeneous rhythms, etc.[32]

According to de Certeau, tactics prioritize time because of the way in which our actions create possibilities that may be favorable to our lives. Yet, it is possible to think how creating such possibilities may allow us to get a sense of connection to a particular location, while we traverse the complicated world of multiplicitous selfhood without necessarily having a particular location designated as our home.

Lugones is right on the mark to expose the weaknesses of de Certeau's characterizations of strategies and tactics in light of the possibility of a more sustained liberatory project or a "spatial politics." While an in-depth analysis of the virtues and the pitfalls of Lugones's account of the doings of the tactical strategist is beyond the scope of this paper, I welcome her proposal for a more intersubjective fluid, spatial, politics attentive to difference and leery of clearly marked dichotomies. My account of hometactics does not emphasize a larger spatial politics, not because of lack of interest but because of my desire to bring to light the more personal day-to-day practices of multiplicitous selves as they struggle with the home question. While I realize the connection between the personal and the political, here I am pointing to daily practices connected to the home question that are not necessarily aligned to an explicit political project.

Importantly, Lugones does not have any affinity to the notion of "home." Consider a footnote in her tactical strategies chapter:

> Streetwalkers include women who are at odds with "home." The home-shelter-street-police station/jail/insane asylum-cemetery circle, in ever so many permutations, is their larger understanding of home. Home is lived as a place inseparable from other places of violence, including the street. One could punctuate any other place in this circle. I count myself more skillful at dodging violence in the street.[33]

For her, home is more reminiscent of violence. There are no magical conjurations in this concept, no appeal to comfort and ease. It is another chapter in the yet another unfortunate dichotomy of public/private that Lugones also wishes to dismantle in her analysis of tactical strategies. For me, however, the question of home and the will to belong associated with it are still issues, deeply personal issues, despite my clear understanding of the dangers of the myth of home and my understanding of the larger political questions associated with the home question. It is precisely this paradoxical position that motivates this investigation. My account of hometactics is both my response to the paradoxical will to belong while understanding the mythical, magical, and thus unreal, aspects of home. It is also my disclosure of what multi-plicitous selves are already doing in their everyday experience. I clearly do not oppose grander and more sustained political projects, but I do not wish to overlook or forget those moments when multiplicitous selves tackle with everydayness and find ways, yes, to "make do," to feel comfortable in spite of a clear understanding of the ways in which power relations are bound to undermine, hurt, and alienate.

In my view, hometactics can be deployed at a personal or relational level. They are everyday practices that multiplicitous selves can carry out in order to have a sense of familiarity, ease, or belonging in a space or location, even though that space is a new or foreign one, or in a social gathering or commu-nity, despite the fact that a community may be made up of members claiming different identities. Hometactics are practices that we may suddenly recog-nize as granting us new possibilities of belonging in a location and a sense of identification with others with whom we may or may not share social identities, all without the appeal to a fixed home location, an intentional self-integrating life project or a set of so-called authentic identity markers.

Since hometactics are everyday practices in which we literally "make do" with what we have, they do not form a robust sense of belonging or famil-iarity, whether it is associated with a location or a group and thus may not be capable of forging strong political coalitions that can establish practices of resistance. Yet, what can be viewed as a lack of political functionality or strength does not undermine their importance in terms of the lived experi-ence of multiplicitous selves. The sense of individual or group "belonging" that they may provide is a great source of comfort in the midst of the com-plex, sometimes ambiguous, sometimes contradictory lives of multiplicitous selves. Such a comfort is not based in a great myth or conjuration, such as the traditional notion of home, or in a grand self-integrating life project, but in particular everyday practices of "making do" with the incredibly complex and thorny, yet creative and resourceful lived-experience of the multiplicitous self.

How multiplicitous selves "make do" in their everydayness with the use of hometactics is an important issue that we need to analyze further if we are to understand the phenomenology of multiplicitous selfhood. What I am calling hometactics, microtechniques of lived experience, is already being put into practice by these selves and might prove to be useful for those who are not already doing it. Important questions as to the extent to which such hometactics may be found to be too opportunistic within dominant sche-mas, may be representative of not just making do but of "selling out," may be too passive, may be too complicit in dominant schemes, and may or may not preclude the possibility of more sustained political projects remain to be examined. Yet, given the open-ended and unmappable character of these practices, it is not possible to make a priori claims regarding what multiplicitous subjects are up to or what they always ought to be doing when they deploy these hometactics. For me, hometactics have been a way of not just surviving in my travels across different worlds but of feeling a sense of much needed familiarity and relief in the midst of an existence filled with contradictions and ambiguities that lead both to moments of intimate terrorism—or of cactus needles embedded in the skin—and exciting moments of creativity and resistance.

I would like to conclude with another confession. I am a philosopher working in an academic environment that continues to privilege maleness and whiteness and writing by maleness and whiteness, the two attributes still considered by many as the bearers of philosophical excellence. Recall how Hegel wrote that women are like plants, and Africans could not arrive at *Geist*—Hegel's view of women and people of color being just one of so many reminders of the narrow, restricting, and alienating intellectual space of philosophy, a space that I precariously inhabit. There have been changes; there has been growth, talk of inclusiveness, talk of justice. But the writing that comes from the white female hand is still more important even within feminism, the movement pushing philosophy and others to see further, to understand more. So what can I do? I take what is given to me and make it my own . . . with words, with ink, with my lived experience. I offer you these words, these thoughts. I carve out a space for me in this philosophy that was never meant to be a home for me—this is one of my hometactics.

Acknowledgments

I would like to thank Alia Al-Saji, Nicole Garner, and Kyoo Lee for helpful comments and suggestions on an earlier draft of this paper. I would also like to thank Emily S. Lee for inviting me to participate in the Fortieth Cal State Fullerton Annual Philosophy Symposium on Phenomenology, Embodiment, and Race, in which I presented the first draft of this paper.

Notes

1. bell hooks, *Belonging: A Culture of Place* (New York: Routledge, 2009), 215.
2. Caren Kaplan, *Questions of Travel, Postmodern Discourses of Displacement* (Durham, N.C.: Duke University Press, 1996), 39.

3. I moved from Nicaragua to the United States in 1979, and after all these years I continue to return to the question of home.
4. Chandra Talpade Mohanty, *Feminism Without Borders: Decolonizing Theory, Practicing Solidarity* (Durham, N.C.: Duke University Press, 2003), 126.
5. Bernice Johnson Reagon, "Coalitional Politics: Turning the Century," in *Home Girls: A Black Feminist Anthology*, ed. Barbara Smith (New York: Kitchen Table: Women of Color Press, 1983), 356–369.
6. Aimee Carrillo Rowe, *Power Lines: On the Subject of Feminist Alliances* (Durham, N.C.: Duke University Press, 2008), 29.
7. The notion of a "politics of location" was coined by Adrienne Rich in her analysis of her own positionality as a white, Jewish, lesbian, privileged woman (*Blood, Bread, and Poetry: Selected Prose*, 1979–1985, [New York: Norton, 1986], 210–231). It has become a crucial idea in feminism, as feminists carry out investigations about their own spatial and social positionality and how this positionality informs their political responsibilities. Various feminists, including bell hooks, Chandra Talpade Mohanty, Rosie Braidotti, and others have elaborated on this important notion.
8. Carrillo, Rowe, *Powerlines*, 25-46.
9. Mohanty, *Feminism Without Borders*, 117.
10. Such "nurturing" spaces might not always become unsafe for those inhabiting them. However, given the heterogeneity of groups, it is likely that questions about belonging might arise.
11. Johnson Reagon, "Coalitional Politics," 359.
12. Gloria Anzaldúa, *Borderlands/La Frontera: The New Mestiza* (San Francisco, Calif.: Aunt Lute Books, 1987), ch. 7.
13. María Lugones, *Pilgrimages/Peregrinajes, Theorizing Coalitions Against Multiple Oppressions* (Lanham: Rowman & Littlefield Publishers, Inc., 2003). While I have been deeply inspired by Lugones's account of world traveling I do not follow all of Lugones's characterization of world travel. See Mariana Ortega, "'New Mestizas,' 'World'-Travelers,' and 'Dasein': Phenomenology and the Multi-Voiced, Multi-Cultural Self," *Hypatia* 16, no. 3 (Summer 2001): 1–29. My view is that world traveling does not have to entail "self-traveling," and thus we can understand the "I" as a *multiplicitous* self rather than a *multiplicity* of selves.
14. I must be clear here and add that by appealing to a "will to belong" I am not appealing to some metaphysical or psychological aspect or drive of humanity that we all must have by virtue of being human. It would be incredibly pretentious for me to make such a claim. Perhaps Shopenhauer and Nietzsche knew more when they made their appeals to the "will to live," the "will to truth," and "the will to power," respectively.

I am simply naming a feeling, perhaps an attitude that I find in myself, as well as many other people, whether they are immigrants or exiles or not, although many exiles certainly discuss it more. I am making explicit something that is already there in my lived experience as well as in the experience of others. It is not my wish to reify, naturalize, or generalize from such an experience, but I do wish to engage this feeling in light of questions of home, location, and multiplicitous selfhood.

15. María Lugones, "Hispaneando y Lesbiando: On Sarah Hoagland's Lesbian Ethics," *Hypatia* 5, no. 3 (Fall 1990), 138–146, esp. 142.
16. Lugones, "Hispaneando y Lesbiando," 144.
17. Ibid., 143.
18. Edwina Barvosa, *Wealth of Selves: Multiple Identities, Mestiza Consciousness, and the Subject of Politics* (College Station: Texas A&M University Press, 2008).
19. Barvosa, *Wealth of Selves*, 141.
20. Ibid., 151.
21. I thank Kyoo Lee for her comments regarding the possibility of being without longing, or as she puts it, "without being forced to choose sites/sides of be-longing." I realize that I am still invested in being "with longing," even when the sites of belonging and belonging itself are being problematized.
22. Here I am using *praxis* as in "practice" or "activity."
23. Michel de Certeau, *The Practice of Everyday Life* (Berkeley: University of California Press, 1984), 37.
24. de Certeau, *The Practice of Everyday Life*, 38.
25. Ibid., 30.
26. Lugones, *Pilgrimages/Peregrinajes*, Ch. 10.
27. Ibid., 216.
28. Ibid., 207–209, 216.
29. Ibid., 218.
30. Ibid., 221.
31. Ibid., 220.
32. de Certeau, *The Practice of Everyday Life*, 38.
33. Lugones, *Pilgrimages/Peregrinajes*, 209.

EIGHT

WALLING RACIALIZED BODIES OUT

Border versus Boundary at La Frontera

Edward S. Casey

An international border wall serves very diverse purposes. Some of these purposes are inclusive, some exclusive. Among the most pronounced of claims to inclusion is the assertion of national sovereignty. This assertion often takes the form of a territorial claim: on this side of the wall, the land is entirely ours to dispose of as we wish. All that is located here, up to the locus of the wall, is controlled by us: we own it, it is ours to manage and shape, and we have the right to determine who can stay inside this wall as a legitimate resident, a national citizen with papers to prove it. But the very same wall also acts to exclude, beginning with those on the other side of the wall who do not count as citizens, who belong elsewhere and should stay there—over there, out there. Crossing over the wall without permission is to be, by definition, an "illegal alien"—where "alien" signifies a stranger to this nation, someone who has no right to be over here, within the precinct of legal citizens.

Excluded by the same gesture are also those of other races. Whatever the political discourse of the country that has built and now maintains the wall—no matter how Enlightened it purports to be—it acts to exclude others whose bodily characteristics are taken to confirm their alien status, their proper standing as extramural. Race as a distinctive mark of these bodies is a primary indicator of their rightful proper place—which is outside the wall, on the other side. Even if not thematized as such by the nation that erects the wall, race comes into play at the border as a tacit criterion for determining who is to be allowed across the wall and who is to be forbidden entry. However subjacent it may be to the official political discourse, the exclusion of those of other races is deeply consequential for the historical and cultural matrix that is generated by the border and that accrues to the nations on either side of it.

Walls at international borders would not be built in the first place unless they served several aims at once—some of which reflect an effort to preserve the integrity of those with established and legitimated status in the wall-building society, others of which betray a motive to bar those whose very bodies are grounds of suspicion: racialized bodies who provide reason for wanting to keep them out of the privileged compound of the nation and its favored race.

In this essay, I characterize the international wall recently erected along a long stretch of the U.S.–Mexico border (also referred to as "La Frontera") by invoking the terminology of edge, especially its two main species, borders and boundaries. By so doing, I hope to gain increased precision for what I have so far been labeling merely as the "exclusion" and "inclusion" that all international walls bring with them. This will put us in a better position to return at the end of this essay to the question of racialized bodies at La Frontera—in particular, Latino bodies in their intense involvement and suffering there.

Edges Matter

Edges are where matter runs out or runs thin, whether this is the dense matter of solid things or the stretches of space that we call "regions" and "territories." They mark the place where things lose their dense consistency and land its sheer spread-out-ness. They are where material substance or physical landscape comes to a finish. They are where matter peters out.

Nevertheless, *edges matter*—they make a decisive difference in how we distinguish one thing from another, one place from the next, one woman from her sister, one man from his son. Despite their abrupt or eventual vanishing, edges make it clear where one thing, place, or person begins and another ends. Edges matter to matter; they embody crucial differences in and between material things. More generally, they can be considered the primary means by which the differences between things and places, events and persons get established and expressed—sorted out, we might say.

A striking instance of the way that edge matters is found in the current circumstance at La Frontera, at the U.S.–Mexico border. This international edge has become emblematic of such burning issues as immigration, national security, drug traffic, and the natural environment. I shall not discuss any of these vexing issues in detail—only enough to suggest that edges form an integral part of their fate in dimensions that are at once "placial" and political: namely, as boundaries and as borders.

Two Main Forms of Edge

So far, I have been talking about what edges are not: they are not parts of matter or space (if anything, they mark the moment when matter gives way to empty space) and they have mainly to do with the differences between things. But what are they, positively put? They are the point where things exfoliate and enter into their surroundings. At least this is so for the external edges of things: which we tend to take as paradigmatic for all edges. But there are also internal edges in the form of folds and creases, cracks and crevices. If external edges serve to terminate something, internal edges complicate it from within. In this latter capacity, edges may indicate still deeper structures that are themselves hidden from view: think only of the way that the outlines of the rib cage in the chest area of higher vertebrates disclose bone structures otherwise concealed under the skin.[1] In neither of these two basic avatars, internal and external, are edges adventitious—as we might be tempted to think if edges are regarded as the merely contingent outcroppings of things. Edges are not just peripheral presences but go to the core of what things are (and not just how they appear, though they are crucial for this as well).

Edges so understood come in a number of major forms. These include (but are not limited to) borders and boundaries. By my current count, there are seventeen distinct kinds of edges, among them: brinks, rims, margins, thresholds, frames—and the list goes one. Brinks (for instance, precipices) are edges that lead directly to certain dramatic or dangerous situations: as when we say that we are "on the brink of disaster" or "on the brink of a decision." Rims are the strictly enclosing edges of containers like metal cans or of certain geological formations such as the North Rim of the Grand Canyon: they are characterized by their comparative rigidity or persistence. Margins (as well as peripheries) are edges in the form of bands that surround a given piece of land or a printed text—bands that are variable in breadth but always more extensive than a rim or a brink. Thresholds also possess a broadband quality, but they often serve as the initiatory phases of established rituals such as welcoming someone into one's home or (in an earlier American custom) carrying a bride through the main entrance to the domestic space of a new home. Frames share with thresholds a conventional character, being determined on the basis of social or cultural (and sometimes specifically artistic) criteria. But unlike thresholds, frames act to enclose or limit from the outside—from just beyond that which they surround as a frame, whether this be a painting, an idea, or a text.

Borders and boundaries are in a class of their own. Both act to demarcate a given place or region—to set it off from other places or regions. In this capacity, each is decidedly two-sided: we talk of being "on this side" or "on the other side" of boundaries and borders. Indeed, we must do so, since straddling a border or boundary is a transitory action only: eventually, one must go one way or another—you can teeter on it only so long.

Despite this similarity, borders diverge from boundaries in certain ways. A border is a clearly and crisply delineated entity, and is established by conventional agreements such as treaties or laws; thus it is a product of human history and its vicissitudes, though it has parallels in animal populations (such as territorial markings). A boundary, too, can have cultural and historical parameters; but it may also be altogether natural in status, as with the boundary of a forest. It is rarely demarcated with any precision, varying in contour and extent depending on environmental or historical circumstances. Most importantly, it is porous in character (like the human skin), admitting the passage of various substances through it—not just for ritualistic reasons (as with a threshold) but because of its very structure—whereas a border is designed to be impervious. Also, while a boundary lacks exact positioning (hence is difficult to map), a border is located *just here* and nowhere else: somewhere in particular. It is at once securely fixed in place and unyielding (thereby facilitating its cartographic representation as well as its designation in terms of such precise parameters as miles and meters). Whatever the confusion between "borders" and "boundaries" in much ordinary English parlance, I take them to be quite different in kind.

Border Versus Boundary in the Evolution of La Frontera

What do edges so arrayed, and borders and boundaries in particular, have to do with La Frontera? Well, just about everything. . . . I shall indicate how this is so by a series of brief sketches in which I describe the ways La Frontera can be considered first as a border and then as a boundary in the basic senses of the two terms I have just pointed out, with a special focus on the wall that has been built at La Frontera during the last fifteen years.

The *border* aspect of La Frontera is massively evident: hence the common appellation "U.S.–Mexico *border*." Originally, "the border" was the result of the Treaty of Guadalupe Hidalgo in 1848, and it has never changed location except for the modifications introduced by the Gadsden Purchase of 1853, and one sliver of land called "El Chamizal" just north of the Rio Grande in El Paso. The creation of the border itself was the conjoint product of people of very different job descriptions: opposed armies who, though in retreat from outright war of the kind that had been so devastating in the 1840s to the northern provinces of Mexico, were still on the ready; politicians, ranging from President James Polk to diplomats who carried out the treaty negotiations in the presence of generals from both armies; surveyors and cartographers, who were charged with the determination of the actual location of the border and who, accompanied by astronomers and artists, spent arduous months getting acquainted with the terrain on which the border was to be imposed; and, a little later, stone masons (who laid down the marker stones that designated it), fence builders, and (150 years still later) construction workers who built the imposing wall that was initiated after 1993 with Operation Blockade and Operation Gatekeeper; and, more recently, a new army of border guards (all too aptly called Border Patrol), special interrogators, those who work at the checkpoints, and those who are employed in the 24/7 surveillance operation that overlooks large stretches of the wall.[2]

In short, it has taken a veritable phalanx of specialists and workers of diverse descriptions to lay down, build, and maintain the border, culminating in the current border wall. This wall, begun in the mid-1990s at discrete locations (first of all, just west of El Paso), now stretches for some 650 miles, covering most of the U.S.–Mexico border in the southern and southwestern states contiguous with Mexico. The events of 9/11 brought massive extensions and reinforcements of the discontinuous wall that had first been constructed to deal with the influx of Mexican workers after the institution of NAFTA. It is as if the very nature of La Frontera, in living up to its designation as a "border" and as reflecting its vexed history, has called for strenuous effort and special vigilance at every point of its century and a half lifetime. A multidisciplinary force was mandated from the start to ensure that this border be true to its essence as a precisely determined, tightly fitting edge, with durable markers and highly fortified means of enclosure positioned strategically to shore up its status as an artifact designed to contain efficiently and to keep out forcefully. That these efforts resulted in the current massive wall seems predictable in retrospect: the wall was just the last step in actions of sealing off the southern border of the United States, motivated not only by economics and terrorism but racism. (Canada, which has never considered building a wall, has no agenda of racial purity—an agenda that is all the more powerful for being unstated on the part of the United States.)

At a deeper level, this entire enterprise has been an expression of state power on the part of the United States, which dictated the terms of the original treaty that brought La Frontera into existence. This treaty was an unvarnished articulation of sovereign power that sought territorial expansion—and claimed the right to determine the exact extent and shape of the new territory. What Foucault held to obtain in circumstances of nationalist imperial power was true for La Frontera from the start: here "sovereignty is exercised within *the borders of a territory*."[3]

Nevertheless, despite its origins in the naked assertion of national sovereignty in the flush of a military victory, during the first century of its existence La Frontera was a relatively relaxed circumstance. There are early photographs of the towns that straddled the border on either side, with only a milestone or commemorative marker in the town square to remind people that this was indeed a "border town" as the phrase went. Citizens of both nationalities could wander back and forth freely and with nonchalance. One famous saloon prided itself on being located literally "on" the border, and painted a symbolic "border line" down the center of the bar to underline this geographical fact, serving certain kinds of drink on one side and different ones on the other side. (I leave it to your imagination as to which was mixed on which side.) Indeed, living residents of Nogales, Arizona, recall fondly the ease with which as children they walked back and forth between the American city and its Mexican counterpart, "Nogales Sonora."

All of this changed drastically after NAFTA and 9/11: the former highlighting issues of immigration control (after NAFTA went into effect, increasing numbers of Mexican farmers were forced off their lands, where they could not produce crops to compete with the grains from America that flooded Mexican markets at extremely low prices as subsidized by the U.S. government; hence they were forced to find work elsewhere), the latter emphasizing questions of national security thanks to the fear of "foreign terrorists" that was so rampant in the immediate wake of 9/11. The wall at La Frontera was a direct response to the first of these two developments; but its extent and associated reinforcements were modest compared to the vast extensions that have been instituted since 9/11. At this point in history, the wall is found at every major, and many middle-sized and even small towns along the border—and at many points in between. With it comes a formidable array of those charged with its construction and upkeep, and with the enforcement of rigorous strictures on rights of passage through its checkpoints. An entire industry, indeed an entire culture, has grown up around the wall—to the point where the border itself is often identified with the wall in the popular imagination, even though for reasons of local topography the actual position of the wall sometimes deviates significantly from the original (and still officially recognized) border line itself.

All the personnel employed at or near the wall are expected to pursue certain goals in common, each of which bears directly on the reliability and strength of the wall as a safeguard for vested interests of the United States—interests that are commercial or military or (most especially) concerned with the flow of migrants (as I prefer to call those who attempt to enter the United States for whatever reason, usually to find work, without "proper papers"). These goals include accuracy in the demarcation of the border; the policing and surveillance of the entire border region in the pursuit of increasing national security, preventing illegal drug importation, and controlling undocumented migrants. All of these fiercely held goals converge in making the border itself ever more definite and known as something that is objectively and unquestionably *there*—and presented as such. In all this concerted activity, it is as if La Frontera has been fetishized as an object in itself—finally, more an ideal object, an asymptote or regulative ideal, a sheer limit, than a material entity.[4] The wall bears the brunt of the materiality, even if the border itself, insofar as it is distinguishable from the wall, is regarded as untouchable and invisible—as is true of any pure border. Such a border is an ideal object that acts to safeguard vested interests. It is as if these interests were legitimated by this very act of idealization. So as not to keep the border entirely in the ideal realm, such concrete entities as barbed wire fences, border markers, and walls are created and continually invoked, anchoring what would otherwise be abstractly structural as ideal.

The *boundary* aspect of La Frontera is much less conspicuous than its border-like character—especially since 1995—yet it is always present and cannot be overlooked in any full assessment. To begin with, despite its pretension to imperviousness in recent times, La Frontera has proven to be chock-full of holes and openings: not only in the official portals at checkpoints (much more easily passable if one drives from north to south rather than in the reverse direction), but also in the wide spaces between parts of the wall, where the only obstacles are easy-to-climb fences and natural obstacles such as gullies, precipitous hills, and wild deserts with intense heat and high aridity. Many migrants opt to pass through these desert areas, with great peril to themselves and their families. Wild animals are better adapted to these open regions, but they are stopped short by the wall itself, which chokes off *their* migration paths and precipitates sudden confusion: Can you imagine a wildcat coming up against the wall and staring at it in disbelief? How can it know where there is a way around the end of the wall—which may be many miles away? Indeed, how can it know that the wall *has* an end? (In fact, there have been serious problems with animal movement and with plant cross-fertilization across the wall—with damage to waterways and marshlands.) Only birds fly free over the wall: an action mimicked by protesters at Tijuana a few years ago who shot a human being from a canon over the wall, as if to say that this is as close to being a bird as humans can come in the circumstance. On another occasion, balloons were released over the wall to demonstrate that only for wholly airborne objects such as these is unfettered movement across the wall possible.

Undeniably, the wall at La Frontera has become resistant to easy, open entry and traversal by human beings, including drug traffickers but also the many more Mexican and Central American migrants who wish to find work in the United States. Still, despite its prohibitory and exclusive character, this wall is not unyielding to modes of passage, even if many of these are realized in states of desperation and as "illegal" actions. However fiercely defended or surveyed it may be, the border wall at La Frontera cannot stanch altogether the flow of land animals and humans, whatever their reasons for crossing over may be.[5] In the end, many assorted creatures, human and nonhuman, *find their way over the wall*; they make their way across it—often with considerable effort and ingenuity, and always with definite danger.

This is not to mention more subtle forms of transgression such as Internet transmission and, in particular, artworks that are transgressions in the very face of the wall. For the last several decades, the Taller de Arte Fronterizo (Border Arts Workshop, founded in 1984) has brought together American and Mexican artists who live on both sides of the border for collaborative projects of remarkable variety and scope.[6] For these artists, and ourselves when viewing their artwork, the border becomes a boundary, with all that this implies of the passable and the permeable. Here, in the wall's stern face, the freedom of artistic expression and protest, evident for those who have eyes to see, ironically rejoins the ubiquity of the climate and the weather—all of which belong equally to everyone on both sides of the wall, animals and humans alike. Art may not be able to save this desperate situation, but it certainly alleviates some of the tension: "we have art so that we shall not perish from truth."[7]

Despite these instances of transgression, intrinsic boundary features of La Frontera are as exceptional as they are marginal, as inconspicuous as they are intermittent. But this only makes the occasional occurrence of boundary-like events all the more welcome when it does happen. These events allow the border to breathe—to open itself to flows of several kinds. It would certainly be too much to proclaim of this situation that in it *panta rhei* ("everything flows": Heraclitus). But *some things do move*: they move under, over, and through a border wall that has been designed to be impenetrable.

Constituting the Full Spectrum

If it is true that any adequate description of La Frontera requires us to consider it as both a border and a boundary, then a first consequence is that we cannot think of it as a single, simple kind of edge, for it is both at once, thus literally ambiguous. This minimal realization is important if we are to fend off the inveterate tendency to reduce what is in fact a very complex situation to an oversimplified image or interpretation of it. An earlier but parallel reductive error was to regard the U.S.–Mexico border as consisting in the set of marker stones and the fencing that marked its trajectory from the middle of the nineteenth century onward. Both the present "security wall" (as it is sometimes referred to euphemistically) along with the surviving marker stones and stretches of fence, stake out and shore up La Frontera, but they do not constitute it as a border. At the most, they support its formal status as a border while neglecting (indeed, actively denying) its being as a boundary. In fact, they are not to be confused with the border line that is another aspect of La Frontera: the border line is a cartographic entity: a graphic representation of an ideal limit.

This suggests a preliminary clarification: the border, considered in the way I have proposed (i.e., as a constructed and conventional entity), is situated *between a boundary and a border line* on an imaginary scale of terms that specify an edge like La Frontera. A border lacks the permeability of a genuine boundary; yet it is not reducible to something strictly linear either. An exemplary boundary is found in the Río Grande, which serves as the basis for the U.S.–Mexico border itself for two-thirds of its entire length. But *as a river*, its exact size is constantly changing with the passing of seasons, waxing in width in the (all too brief) rainy season and contracting to nothing but a flat river bottom in drier times. Any attempt to regard the Río Grande as a precisely determinable entity like a border is foredoomed—as would be (and even more so) considering it a border line.[8]

Another term that also belongs on this imaginary model is *borderlands*, made famous by the writings of Gloria Anzaldúa but having an extensive history of its own.[9] Let us think of a borderland as the area that flanks a recognized international border—often on both sides. It is an area in the form of a band or strip that cannot be measured in so many meters or miles: we would not even be tempted to do so, in contrast with the border line and the border itself, which we assume to have exact metric properties. In this respect, a borderland is closer to a boundary; yet its semantic resonance differs in that a boundary is always an edge *of*, or edge *for*, something else—an activity, another place, another space—whereas a borderland is bound, conceptually and concretely, to the border it surrounds. Boundaries, moreover, can exist almost anywhere, in any more or less open environment, and have no such dependency on a preexisting and (comparatively) stable entity as a border.

This suggests that we have to do here with a series of five terms that are arranged like this:

boundary/borderland/BORDER/walls (and fences)/border line

At the left end of this spectrum, we have terms that approximate to edges that are porous and malleable, depending on the circumstance: for which the paradigm case is that of boundaries and of which a borderland is an intermediary case. On the right end, closure and exactitude are prized: here the exemplary instance is the border line, which is highly determinable both in terms of actual measurement and cartographic representation. Walls and fences mark and reinforce the border, even if not with the precision of a border line.

In the very middle of this series is the border, which is closer to a borderline in terms of its putative exactitude, yet which is also integral to the very idea of a borderland. The treaty of Guadalupe Hidalgo speaks of "the U.S.–Mexico border" (which it established by means of its literal discourse), *as if it were something altogether definite*—at least definite enough to be counted on in future political discussions, historical accounts, land surveys, and maps. And necessarily so: each of these four latter activities requires a constant point of reference to be effective on its own terms. This suggests that the very notion and term *border* is more of a discursive entity (a matter of words and their meanings) than something materially "real", that is, something one can see, touch, or walk over.

If this is so, it helps to explain the paradox that powerful as is the idea of an international border—not just that at La Frontera, of course, but comparable cases such as the border between East and West Berlin, that between Palestine and Israel at the current moment, indeed between any two or more states or territories—it is *never a visible phenomenon.* Has anyone ever seen La Frontera, whether on the ground or anywhere else? Of course not![10] Its real force is "the force of law": which is to say, something set up by international treaties, continually reinforced by border guards and border patrol, and (increasingly often since 1995) rooted and reified by the building of high walls. Such walls can be said to introduce a factor of physicality that is lacking in the very notion of border itself. This helps to explain the strong temptation to construct them whenever the political will and the funding exist to do so. Quite apart from issues of national security and the enforcement of treaties, much less of so-called illegal immigration, it seems as if something like a wall or its equivalent is called for by the very idea of border. *This* we can see; this we do confront bodily. Or we could say that the counterpart of the rhetorical and theoretical power of an international border—which is so considerable in historical and political domains—is a wall or some other such physical entity (like marker stones), all of which act to transmute an otherwise strictly discursive power into concrete material thinghood.

Borders, then, are rather strange hybrid entities: they are irreal as discursively constructed, but they can be materialized in things like walls. In contrast with boundaries and borderlands, but in common with border lines, borders are ideal and eidetic; they are constituted by words (typically written, though these are often based on prior negotiations conducted orally: in both cases, their meanings are irreal as semantic entities), or by images (as with border lines considered as drawn features in the maps that depict them). At the same time, borders and border lines are conventional and historical—and, just as much, economic and political, social and ethnic—and, in all these various respects, reflective of human beliefs and actions: thus, they could well have turned out differently. As with the discourse that sets them up in the first place or with the images that represent them, their meaning is something intentional, the expression of human needs, desires, and resolutions. This meaning is a product not just of words and images but of such things as economic forces, political struggles, class differences, and racist attitudes. Such meaning is something that is made or posited or agreed on (however tacitly) rather than discovered or found in material reality. In this respect, it is a supervening variable that does not belong to an original order of being that we usually consider physically real—an order that contains the people and animals who try to pass over a border, or the actual local environments, or the materiality of substances chosen to designate and instantiate the border (again: marker stones, barbed wire fences, or metallic walls).

When Borders Become Boundary-Like

Presuming that I am anywhere near right in this analysis, we need to ask ourselves next: What does such bivalency of ideal and real, meaning and matter, image and thing, portend for understanding the situation at La Frontera (and, by extension, at any comparable border circumstance, especially those that are marked by walls)? One straightforward thing it portends is that borders, despite their ideality, evolve and are subject to birth and decay—a cycle that is especially manifest in a case such as the Great Wall of China, which by now has become nothing but a tourist site. Borders have a life and death of their own, whose history can be traced in exquisite (and sometimes excruciating) detail. The mutability of borders (and all the more so that of the walls that materialize them) is, then, a species of the finitude of all cultural and physical constructions and is hardly peculiar to borders alone. But it is important to underline such mutability, given the many contemporary political discussions, which all too often assume that this particular border is here to stay, that it is somehow "natural" or "right" in its exact current avatar, and that its continued existence provides an anchor for issues of homeland security and immigration and drug control—that it is something we can count on as a precise physical phenomenon.

Yet this is simply not so. The factor of drug-war violence, for example, has come to the fore in the last several years, altering the public perception of the fact and function of La Frontera. Immigration is being eclipsed in the public mind by the widespread violence that is happening at border towns such as Juarez and Tijuana and that is spilling over into cities on the American side like Tucson. The walls built near these places now show themselves to be woefully inadequate for coping with the illicit drug (and associated arms) traffic that manages to get through: if not by way of ruses and bribes at the checkpoints, then by extensive underground tunnels that have been built by the drug cartels under the existing wall.[11] Not entirely unlike the overwhelming of the Great Wall of China by Mongols and other nomads, a supposedly secure wall that was built quite recently is proving so vulnerable that it will soon not count as a border at all—if "border" entails a strict enclosure that is effective in preventing unchecked entry into what lies on the other side of it. With respect to the drug traffic, the U.S.–Mexico border is ironically becoming more like a boundary—a highly permeable edge that offers little resistance to its being crossed in one direction or the other. Drugs flow into the U.S. from the south at various points, while arms are brought back in the opposite direction from gun dealers in Arizona and Texas. As a result, the very meaning of *security*, including that at stake in the much-vaunted "homeland security," is changing before our eyes. What was intended to be a tight container in the erection of a tall and metallic wall with a thick and deep concrete base that has now cost hundreds of millions of dollars has become a leaking vessel. Neither does the high-tech surveillance equipment (Klieg lights, 24/7 panoramic cameras, patrol cars on the ground, drones overhead) seem to make any serious difference in the current predicament. And this is also so for the crossing of the undocumented over the border: new ways around and over the wall continue to be devised. (Just yesterday, as I write these lines, the *New York Times* carried an article detailing how the use of cell phones by coyotes leading groups of migrants has come to be effective in avoiding discovery by the Border Patrol.[12])

The situation is in effect returning to the state of affairs before the wall began to be built in the mid-1990s, in the immediate wake of NAFTA, exhibiting a vulnerability not unlike the string of fences that then stretched out between the original marker stones—fences that were never a serious deterrence to the movements of humans; only cattle were held back. The fences and marker stones constituted what has been called a "soft border" that resembled nothing more than . . . a *boundary*; the differences between the two sorts of edge here becoming ever more slim in practice.[13] The effort to produce an airtight edge in the form of a wall made of reinforced steel set in a firm concrete base is foundering.

Even if the wall and the various checkpoints arranged along it have proven ineffective for a kind of traffic not originally foreseen, they have been at least partially successful in the effort to stem the flow of migrants who sought jobs in the United States following the institution of NAFTA in the Clinton presidency.[14]

I say "partially successful," since some determined migrants have scaled the wall late at night with ladders from the Mexican side, and a few have tunneled under (though not on the elaborate scale realized by the drug cartels). Many more have gone around the end of the wall as constructed in a given area—though all too often to meet their death on the burning desert that lay before them. Despite the many physical and legal obstacles at the wall itself, undocumented migrants continue to stream across the border near, if not actually *at*, the wall itself. The massive migration (amounting to at least several million migrants who now live, legally or not, in the United States) has not been contained, much less stemmed. Even at its original mission, then, the wall has fallen far short of what it was built for: the prevention of immigration that is deemed "illegal."

The Fate of Borders

I cite these facts of recent history at La Frontera not just to make the point that the U.S.–Mexico border, girded up by its lengthy and massive wall and associated methods of surveillance, have been subject to variations in the border situation that were never fully foreseen, but more importantly to indicate that borders can very quickly lose their protective function—and thereby in effect remit their essence, their very raison d'être.

The putative tightness of the U.S.–Mexico border—based on the all too tempting belief that border walls can achieve genuine security for the homeland—has gone aground, and probably always will. It is not just that "something there is that doesn't love a wall, that wants it down."[15] Robert Frost's famous line goes only part of the way toward what we need to realize about security walls of many kinds: in a certain fundamental sense, they are *built to be breached*. This is not just to say that they engender *resistance*, to use Foucault's technical term for the effect of any strict institutional limit; but they also bring about their own demise as if by a subtle form of self-destruction—of being undermined not only from without (that is, from a failure to hold back overt invasions) but also from within, on their own terms. There is something about a wall, we might say, that does not love *itself*—at least not enough to maintain itself as permanently inviolable. To say it in the primary terms of this talk: *borders are always already in the process of becoming boundaries.*

My point here is not simply about the physical frailty of constructed things such as fences and walls; it bears on the striking way that such limitative and protective entities end by being ineffective at the very thing they were designed to do. They are subject not just to penetration and eventual ruination in historical time, but to a process of self-undermining by which they render themselves unable to perform the very tasks for which they were constructed in the first place. To this very extent, they lose their being as strict borders and approximate to open-ended boundaries, their supposed opposite. In such a situation, borders and boundaries seem to act much like incongruous counterparts that, as with the right and left hands, resemble each other in outward appearance, yet remain decisively different from each other in terms of internal relational structures.

Boundaries, though not permanent either, are much more perduring than borders. This is so despite the fact that their detailed configuration changes all the time, indeed more rapidly and easily than with borders, especially in view of the heavy institutional investment (and resulting inertia) inherent in the latter. Yet their underlying contour or profile, being more closely attuned to the layout of their landscape setting, is more stable, being more reflective of their environmental circumambience. Thus, boundaries are often integral members of entire life-worlds, cultural as well as natural, rather than being artificial intrusions into them, as so many borders manifestly are. Moreover, their perduringness occurs not despite their comparative fluidity and porosity but *because of it*. The basic resilience and resourcefulness of boundaries allow them to retain a fundamental Gestalt over long periods of human history and even through considerable climatological and geological changes.

Borders, in contrast, are at once more contingent in origin (La Frontera would have been a very different reality had the U.S.–Mexico War turned out in Mexico's favor) and more needful of support once established, as is abundantly evident in the case of the border wall there. On the one hand, they can be revised at any moment, if, for example, the international balance of power shifts or a new technology of constructing walls arises. On the other hand, in between these moments of major political or technological change, borders such as La Frontera have to be controlled and policed and supervised intensively, day and night and with many people hired for just these tasks (the number of Border Patrol has more than tripled in the past decade).

Ultimately, once it has outlived its political or economic or symbolic usefulness, every border is destined to become a boundary and to return to an abiding state of nature. This is just what happened in the case of the Great Wall, which, many centuries after its military significance had ceased, rejoined the open landscape of western China, crumbling into the earth that underlies and surrounds it. Animals and humans move over it at their whim. This will be the fate of La Frontera as well—even if, from today's perspective, such an outcome seems a long way—a much too long way—off. Its status as a sheer border concretized in the wall built there is so massively apparent, so brutally salient that we can barely imagine the day of its demise, the day when La Frontera will have become, once again, much more of a boundary than a border, its wall removed or in a state of ruin.

The Intertwining of Borders and Boundaries

Let us retrace our progress: I started by a brief discussion of edge (section I), distinguishing borders and boundaries from other kinds of edge and from each other (in sections II and III). Then I demonstrated how each is operative in a concrete circumstance such as La Frontera (section IV), especially in the border built there; and I began to explore how they interact with each other (sections V and VI) and how they undergo transformations, including radical ones that lead us to redesignate them altogether as "boundaries" when previously they were officially designated as "borders" (section VII).

But these transformations have one very particular limit. Despite the many empirical and historical mutations in the status of a single border like that at La Frontera, one basic sort of change is precluded: there can be no *change of kind* between borders and boundaries as such—no *metabasis eis allo genos*, no "change into another kind of thing," in Aristotle's sober phrase.[16] In short: no metaphysical sea change—no change of category, of kind of being. Between borders and boundaries regarded as distinct types of edge, there will remain an indissoluble difference—whatever the vicissitudes of their actual instantiations and complications at a place like La Frontera, bearing conflicts and inequities as it has been and is likely to remain for some time to come.

It is crucial to indicate how borders and boundaries in the case of La Frontera (and other comparable circumstances) not only arise together in various changing ratios but, more trenchantly, how they are *indissociable* from each other. In other words, I shall raise the philosophical ante by taking the discussion to a more general level. At this level, borders and boundaries, despite their categorial differences, can be seen as two aspects of one situation—aspects that are not only compatible and complementary with each other but that *require* one another. This corequisite status is especially evident when the edges of two nations (indeed, of any two polities: states, counties, cities, boroughs) are contiguous. In this circumstance, border and boundary features are both ingredient, and any adequate analysis must acknowledge their commixture as a base line from which further specification and understanding can emerge.

The fact is that such close collusion between borders and boundaries arises relatively often in the human life-world. It doesn't show up in the animal kingdom, which doesn't possess borders, given that borders on my construal are institutional (that is, social and political) and as such demand explicit agreements that are sealed in words. For borders on this construal are not tacitly established by a practice such as marking the edge of a territory by leaving urinary scents there: which is as close as prelinguistic animals come to constructing borders. For the most part, nonspeaking animals live in a world of boundaries, while humans inhabit a world that is conjointly specified by borders and boundaries: both at once, albeit in changing configurations.

This is not to deny that there are human situations that are sheerly borderlike in character. A case in point is the representation of a border, as this is set down in a line on a map. The line, as I've been arguing, designates nothing but what has been agreed on by those who drew up the terms of a treaty or some other vehicle of political accord. As literally a "border *line*," a cartographically represented border is nonporous; it does not allow passage through it at its own level—even broken lines in maps designate continuous connection. In effect, a border line excludes the very features of permeability by which I have characterized a boundary. At the other extreme, we witness humanly designed edges that count solely as boundaries, say, the edge of Central Park in New York, which offers multiple ingressions by its many gates, none of which are locked.

But in the situation that has provided the focus of this essay, namely, the wall at La Frontera, we witness the intimate and mutual interaction of border and boundary aspects. In such interaction, these aspects retain their own integrity. On the one hand, the border aspects express the historical and institutional character of this literally international edge, beginning with establishing conditions for being permitted entry to a given part of one of the contiguous nations—conditions that take account of immigration and security issues, but also a host of other considerations, including efforts to control drug transmission and the spread of transmissible diseases, or to regulate the flow of agricultural goods or to limit the overall population of the host country. All such factors, and still more (including those that may not figure on any official agenda such as the exclusion of races) bear on La Frontera regarded as a border in my sense of the term. On the other hand, the boundary aspects reflect the fact that accords between nations, however sternly posited or fiercely imposed, require more than words alone to be enacted and effective; something has to happen *on the ground*, something has to be *put in place*. This is to say that more than cartographic inscriptions or verbal pronouncements are at stake; something must be constructed quite concretely—if only a gate or a fence, most certainly a wall—and this must happen *on the earth*. This suggests the following schema of analogical relations, which represents the merging of my preferred terms according to Heidegger's celebrated dyad of *earth* and *world*:

BORDER : WORLD :: BOUNDARY : EARTH

The truth is that borders and boundaries are not opponents, according to the use of the word by which Heidegger describes the relationship between earth and world.[17] Despite their intrinsic differences of character and kind, boundary and border are yoked from the start in a circumstance like La Frontera; neither excludes the other; each colludes with the other at every significant stage of their relationship. They are codeterminate members of the same set.

When border and boundary coexist in this way, they are more like Spinozan attributes of Thought and Extension than strictly separate features like Mind and Matter in Cartesian metaphysics. For they are concomitant attributes of one and the same edge situation. Just as substance for Spinoza is ineluctably extended in space and subject to thought—simultaneously, so the edges that separate nations (and thus peoples and cultures) from each other present both border-like and boundary-like features—even if the exact form of each differs from case to case, as does their relationship. The same thing obtains for any edge situation that we are tempted to call an "international border" in the usual geopolitical sense of the term: not just that between the United States and Mexico, but that between United States and Canada, Ecuador and Peru, Germany and Poland, and India and Pakistan. Along these highly charged edges, walls are sometimes built—and sometimes not. When they are, they serve to reify the border with a special force, a particular twist: to make a point about a line that has become a physical wall.

Racializing and Racialized Bodies at the Border

So far, I have only been able to gesture toward the fact that race is an issue at La Frontera and its wall. The issue concerns the imputed racial identity of Latinos—those from "south of the border," whether from Mexico or Latin America. Too often, it is assumed that this identity is self-evident and that it is somehow explanatory of the efforts of "illegal aliens" to gain entry to the United States—as if their very bodies in their racialized physicality were responsible for these efforts, rather than, say, the much more likely reality that the border crossing is motivated by a desire to seek employment when this is unavailable in the home country.

In the case of Latinos, racializing perception on the part of Anglos acts as the *basso continuo* underlying a history of discrimination and exclusion. Mexicans were routinely lynched in Texas and California in the 1850s, as well as in the next several decades. After 1847, "Californios," those who claimed Spanish descent but were in fact a mixture of Mexican and Spanish stock, were driven off their lands in California. Nor is the history of Latino racism restricted to the nineteenth century: A Ku Klux Klan chapter that aimed at the elimination of Latinos (and other "inferior" races) marched defiantly down the main street of Santa Barbara in 1920. A forced repatriation of Mexican workers went into effect in the 1930s—ostensibly because of the depressed labor market in the United States—and one million "braceros" or guest workers were forcibly deported to Mexico in 1954. There was segregation of classrooms in public schools in California into the post–World War II period, with separate seating and restrooms for Mexicans and white Americans.

In view of this history of racism, it is hardly surprising that the official justification for building the wall— to stem the tide of workers who were fleeing to the United States in the wake of NAFTA—had a racist dimension, with references abounding in the popular press to "little brown men" who were stealing jobs from Americans (read: white working-class Americans). The phantasy of a human tide of brown bodies continues today with fears among a significant number of contemporary Anglos in the southwest United States and California that Latinos will soon outnumber them, especially in view of the belief that Latinos always spawn large families—as if that was a racially based mandate. The barely concealed common premise of both tidal phantasies is that Latinos are bestial and uncontrolled in their impulsive desire to work under any conditions and to breed at any cost.

What better way to stem both feared inundations than to seal it off at its very source—at La Frontera, which all "wetbacks" and "spicks" must cross somehow to get into the United States? The prospect of a wall presents itself, almost irresistibly, as the most effective such seal—or, if it proves less than fully effective once it is built, at least the most visible sign to make to Mexicans and other Latinos that they are *not welcome.*

The situation at the wall is not only one of inhospitality; it is one of extreme surveillance—thanks to the tall Klieg lights, supervisory towers with powerful telescopic cameras, and drone flights. Any moving body is picked up by Border Patrol agents who scan screens that show any physical motion that is the slightest bit out of line. Exposed in this total light of exposure, the skin color of anyone trying to cross over the wall is immediately apparent to anyone charged with such supervision. Not just the movement of the trespassing body but its qualitative coloration is conveyed to those whose eyes are pried on the tell-all screens, the newest form of panopticon: from whose detection there is no escape.

For all these reasons, the wall at La Frontera presents a *clean break*: its constructed reality is designed to separate the undesirables on the other side from those privileged to reside on this side. A significant part of the undesirability of those coming from the other side stems from their perceived racial identity as people of brown flesh, thus inherently suspicious and to be excluded. To think this way is to engage in border logic at another level than that of the official justifications for building the border wall at a cost of more than 2.4 billion dollars (so far and still counting) , which is designed to be impenetrable. Even if the manifest failure of the wall to accomplish its designated mission were to be accepted by those who support it in Congress and elsewhere, satisfaction would still be found in the belief that the wall taken as a gesture of excluding racialized others at least keeps most of them safely at arm's length, on the far side of the wall.

Short of the wall's eventual decommission and demise, one wonders what would happen if La Frontera were imagined as a genuine boundary rather than as that separative edge I have called border and whose materialization is found in the wall constructed there? What then? And what would this bode for racialized bodies at La Frontera? Given that energies collect at edges, very much including those that are borders and boundaries, we can only hope that there would be an emergence of energies for inclusion—not this time that of nationalist-territorial inclusionism (which is dependent on and conterminous with exclusionism), but for an inclusiveness and outreach that reflect boundary rather than border mentality. The bodies that interact at such an edge would still be racialized but, one can hope, less divisively and injuriously so. The exclusivist dyad of us versus them would give way to an open myriad of ourselves-with-others (and they-with-us) in which the perception of bodies might take on alternative and imaginative directions such as that which is apparent in the creative works of the Taller de Arte Fronterizo at Nogales.

———◦———

It remains that La Frontera is part of a complex set of circumstances, as anyone knows who has tried to follow events there in recent times; in truth, it was always complicated, from its first days of establishment and recognition. As with any border, its status is ambiguous and its description often compromised. Adding to this intrinsic complication is the fact that the border at La Frontera was haunted by the shadow of nineteenth-century U.S. imperialism that sought territorial acquisition at any cost and sanctioned any way to realize this, including war, extortion, bribery, and misrepresentation. Little has changed in this respect. Americans are still taking advantage of their neighbor to the south, now in the form of drawing on cheap labor, making massive use of this labor in the United States but failing to support migrants' rights or offering a decent chance for citizenship for those who desire it. This is not to mention using the drugs and supplying the arms that have made Mexican drug cartels so rich and so violent. Running throughout these contemporary extensions of an earlier exploitation is a still rampant racism.

Usually, the complexity of La Frontera is attributed to other, very specific factors such as the U.S.–Mexico War; the tilted terms of NAFTA; the grotesquely unequal flow of global capital across "the border"; the increasing power of the drug cartels; and so on. All of these factors are potent players in life at the border, but in this essay, I have been advocating an alternative approach: to regard the complexity of La Frontera in terms of the mutual interaction of its border and boundary aspects as they meet in the reality of the wall that has been constructed there: as two ways of being an edge in circumstances that are literally geopolitical and economic, cultural and racial.

This interaction has its own history, from 1848 to the present, to which I have only been able to allude in piecemeal fashion. My thought experiment has been to consider this dauntingly complicated situation in terms of two primal parameters, two basic ways of being an edge: very much including an international edge between two nation states. If we think in this vein, I believe that a new way of understanding La Frontera may emerge—one that allows us to put this vexed set of circumstances, including the fate of racialized bodies acting there, in an unaccustomed light that acts to shake up our customary assumptions about this and other comparably complex border situations.

In the case of La Frontera, we see the close imbrication of landscape and history, political force and technology, human interaction and racial perception, and much more. This imbrication is so dense that we need to find a point of purchase on it, a "lever of intervention" in Derrida's phrase. My lever has been the idea, the very fact, of edge, which collects around it such different things as nations and cultures, races and regions. And edge itself is dramatically and fatefully realized in the form of a wall such as that found at La Frontera.[18]

Notes

1. Note that each role for edge is of positive, and often decisive, significance: things must end somewhere (or else they would no longer count as "things"), and it is valuable to know just where this happens; we need to know what inner structures are like for purposes of medical diagnosis and more generally for the perception of all complex objects.

2. "Operation Blockade" was launched in 1993, in the El Paso/Juarez area and "Operation Gatekeeper" after 1995, in the San Diego/Tijuana region.

3. Michel Foucault, *Security, Territory, Population: Lectures at the Collège de France 1977–78*), trans. G. Burchell, ed. A. I. Davidson (New York: Palgrave, 2004), 12. My italics. This is from Foucault's lecture of January 11, 1978. Foucault adds that sovereign power is exercised not just on land but on the "multiplicities" that make up its people and history: "Sovereignty and discipline, as well as security, can only be concerned with multiplicities" (ibid.).

4. On the concept of limit, see the section on "Limit and Edge" in my book *The World on Edge* (forthcoming, Indiana University Press).

5. On the manifest failure to stem migration in the Laredo/San Juan area, see David Spener, "Controlling the Border in El Paso del Norte: Operation Blockade or Operation Charade?" in *Ethnography at the Border*, ed. Pablo Vila (Minneapolis: University of Minnesota Press, 2003), 182–198.

6. On this artwork (especially its centerpiece *The Parade of Humanity*, and its more general significance, see Mary Watkins, "Psyches and Cities of Hospitality in an Era of Forced Migration: The Shadows of Slavery and Conquest on the 'Immigration' Debate," *Spring* 78 (2007): 17–31.

7. Friedrich Nietzsche, *The Will to Power*, trans. W. Kaufmann and R. J. Hollingdale (New York: Vintage, 1968), section 822.

8. When an international border-line is located in rivers by projecting it into the precise middle of a river, an anomalous circumstance arises whenever the banks of the river overflow onto the banks differentially—for

then the middle of the river will change its position in terms of degrees of latitude and longitude, as will happen again as soon as the dry season arrives. What kind of border line is this in which we cannot say for sure just where it is located in world-space? Note also that in 1884, it was decided that whenever the main river channel of the Río Grande changed slowly enough, the border would change with it; but if the alteration was too rapid, the border was to remain in its previous state. But how slowly? how rapidly? There is no determinate answer to these questions—thus demonstrating the contingent character of a border that is based on a boundary.

9. See Gloria Azaldúa, *Borderlands/La Frontera: The New Mestiza*, 3rd ed. (San Francisco: Aunt Lute Books, 2007).

10. A telling instance of this fact is at play in the last scene of Jean Renoir's film *The Grand Illusion*, when the German soldiers stop shooting at the French soldiers who flee to safety over the Swiss border even though they could easily have killed them and even though *the border is hidden under the snow*. Here the border's literal invisibility stands metaphorically for its actual invisibility. (I owe this example to John Protevi.)

11. Such tunnels are discovered every few months, but this has in no way prevented their continuing construction, often at considerable expense and effort: some of the more elaborate tunnels are air-conditioned. As for bribing, this has reached the point where a number of customs officials are known to be working incognito for the drug cartels: see Randal C. Archibold, "Hired by Customs, but Working for the Cartels," *New York Times*, December 18, 2009. Regarding the many ways by which cash comes across La Frontera, see James C. McKinley Jr. and Marc Lacey, "Torrent of Illicit Cash Flows Where U.S. and Mexico Meet," *New York Times*, December 26, 2009.

12. See "Smugglers Guide Illegal Immigrants with Cues via Cellphone," Marc Lacey, *New York Times*, May 9, 2011.

13. I take the term *soft border* from Julie Mostow, *Soft Borders: Rethinking Sovereignty and Democracy* (New York: Palgrave Macmillan, 2008), esp. 56, 123–124, 131, 141, 145–146. "Soft borders" are in effect what I am calling "boundaries."

14. Moreover, the wall is only imperfectly effective for preventing terrorists to enter the U.S. from Mexico (an early fantasy of the Department of Homeland Security): such was the intention, such the promise, especially in the wake of 9/11, when the Department of Homeland Security was established with the express purpose of keeping out "foreign terrorists."

If the current wall does not undercut the transfer of pistols and rifles across it, how can it prevent the transmission of miniscule components for bombs?

15. From Robert Frost, "Mending Wall": "Before I built a wall I'd ask to know / What I was walling in or walling out, / And to whom I was like to give offence. / Something there is that doesn't love a wall, / That wants it down!"

16. This phrase is from Aristotle, *Posterior Analytics*, trans. J. Barnes (Oxford, U.K.: Oxford University Press, 2002), 215, 76 a 22, which is translated as "apply to another genus." I thank Eric Casey for locating this reference.

17. Between earth and world—especially in the artwork—there is a "basic strife" (*Urstreit*) in which "the work-being of the [art]work consists in the battle between world and earth" (Martin Heidegger, "The Origin of the Work of Art," *Poetry, Language, Thought*, trans. A. Hofstadter [New York: Harper, 1971], 49). But Heidegger admits that the strife between earth and world is such that "the opponents raise each other into the self-assertion of their natures" in "the simplicity of [an] intimacy" that attains "repose" (pp. 49–50).

18. An earlier version of this essay has been published as "A Matter of Edge: Border and Boundary at La Frontera," in *Society and Space* 29, no. 3 (2011).

NINE

PRIDE AND PREJUDICE

Ambiguous Racial, Religious, and Ethnic Identities of Jewish Bodies

GAIL WEISS

In addition to a specific set of religious beliefs (which, it must be noted, are not unanimously accepted by all Jews but perpetually in question), physical features, gestures, language, garments, political commitments, and cultural practices have all been viewed, at various times, as central components of a Jewish identity. Indeed, the allegedly "defining" features of a Jewish identity have been, and continue to be, subject to contestation by Jews and non-Jews alike. As Jewish identity debates have continued to rage throughout the centuries, the different answers provided are a reflection, not only of who is asked, but also of who is doing the asking, and most importantly, why they are asking. Ongoing controversies about who is or is not a Jew and what makes a person a Jew amply reveal that the characteristics associated with a Jewish identity have functioned as sources of Jewish pride (and quite often humor!) as readily as lightning rods for anti-Semitism, that is, as simultaneous sources of pride and prejudice.

Drawing critically from the following claims made by Sander Gilman, Jean-Paul Sartre, and Frantz Fanon, each of whom offers important, provocative, and troubling insights about the relationship between a person's body and the Jewish "nature" it supposedly expresses (or fails to express), I argue that the "Jewishness" of some human bodies, even when it is explicitly acknowledged and uncontested, is always a matter of ambiguity and overdetermination and therefore incapable of providing closure to the question of what, exactly, constitutes a Jewish identity.[1] It is crucial, I maintain, that we recognize this essential indeterminacy as a constitutive and positive feature of Jewish identity in order to counter the rigid, reductive descriptions of Jews offered not only by anti-Semites but also by many defenders of Jews and Jews themselves. Let us turn first to Gilman's observation regarding the social construction of Jewish bodies:

> Where and how a society defines the body reflects how those in society define themselves.[2]

Here is Sartre:

> We must therefore envisage the hereditary and somatic characteristics of the Jew as one factor among others in his situation, not as a condition determining his nature.[3]

And finally, Fanon:

> All the same, the Jew can be unknown in his Jewishness. He is not wholly what he is. One hopes, one waits. His actions, his behavior are the final determinant. He is a white man, and, apart from some rather debatable characteristics, he can sometimes go unnoticed.[4]

Though Gilman, Sartre, and Fanon all acknowledge that the negative stereotypes held by anti-Semites (stereotypes that have been both publicly and privately promulgated for centuries, across a variety of countries and cultures), are internalized by Jewish people, producing a Jewish inferiority complex that can be almost impossible to overcome, they offer strikingly different analyses of "the problem" and of its solution. More specifically, these statements by Gilman, Sartre, and Fanon express different ways of understanding what I would call the *intercorporeal* dimensions of Jewish experience. With the term *intercorporeality*, I am invoking Maurice Merleau-Ponty's notion that my bodily experience is shaped (and continuously reshaped) by the innumerable and ever-changing relationships I sustain with other bodies, human as well as nonhuman, animate and inanimate, throughout my life. Gilman, like Merleau-Ponty, foregrounds the centrality of the body in all aspects of our experience in the passage above, when he asserts that a person's self-definition arises out of how his or her body is viewed by the society in which he or she lives. While Merleau-Ponty, like Husserl before him, tends to portray intersubjective encounters in very positive terms, most often depicting my own spatial and temporal horizons as not only expanded but immeasurably enriched by my encounters with other people, it is also clear that the internalization of racial, sexual, religious, ethnic, class, able-bodied, and other types of prejudices prevents our encountering other bodies in the genuine spirit of open exchange that Merleau-Ponty poetically describes in the following passage from his late work, *The Visible and the Invisible*:

> . . . for the first time, through the other body, I see that, in its coupling with the flesh of the world, the body contributes more than it receives, adding to the world that I see the treasure necessary for what the body sees. For the first time, the body no longer couples itself up with the world, it clasps another body, applying [itself to it] carefully with its whole extension. . . . fascinated by the unique occupation of floating in Being with another life. Of making itself the outside of its inside and the inside of its outside.[5]

Though it certainly would be wonderful if all, or even most of our experiences of perceiving and being perceived by others, provoked and even increased our sense of fascination and profound respect for the mysterious alterity of the other, thereby creating invaluable opportunities for learning from our similarities and our differences, the long, insidious histories of anti-Semitism, anti-Black racism, homophobia, and sexism (to name but a few) offer much more sinister accounts of how other people's views of one's body as an object of disgust, pity, horror, as diseased, as innately and therefore irremediably inferior to the bodies of others, mediates an individual's view of him- or herself as well as others. While these histories are themselves full of ambiguity concerning exactly which qualities separate these stigmatized bodies from other bodies (e.g., physiological, psychological, or, most often, a mixture of the two), what seems to be quite unambiguous is the persistence and vehemence of the persecution itself and its pernicious effects on those who are its targets. And yet, I would argue, these effects themselves must also be seen as ambiguous insofar as prejudice can produce pride (as one of its most perverse, unintended effects) as readily as shame.[6] Indeed, the very expression, "the Chosen people," a term used most often (but not only) by religious Jews to describe their positive sense of belonging to a group that has historically been mistreated by others, not only emphasizes but even seeks to increase the chasm that the anti-Semite believes divides Jewish bodies from non-Jewish bodies. However, as Chaim Potok's novel *The Chosen* amply illustrates, this is itself far too simplistic a picture, for when the term "the Chosen people" is invoked by very observant Jews, it is also frequently used to demarcate "proper" or *authentic* Jews from allegedly "improper" or inauthentic Jews who have "failed" to live up to their Jewish heritage and the religious responsibilities that are deemed to be inseparable from it.[7]

Even if one was to agree with Sartre that "[i]t is society, not the decree of God, that has made him a Jew and brought the Jewish problem into being," not surprisingly, it is Jews who must deal with the "Jewish problem," Blacks who must deal with the "Black problem," and homosexuals who must deal with the "homosexual problem."[8] Despite his best efforts to place the Jew on an equal footing with the rest of humanity, thereby dissolving the abyss that the anti-Semite posits between them, what is especially striking about Sartre's statement, "[i]t is society, not the decree of God, that has made him a Jew and brought the Jewish problem into being," is how effortlessly Sartre moves from the Jew to the "Jewish problem," that is, how the experience of being Jewish is so quickly conflated with the experience of anti-Semitism. Indeed, a similar claim can be made about the common tendency to equate Black experiences with the experience of anti-Black racism, and homosexual experiences with the experience of homophobia.[9] In fact, Sartre goes so far as to proclaim that "it is not the Jewish character that provokes anti-Semitism but, rather . . . it is the anti-Semite who *creates the Jew*."[10]

While it is almost unfathomable to conceive how one can be Jewish, Black, or homosexual in the West without becoming aware of the discrimination that has been directed at each group, it is nonetheless extremely problematic to identify too closely the depth and diversity of Jewish, Black, and/or homosexual experiences with the history of their discrimination. Crediting the other with the ability to define one's identity (and in such overwhelmingly negative terms!), not only eviscerates the agency of those who are oppressed by the other's essentializing descriptions, but also forecloses some of the inherent ambiguity that, I am claiming, always attends each of these identities, giving too much power to the hostile other to define the parameters of one's embodied existence, thereby denying the spontaneous, unpredictable, and life-affirming dimensions of these experiences even when they are also attended with great suffering.

In the initial quote from *Anti-Semite and Jew*, with which I began, Sartre offers one important consolation to the Jew for the devastating, totalizing judgment of inferiority that is conferred on him[11] in one fell swoop by the anti-Semite, whether in actual or hypothetical encounters. The Jew's "hereditary and somatic characteristics," Sartre informs us, are merely "one factor among others in his situation," not in any way to be considered "as a condition determining his nature."[12] Sartre's well-meaning defense of the Jew against the anti-Semite, emphasizes that the anti-Semite's view of the Jew is entirely socially constructed; he argues that Jewish people lack the *Jewish essence* attributed to them by the anti-Semite. Like all other human beings (each of whom Sartre identifies as a "being-for-itself"), a Jew too, "is what s/he is not, and is not what s/he is."

While we might reproach Merleau-Ponty for offering an overly idealistic account of intercorporeal encounters between human beings (and it is significant that his most eloquent and even erotic accounts of these encounters in *The Visible and the Invisible,* occur between two bodies, a duo already open to being transformed, in new and interesting ways, by one another), Sartre's assertion that inherited and bodily characteristics, while undoubtedly part of our facticity, make only a small contribution to the total situation in which we find ourselves, is also problematic insofar as it suggests that the reality of how our bodies are responded to by others is something that can and should be transcended in favor of the broader perspective provided by considering our "total situation." Whether one adopts the Merleau-Pontian approach, focusing on the positive possibilities for self-discovery through intimate encounters with the embodied other to the exclusion of the destructive ways in which individuals often regard and treat one another, or whether one affirms Sartre's view that one's "somatic and hereditary characteristics," even if misconstrued and viewed negatively by others, shouldn't ultimately be attributed with too much significance because they do not capture the entirety of an individual's situation, neither strategy seems overly helpful to an individual or group who has been infected with a "contaminated identity" because of the alleged presence or absence of specific bodily characteristics that are seen as marking the irremediable inferiority of one's very way of being-in-the-world. Given the nonviability of either of these strategies, and yet keeping in mind Gilman's trenchant observation that "all aspects of the Jew, whether real or invented, are the locus of difference," we must also examine the option proffered by Fanon, one that I believe is equally problematic but that has a specific history of its own.[13]

The Overdetermination of Jewish Bodies

Before addressing Fanon's view of how the Jew might respond to what he, following Sartre (using explicitly Freudian language) refers to as the Jew's "overdetermination," it is important to stress that, despite significant differences in their respective understandings of "the problem of the Jew," my opening quotes by Gilman, Sartre, and Fanon, like many other claims about Jews, begin with reference to his (and, much more rarely her), "Jewish body." The presumption is that "we all know" what such a body is, or at least should be, and yet, I would argue, it is this very appeal to the concreteness of embodied experience that, paradoxically, supports the ambiguity or indefinability of Jewishness.[14] Where does this Jewishness or "Jewish essence" reside exactly? For, even when the anti-Semite seems closest to "pinning it down," for example through the possession of a specific type of nose, hair texture, complexion, or even penis, there are always non-Jews who turn out also to possess these features and Jews who do not.[15] Moreover, the identification of who is Jewish and who is not is complicated by the sheer variety of ways in which individuals may identify as Jews, including religiously, ethnically, and/or racially. Rather than viewing this indeterminacy that frustrates attempts to define Jewishness negatively, the ambiguities that accompany any and all attempts to "pin down" or "fix" Jewish identity once and for all, I am suggesting, can and should be seen as productive possibilities, expanding the range of potential ways one can access, engage, and ultimately transform Jewish experience.

While Gilman suggests that Jewish people's identities in the Western world are inevitably mediated by the dominant historical view of their bodies as corporeal signifiers of physical, psychical, material, and spiritual inferiority, a claim with which Sartre agrees, at the same time, Sartre is quick to emphasize, as we have seen, that "the hereditary and somatic characteristics of the Jew" are together only "one factor among others in his situation, not . . . a condition determining his nature."[16] It is striking that even though Sartre, like Gilman, denies that the Jew's body is an unambiguous marker of his or her Jewishness, much less his or her inferiority, Sartre nonetheless feels compelled to minimize the significance of corporeality in the assumption (or even the rejection) of a Jewish identity. Such a claim affirms a central insight of *Being and Nothingness*, namely, that the inherited and bodily characteristics that help to constitute our facticity, our concrete presence in the world, are never sufficient to define us. For the Sartre of *Being and Nothingness*, it is not our facticity but the *choices* we make in light of our *entire* situation, a situation that includes not only our past and present, but also the open-ended future, which alone can provide definition to the indefinable beings that we are. He describes these choices as expressing our human transcendence, and claims that this transcendence is exactly what makes it possible to redefine ourselves even and precisely when the other is trying to "pin a person down" in his or her facticity.

Despite the consistency of this message in *Being and Nothingness*, and the multiple arguments and examples Sartre appeals to throughout the text to explain and support it, it is not very surprising that, just a few years later, in his 1946 postwar publication, *Anti-Semite and Jew*, Sartre feels an even more urgent need to argue that an individual's "nature" cannot be reduced to physical or even psychical characteristics. For, in the three-year gap between these two texts, the depth of the Nazis' anti-Semitism, and their twentieth-century "final solution" to the "Jewish problem" was horrifyingly revealed through the remarkable success with which they undertook the mass extermination and physical elimination of Jewish bodies.[17] Sartre implies, though never states outright, that this "solution" was only capable of being carried out not only on six million Jews but also on millions of other people (e.g., disabled individuals, homosexuals, gypsies, etc.) who were similarly stigmatized for their alleged corporeal deficiencies, because of what he calls the "involuntary complicity" of millions of non-Jews who tacitly acquiesced to the egregious injustices taking place before their eyes.[18] And, one of the most serious injustices committed by the anti-Semite, in Sartre's view, is to ascribe a fixed nature to the Jew that depends exclusively on "inferior" corporeal attributes that are allegedly possessed by Jews alone.[19]

Fanon, in my opening quote, complicates this picture by reactivating the notion of choice or agency that is seemingly in danger of evaporating as a result of the anti-Semite's view that all Jews share the same essence or "nature." Specifically, Fanon claims that it is possible for these "hereditary and somatic characteristics" that allegedly define one's "Jewishness," to remain invisible to others and that, therefore, the Jew, unlike a person of color, can elect to "hide" (or at least *attempt* to hide) his or her stigmatized identity from a hostile world. While Sartre suggests that our bodily facticity does not and should not have overarching significance in our lives because it is only one component of our entire situation, Fanon states that the Jew (unlike the Black person) can always engage in dissimulation, disguising the facticity of his or her Jewishness altogether because he or she shares the skin color of the dominant, non-Jewish majority.

Though we might reproach Fanon for the false assumption that all Jews are white, even if he had acknowledged the existence of Jews of color, he would have undoubtedly affirmed that in their case, too, skin color "trumps" (and therefore can easily hide) one's Jewish identity. The fact that Fanon overlooks (or perhaps may well have been unaware of) the existence of Black Jews and other Jews of color, is not as striking, especially given the time period in which he wrote, I would argue, as his failing to acknowledge the very visible bodily markings (e.g., religious garments, hairstyles, etc.) that have historically signified Jewish identity as readily as skin color has signified Black identity. Of course, Fanon might have quickly (and rightly) pointed out the important difference between what Colette Guillaumin refers to as "voluntary markings" such as clothing and hairstyles that can fairly easily be altered versus "involuntary markings" such as skin color, which are more permanent, but, I would argue, this distinction itself starts to break down once one realizes that "voluntary markings" are rarely a purely individual choice but are frequently chosen for one by one's parents, peers, and one's larger community and, hence, may not be so voluntary after all, and even "involuntary markings" do not have static meanings across time and space but rather take on different meanings in different social, political, historical, and cultural contexts. Indeed, it is the very multiplicity of the (sometimes conflicting) meanings produced through these "voluntary" and "involuntary" markings, I would suggest, that enable us to understand Jewish bodies as ambiguous in a Merleau-Pontian sense and overdetermined in a Freudian sense.

In the chapter, "The Charge of Anti-Semitism: Jews, Israel, and the Risks of Public Critique," in *Precarious Life: The Powers of Mourning and Violence*, Judith Butler depicts this overdetermination as a form of excess that resists any and all attempts at precise definition. Rejecting reductions of Jewishness to Zionism, on the one hand, or the shared experience of anti-Semitism, on the other, Butler claims:

> The "Jew" is no more defined by Israel than by anti-Semitic diatribe. The "Jew" exceeds both determinations, and is to be found, substantively, as this diasporic excess, a historically and culturally changing identity that takes no single form and has no single telos.[20]

In *Difficult Freedom: Essays on Judaism*, Emmanuel Levinas articulates what Butler is calling the Jew's "diasporic excess," as follows:

> For millions of Israelites who have been assimilated into the civilization around them, Judaism, cannot even be called a culture: it is a vague sensibility made up of various ideas, memories, customs and emotions, together with a feeling of solidarity towards those Jews who were persecuted for being Jews.[21]

It is not incidental, I think, that Butler and Levinas, both of whom are Jewish, emphasize the dynamic, indeterminate qualities of Jewish experience to counter essentialist understandings of Jews (and, in Levinas's case, of Judaism), while Sartre and Fanon, neither of whom are Jewish, appeal to the Jew's ability to transcend or even "hide" his or her Jewishness as potential strategies for dealing with anti-Semitism. That is, while Butler and Levinas turn to the rich ambiguities of Jewish experience to "deconstruct" fixed understandings of both Jews and the "Jewish problem," Sartre and Fanon invoke a universal quality they claim is shared by Jews and non-Jews, namely our capacity for transcendence, or, our ability "not to be what we are." Through the exercise of human transcendence, on this Sartrian account, Jewishness can be recognized as merely one aspect of an individual's entire situation (and Fanon reminds us, one can even choose to hide it altogether), and therefore it cannot be seen as its determining factor. Thus, deemphasizing the Jew's Jewishness and affirming his or her humanity becomes the antidote to anti-Semitism that will finally enable Jews to take their place as equals (and therefore no longer as Jews!) in the larger social world.

Although the concept of overdetermination seems particularly apt to address the many different kinds of meanings, both positive and negative, that have been ascribed to Jewish bodies within and across cultures throughout the centuries, there are significant differences between how Freud deploys this concept, and how it is subsequently taken up and transformed first by Sartre, and then by Fanon. Unlike Sartre and Fanon, who posit the Jew's "overdetermination from within," an expression that itself requires careful unpacking, Freud uses the term *overdetermination* primarily in reference to specific experiences (and, on occasion, objects), rather than people. Thus, in his famous case study of "Dora," "Fragment of an Analysis of a Case of Hysteria," Freud argues that Dora's experience of "wandering about in a strange town" in one of her dreams "was overdetermined."[22] The first explanation he provides for this overdetermination is that Dora's experience extends beyond her dream to an event that actually happened in her life, namely, her first visit to Dresden, when she had the opportunity to tour the city with a cousin but *"she declined and went alone."*[23] The connection between Dora wandering on her own in an unknown environment in her dream and her recollection of actually visiting an unknown city by herself is not initially made by Dora or by Freud, but is itself established only after Dora recounts a more immediate memory of being asked to take a cousin from out of town, who was staying with Dora's family for the holidays, sightseeing in Vienna.

It is precisely because our memories are not self-contained, insofar as one memory has the power to immediately produce another memory—the power of "free association" as Freud suggests—that we can understand Dora's experience of "wandering about in a strange town" as overdetermined. Freud reveals, moreover, that the overdetermined quality of this experience is due to much more than its repetition in two different landscapes (the landscape of the dream and the city of Dresden, respectively) when he quickly changes the focus of his questioning of Dora from these experiences of wandering to the destinations sought through that wandering: in the case of Dresden, pictures in an art gallery (and a picture of a Madonna, in particular), and in the case of the dream, a train station. Through a very rapid and not entirely convincing series of associations, Freud concludes that these destinations turn out to have overlapping meanings: station, he tells us, actually signifies "box" and the picture of the Madonna in Dresden signifies "woman," and, despite these less than obvious connections, he states that now "the notions begin to agree better."[24] The agreement he has not yet adequately established (since it is not evident at this point exactly how and why "box" and "woman" are so closely linked) is procured through a missing "key," namely the key to the box.[25] The question, "Where is the *key*?"' Freud suggests, can be understood as "the masculine counterpart to the question, 'Where is the *box*?"' and, he tells us, both are "therefore questions referring to—the genitals."[26]

Freud's readers have had a field day discussing the significance of the less than obvious equivalences he establishes between such disparate images/objects, namely, station = box = virgin mother = woman = key = [access to] female genitals, with some of the more skeptical critics seeing these latter as more revelatory of his own sexual desires and experiences than Dora's. While many of his commentators have pointed out that it is no surprise that Dora herself was resistant to his interpretations of her experiences, and that even Freud himself acknowledged this to be a failed case study, it is nonetheless instructive to see how Freud explains the concept of overdetermination by means of what I would call his "cross-fertilization" (pun intended) of meaning. More specifically, through a wide variety of associations/connections/substitutions that he establishes (via his patient's recollections) between one of the analysand's experiences and several of her other experiences, Freud demonstrates that the significance of any given experience can never be understood in isolation from the rest of our experiences. The larger lesson "Dora" teaches us, I would argue, whether or not we accept Freud's questionable interpretation of the etiology of her hysteria, is that any and every human experience can be overdetermined or, in Merleau-Pontian language, rendered ambiguous, to the extent that the capacity for free association that establishes the links among even very diverse experiences (occurring across space and time and even across the divide between dreams and waking life), is actually being concretely enacted by oneself, others, or both.

Merleau-Ponty's emphasis on the intercorporeal dimensions of our encounters with others counters an understanding of free association as a primarily psychic phenomenon that is particularly efficacious at the level of an individual's unconscious. His own interpretation of the overdetermination produced by the power of free association could, I think, be better described as a spontaneous production of concatenated intercorporeal experiences that are themselves inscribed within and worked out through our everyday interactions with others in the world. Strikingly, he works out this new account of overdetermination as a constitutive feature of all perceptual experience in a critical analysis of Freud's case study of Dora.[27] Here Merleau-Ponty suggests that every perception exhibits the same "promiscuous" quality because "each perception is a vibration of the world, it touches beyond that which it touches, it awakens echoes in all of my being to the world [être au monde], it is an excess of meaning [sursignifiante]."[28] Thus, as Emmanuel de Saint Aubert compellingly illustrates in his own close analysis of Merleau-Ponty's reading of Freud's reading of Dora, Merleau-Ponty sees in the specific psychic situation of Dora "a universal characteristic," whereby this promiscuous excess of meaning is not somehow contained *within* an individual psyche but unfolds and is expressed "in an acting drama with others, with acting/active partners [avec (des) partenaires agissants]."[29]

Turning now to Sartre's reference in *Anti-Semite and Jew* to the Jew's alleged "overdetermination from within" and Fanon's extension of this concept in *Black Skin White Masks* to Black people's alleged "overdetermination from without," it is evident that they are both using overdetermination quite differently than Freud or Merleau-Ponty. This is not only because Sartre and Fanon claim that people (e.g., Jews and Blacks) rather than events, objects, or perceptions can be overdetermined but, more importantly, because both Sartre and Fanon are referring to ways in which the significance attributed to one's own or another's action, is *reduced* from a potential multiplicity of meanings to a purely negative construction or singular interpretation that is demeaning and therefore oppressive. Thus, the Jewish man (or woman) who worries that the tip he is planning to leave after a restaurant meal may be perceived by his potentially anti-Semitic companions as too small and who therefore decides that he must enlarge the amount to avoid having his "nature" as "stingy Jew" be "confirmed" by others, is overdetermined from within in the Sartrian and Fanonian senses. This is because the amount of the tip can no longer signify a generous response in light of his straightened financial circumstances, a justified response to bad service, an unfamiliarity with the tipping customs of this particular country, or even a perfectly adequate reward for services rendered, but is viewed by himself and the anti-Semite as a potential indicator of (or, if he doubles the proposed tip, as a refutation of), his "acquisitive, hoarding" nature.

Sartre offers several poignant descriptions of the Jew's psychological experience of being "overdetermined from within" throughout *Anti-Semite and Jew.* It is notable that he never once provides us with a Jewish person's own description of this subjective experience but presupposes that his own anti-anti-Semitism, as Jonathan Judaken calls it, is what enables him to give us a direct account of the experience. In one such description, Sartre informs us that the Jew,

> is haunted by that impalpable and humiliating image which the hostile mob has of him. . . . Ill at ease even inside his own skin, the unreconciled enemy of his own body, following the impossible drama of an assimilation that constantly recedes, he can never have the security of the "Aryan," firmly established on his land and so certain of his property that he can even forget that he is a proprietor and see the bond that unites him to his country as natural."[30]

Overdetermination from within, as Sartre depicts it, is indeed like a "haunting," insofar as it forces the Jew to reckon continuously with the "humiliating image which the hostile mob has of him." More concretely, Sartre argues that Jews internalize negative anti-Semitic stereotypes about the alleged motives for their actions (e.g., stinginess, greediness, acquisitiveness, etc.), and suggests that this "infects" their very way of being-in-the-world, producing, often against their will, a reactive response (even before they have in fact acted) to the anti-Semite's construction of their "essential" Jewishness.

The authentic response to this unpalatable situation in which the stereotypes of hostile others establish parameters for how one evaluates one's own most intimate desires, motives, and behaviors, is, Sartre implies, not to reject but actually to *acknowledge and take responsibility* not only for one's own Jewishness but, at the same time, for all other Jews as well.[31] Such a person recognizes, Sartre informs us, that: "To be a Jew is to be thrown into—to be *abandoned* to—the situation of a Jew; and at the same time it is to be responsible in and through one's own person for the destiny and the very nature of the Jewish people."[32]

In contrast to Sartre's position as a sympathetic bystander (who has a long, albeit mostly secondhand familiarity with anti-Semitism insofar as he is not its target) who assumes the authority to describe not only the attitudes, beliefs, and bad faith of the anti-Semite, but also the impact of the anti-Semite's behavior on the Jewish psyche (and he often invokes this psyche in universal language despite his distinction between authentic and inauthentic Jewish responses to anti-Semitism), and in contrast to Freud's "outsider" (neutral?) position as the analyst whose job it is to construct a coherent narrative that ties together the fragmented and often traumatic memories of the patient into a form that the patient can eventually accept as the *true meaning* of his or her own experience, Fanon describes a person of color's experience of being overdetermined from without from an insider's perspective. For this reason, his phenomenological account of this experience and his implicit critique of Sartre for failing to recognize that there are different ways a person can be overdetermined (i.e., from within and from without) is, I would argue, more powerful and ultimately more compelling, even though, as noted earlier, there are serious problems with his view of the Jew as easily able to "hide" his or her Jewishness from the anti-Semite (and I think at least part of the reason for these difficulties is that he, like Sartre, is rushing too quickly to psychoanalyze an experience he himself has not had).

Rather than dwelling further on the controversial assumptions about Jewish experience and the "Jewish psyche" that are implicit in both Sartre's and Fanon's accounts of how the Jew is overdetermined from within, let us turn our attention to a more productive line of inquiry, namely, Fanon's all too brief, but nonetheless extremely powerful account of how the Black person is overdetermined from without.[33] It is notable that Fanon develops the notion of being overdetermined from without by an explicit contrast with the Jew's (alleged) experience of being overdetermined from within. "The Jew," Fanon maintains in this well-known passage, "is disliked from the moment he is tracked down. But in my case everything takes on a *new* guise. I am given no chance. I am overdetermined from without. I am the slave not of the 'idea' that others have of me but of my own appearance."[34]

The Black person is overdetermined from without, according to Fanon, because the very visibility of his or her dark skin color means that, unlike the Jew who is presumably free to remove any "voluntary markings" that designate his or her Jewishness (we will leave the questions of whether or not there are involuntary markings of Jewishness and whether the "voluntary markings" are as easy to eliminate as Fanon suggests, open for now), the person of color cannot escape the stigma of being viewed as possessing a "contaminated identity" by the anti-Black racist. Thus, while some Jews at least, have successfully hidden their Jewishness, and, according to Fanon, merely had to contend internally with the negative judgments of the anti-Semite without the anti-Semite ever realizing in point of fact that he or she is actually encountering a Jew, Fanon maintains that Black people do not have this "luxury," because the involuntary marking of their skin color makes them the direct target of the anti-Black racist's prejudice, and therefore makes any form of escape from it virtually impossible.[35]

Despite Fanon's relatively clear distinction between the Jew's overdetermination from within and the Black person's overdetermination from without, it is clear that the situation is much more complicated. For, if overdetermination from within occurs when a Jew internalizes negative stereotypes about Jews that offer a series of unflattering, essentializing descriptions of the character traits that supposedly mark one's racial identity, religious beliefs, and/or ethnicity (however one defines the essence of Jewishness), and overdetermination from without occurs when people of color are immediately assumed to be biologically inferior to other human beings before they have even uttered a word or performed any action, then it is evident that the experience of being Black involves not only overdetermination from without (as if this was not enough in itself!), but also overdetermination from within as the Black person internalizes an anti-Black person's view of him or her as a "phobogenic object, a stimulus to anxiety." Indeed, Fanon poignantly depicts his own overdetermination from within, his inability to escape the fear of conforming to racist stereotypes, in the following passage:

> It was always the Negro teacher, the Negro doctor; brittle as I was becoming, I shivered at the slightest pretext. I knew, for instance, that if the physician made a mistake it would be the end of him and of all those who came after him. What could one expect, after all, from a Negro physician? As long as everything went well he was praised to the skies, but look out, no nonsense, under any conditions! The black physician can never be sure how close he is to disgrace. I tell you, I was walled in: No exception was made for my refined manners, or my knowledge of literature, or my understanding of the quantum theory.[36]

To be walled in, Fanon suggests, is to be trapped within the prison constituted by the racist other's judgment of who one "really" is, a form of psychic incarceration that is impossible to escape from the inside because the prisoner does not and never has possessed the key. If liberation is possible in this scenario, it seems that it will have to come from the outside; ultimately, for Fanon (though he doesn't develop the point in much depth), overcoming overdetermination from within must involve an affirmation of the Black person's fundamental humanity by antiracist others.

Even if one argues that anti-Semitism and anti-Black racism might, along with other forms of discrimination, share what David Theo Goldberg calls a "deep grammar," namely a "principle of differential exclusion," it is nonetheless evident that the stereotypes promulgated by anti-Semites and anti-Black racists, respectively, differ in important ways, and that, as a result, they impact Jewish embodied experience and Black embodied experience differently. As Fanon observes, many of the insulting accusations hurled at Jews by anti-Semites (such as the all-too-common stereotype of the cunning Jew who seeks to "take over the world") paradoxically credits the Jewish person with above-average intelligence. This is hardly the case, Fanon reminds us, for the Black man whose overdetermination by the anti-Black racist takes the form of reducing him not only to his "animal-like" body, but quite frequently to a particular body part, namely, his penis. Or, in the shorthand that characterizes what Fanon identifies as the "myth of the Negro . . . "Negroes are savages, brutes, illiterates."[37]

It is not only dangerous, but ultimately, I would argue, divisive and self-defeating to enter into comparisons of which types of prejudice are worse than other types of prejudice. Such an attempt only does the oppressors' work for them, because it turns groups that are targets of oppression into enemies who attack each other instead of joining to attack the cycle of discrimination at its source. All forms of prejudice are evil, even if we acknowledge, as we must, that they harm each of us in different ways, and therefore leave different types of marks on their victims.

In *Intersecting Voices: Dilemmas of Gender, Political Philosophy, and Policy*, Iris Young argues that "A condition of our communication is that we acknowledge the difference, interval, that others drag behind them shadows and histories, scars and traces that do not become present in our communication."[38] While some of these shadows, histories, scars, and traces are undoubtedly due to ways in which we have been overdetermined in the Sartrian sense, that is, the ways in which the possibilities for giving a variety of interpretations of our thoughts, our bodies, and our actions have been foreclosed in advance by others, Young also points to the ongoing possibility of beginning again by committing ourselves to communicating differently. By attending to "the difference, the interval" that separates my experiences and my expectations from those of others, and by returning, as Merleau-Ponty invites us to do, to the inexhaustible possibilities for creating new meaning and new depths to our experiences that challenge and transform the fixed interpretations of others, perhaps it will be possible to realize the more positive sense of overdetermination that is implicit in Freud's account of the power of free association, even though Freud himself fails to enact it in his very restrictive interpretation of the "hidden" meaning of Dora's experiences. The overdetermination of one's experiences, I am suggesting, arises out of the fundamental ambiguity of those experiences, and this can and should become a source of mutual respect and pride, rather than resulting in an attempt to eliminate the ambiguity through the creation of discrete and fixed identity categories to which each of us is supposed to belong, and whose rigidity and lack of depth is itself the product of hatred, suspicion, and prejudice.

Notes

1. This is not to say that *ambiguity* and *overdetermination* are synonymous terms. As I will go on to show, if a given phenomenon is overdetermined, for Freud, this means that it has multiple meanings, not just a singular meaning, and that therefore the phenomenon can be understood in a Merleau-Pontian sense, as ambiguous. However, it is also possible for ambiguity to be present without the overdetermination that Freud claims arises through processes of free association, though it is beyond the scope of this analysis to address these latter cases.
2. Sander Gilman, *The Jew's Body* (New York: Routledge, 1991), p. 170.
3. Jean-Paul Sartre, *Anti-Semite and Jew*, trans. George J. Becker (New York: Schocken Books, 1965), 64.
4. Frantz Fanon, *Black Skin White Masks*, trans. Charles Lam Markmann (New York: Grove Press, 1967), 115.
5. Maurice Merleau-Ponty, *The Visible and the Invisible*, ed. Claude Lefort, trans. Alphonso Lingis (Evanston, Ill.: Northwestern University Press, 1968), 144.
6. This should not be at all surprising from a Foucaultian perspective, given Foucault's analysis of how even the most repressive exercise of power

generates unanticipated, and for that very reason, often highly efficacious resistances.

7. For instance, one day when the orthodox teenager and future rabbi, Reuven Malter, is at the home of his Hasidic friend Danny Saunders studying the Talmud with Danny and his father, Reb [Rabbi] Saunders, Reb Saunders waits until he and Reuven are alone and says, "Reuven, you and your father will be a good influence on my son, yes?" Before Reuven can respond, he anxiously demands: "You will not make a goy out of my son?" (Chaim Potok, *The Chosen*. New York: Ballantine Books, 1967). A few years later, Danny and Reuven are college students at the same Yeshiva (both enrolled in a joint program to receive rabbinic degrees along with their bachelor's degrees). To express his outrage at Reuven's suggestion that the creation of a Jewish state in British-occupied Palestine might be an important refuge for Jewish Holocaust victims flee-ing the anti-Semitism, Reb Saunders refers to the leaders of the Zionist movement as Jewish goys (Jewish non-Jews) and yells at Reuven: "The land of Abraham, Isaac, and Jacob should be built by Jewish goyim, by contaminated men? . . . Why do you think I brought my people from Russia to America and not to Eretz Yisroel? Because it is better to live in a land of true goyim than in a land of Jewish goyim!" (Potok, *The Chosen*, 198). Not long afterward, Reuven's father's Zionist activism leads Reb Saunders to ban his son Danny from any contact with his best friend for two full years, so powerful is his fear that his own son will be contami-nated by contact with an aspiring orthodox Rabbi whose very Jewishness has, in Reb Saunders's eyes, been completely compromised by his sup-port for "Jewish goys."

8. Sartre, *Anti-Semite and Jew*, 134.

9. This is by no means intended to be an exhaustive list!

10. Sartre, *Anti-Semite and Jew*, 143 (my emphasis).

11. That this unfortunate Jew is almost always depicted as a man is not meant to suggest that Jewish women escape this "fate" though clearly the corporeal effects of anti-Semitism are registered differently by men and women. While it is not possible within the confines of this discus-sion to take up the specific gender presuppositions that are both implic-itly and explicitly invoked in anti-Semitic diatribes, including the all-too-frequent feminization of Jewish male bodies, their very presence under-cuts simplistic analyses of the different bodies allegedly possessed by Jewish women and men as contrasted with non-Jewish women and men.

12. Sartre, *Anti-Semite and Jew*, 64.

13. Gilman, *The Jew's Body*, 2.

14. Ironically, even the anti-Semite who has perhaps most vociferously proclaimed that one's "Jewish essence" is marked on one's body, has had difficulty, historically, in determining who exactly has such a body and who does not. As Gilman (1991) observes, it was due to this fundamental undecidability that the Nazis required that those they identified as Jews wear yellow stars in order to make visible the Jewish essence the former viewed as always already corporeally present, even if invisible to the naked eye.

15. Indeed, this is precisely what saved many blond and blue-eyed Jews' lives during the Holocaust, including that of my cousin, Lala Fisher, who survived World War II in Poland by "passing" as a Polish Catholic while her more traditionally Jewish-looking mother and sister, who were not good candidates for passing, ended up being captured and killed by the Nazis.

16. Sartre, *Anti-Semite and Jew*, 64.

17. For clearly killing Jews was not enough; their corpses had to be cremated so that all traces of their contaminating physical existence (intensified all the more by their deathly and deadly putrefaction) could be eliminated.

18. Sartre, *Anti-Semite and Jew*, 151.

19. Although it is clear that by referring to "somatic and hereditary" attributes, Sartre is including psychological as well as physical characteristics that are claimed to mark the Jew as a Jew, to the extent that the former are regarded as capable of being "read off" the Jew's body, they seem to be equally inseparable from the Jew's corporeality.

20. Judith Butler, *Precarious Life: The Powers of Mourning and Violence* (London: Verso, 2004), 126.

21. Emmanuel Levinas, *Difficult Freedom: Essays on Judaism*, trans. Seán Hand (Baltimore: The Johns Hopkins University Press, 1990), 24.

22. Sigmund Freud, *The Freud Reader*, ed. Peter Gay (New York: W. W. Norton and Co, 1989), 222.

23. Ibid.

24. Ibid.

25. Freud justifies the substitution of the key for the box through Dora's recollection of seeking the key to the liquor cabinet the previous evening in response to her father's request for brandy.

26. Freud, *The Freud Reader*, 223.

27. This analysis appears in the lecture notes for his 1954–1955 course on passivity [La Passivité] held at the Collège de France.

28. Maurice Merleau-Ponty, *Le Problème de la Passivité: Le Sommeil, L'Inconscient, La Mémoire. Notes des cours au Collège de France (1954–1955)*, eds. Dominique Darmaillacq, Claude Lefort, and Stéphanie Ménasé (Paris: Belin, 2003), 217.

29. Emmanuel de Saint Aubert, "La 'promiscuité: Merleau-Ponty à la recherché d'une psychanalyse ontologique," *Archives de Philosophie* 69 (2006): 11–35.

30. Sartre, *Anti-Semite and Jew*, 132–133.

31. It should be noted that this claim seems to be somewhat in tension with Sartre's earlier suggestion that Jews need to recognize that their Jewishness is just one part of their total situation.

32. Sartre, *Anti-Semite and Jew*, 89.

33. It is important to acknowledge, despite my claim that both Sartre and Fanon make far too hasty, and therefore problematic, overgeneralizations about Jewish experience, that this does not mean that one can do justice to the rich diversity of Jewish experience if one ignores the broader anti-Semitic context in which it is most often expressed, as more recent books on Jewish experience such as Jon Stratton's *Coming Out Jewish* and Gilman's *Jewish Self-Hatred: Anti-Semitism and the Hidden Language of the Jews* and *The Jew's Body* all emphasize. Cixous rhetorically presents the case as follows in her *Portrait of Jacques Derrida as a Young Jewish Saint*: "So with or without God how does one become Jewish? If not first of all by Jewsay" (Hélène Cixous, *Portrait of Jacques Derrida as a Young Jewish Saint*, trans. Beverley Bie Brahic [New York: Columbia University Press, 2004], 75). Or, in Sartre's words, "The Jew is one whom other men consider a Jew: that is the simple truth from which we must start" (Sartre, 1965, 69). My point is that this observation can only be a starting place for interpretation, not the place we end up if we are to avoid reducing Jewish experience to the experience of anti-Semitism. Overemphasizing the role of the anti-Semitic other in defining one's Jewishness leaves room for the more positive role so frequently played by feeling that one shares ancestral, familial, religious, ethnic, linguistic, culinary, geographical, and/or other cultural and historical bonds with other Jewish people; in short, feeling that one is part of a heritage that is much larger than oneself or one's immediate family.

34. Fanon, *Black Skin White Masks*, 1967, 115–116.

35. Perhaps Fanon would tell a somewhat different story if he wasn't primarily referencing the experience of the natives of his own island of Martinique who tended to share a very dark skin color, but rather was

including the experience of the millions of light-skinned African Americans in the United States (and African Europeans more generally), quite a few of whom can pass as white just as he claims the Jew can pass as a non-Jew. Presumably, Fanon would view such light-skinned Blacks as overdetermined from within, like the Jew, and not necessarily overdetermined from without, like their darker-skinned brethren.

36. Fanon, *Black Skin White Masks*, 117 (my emphasis).
37. Ibid., 117.
38. Iris Young, *Intersecting Voices: Dilemmas of Gender, Political Philosophy, and Policy* (Princeton: Princeton University Press, 1997), 53.

TEN

BODY MOVEMENT AND
RESPONSIBILITY FOR A SITUATION

EMILY S. LEE

Introduction

In place of the impossible impasse between the body as object and the mind as subject, perhaps Maurice Merleau-Ponty's most important and radical proposal remains that the subject is embodied. Between the facticity of the material world and the ideality of meanings, Merleau-Ponty recognizes that the body-subject epitomizes the complex relation between the two spheres without splitting into duality and without positing a monadology. This integration of the matter of the body and the consciousness of the subject—this reconceptualization of the subject as embodied or the body as conscious—undergirds the inextricable tie between our subjectivity and the world. We interact with the world far more intimately because of the intricate and inherent condition of always, already, immediately being-in-the-world.

In trying to understand the meaning and the implications of such intimacy between subjectivity and the world in the *Phenomenology of Perception*, Merleau-Ponty argues that the body in its movement generates space and time. Body movement *generates phenomenological space and time*. Within this paper, I clarify this, as yet, underappreciated position in the *Phenomenology of Perception* to tie this position with Merleau-Ponty's conception of freedom. Understanding that body movements generate space and time explains Merleau-Ponty's position (following Martin Heidegger) that for human beings, to claim responsibility, they must accept their entire situation. One cannot truly

233

claim freedom and blame fate; one can only claim true freedom by accepting responsibility for one's own individual actions and situations.

Responsibility for one's situation is especially presently poignant for whiteness studies to recognize the current position whiteness occupies in society. Studies on whiteness explain the existence of ineffable privileges in simply being white or possessing a white body and the comportment of white bodies. Such experiential privileges with real social-structural benefits come from a particular history, a history of colonialism, slavery, and segregation. Because the privileges emblematize this history, in a controversial and radical move, whiteness theorists recognize the responsibility for situations not of one's own making and do not limit responsibility to only the results from one's immediate personal decisions and acts within one's lifetime. Radical whiteness theorists advocate responsibility for one's situation, not simply the situation one creates for oneself through a series of actions, but including the history into which one is born. But this position has not received widespread acceptance, and without accepting this position, one of the strongest arguments against affirmative action policies has been that whites today should not be held accountable for the sins of their forbearers. The recognition that freedom includes responsibility for the situations in which one finds oneself, including the situations of one's birth, posits that whites today should be held responsible for their forbearer's actions. Merleau-Ponty's analysis that body movements generate space and time fills in some of the details to substantiate this responsibility for the situations of one's birth.

Phenomenology and the Body

Let me begin with Merleau-Ponty's position on the centrality of the subject as embodied. He writes, "the alleged facts, the spatio-temporal individuals, are from the first mounted on the axes, the pivots, the dimensions, the generality of my body." The body "is the measurant of all, Nullpunkt of all the dimensions of the world"; the body is "a heavy signification."[1] As phenomenally experienced, embodied subjectivity is ambiguous. But in order for embodied subjectivity to be ambiguous, the body defies the law of noncontradiction. The body is matter and is not matter.[2] The body is mechanistic and intentional; the body is sentient and sensible. These contradictory ambiguities reflect embodiment as reflexive; one can feel oneself touching oneself and see oneself looking at oneself.[3] The subject is reflexive in the intertwining of the psychological, intellectual, and subjective with the material, biological, and natural features of embodiment. This intertwining of the body and the world explains that our bodies intertwine with others in the world and why intersubjectivity is not a problem for Merleau-Ponty.[4]

Instead of getting caught in the debate and confusion about exactly what constitutes body image and body schema,[5] let me turn to a less attended discussion on body movement. Attending to body movement facilitates an appreciation of the intimate relation between embodiment and the world. I begin with what body movement is not. Body movement does not occur solely as the result of physical causality—such a depiction treats the body as only matter. Body movement does not occur like the movement of physical materials, which relies on an alternative exterior physical force. Alternatively, body movement does not result simply from conscious intentions because body movement does not directly fulfill conscious aims. The mind does not function as the sole originator of body movement. Such a belief errs toward a psychological or cognitive conception of the subject that persists in conveying the body as simply a vehicle that carries forth the decisions and desires of something internal to itself. For as much as one may aim to run a mile within a specific time, most people cannot directly fulfill such an aim without much bodily conditioning. Merleau-Ponty recognizes body movement as "something between movement as a third person process and thought as a representation of movement—something which is an anticipation of, or arrival at, the objective."[6]

Dismissing the traditional explanations for body movement, Merleau-Ponty offers the idea of body motility. Merleau-Ponty proposes that the body retains its own intentionality.[7] Appreciating the idea of body intentionality requires understanding the difference between act intentionality and operative intentionality. Act intentionality refers to the common understanding of intentionality—the intentionality of conscious judgments culminating in individual actions.[8] Such an intentionality is familiar to liberal political theorists as *agency*. Operative intentionality, first introduced by Edmund Husserl, refers to an intentionality already functioning within the world. Merleau-Ponty describes operative intentionality: "the life of consciousness—cognitive life, the life of desire or perceptual life—is subtended by an 'intentional arc' which projects round about us our past, our future, our human setting, our physical, ideological and moral situation, or rather which results in our being situated in all these respects."[9] Operative intentionality depicts an intentionality always already present in the world because we occupy a specific spatial and historical location within a community. Merleau-Ponty eventually relies less heavily on the notion of intentionality, both act and operative. Intentionality evokes too much of an affinity with consciousness, and

Merleau-Ponty aspires to understand embodiment in both its materiality and cognitive ability. He continues to explore the notion of operative intentionality in other forms. For although Merleau-Ponty recognizes the limitations of the notion of intentionality, he appreciates the idea of a guiding influence from and within the world.[10]

Within the relationship between act and operative intentionality or the relationship between the significance of an individual act to the meanings operative in the world lies body motility. Merleau-Ponty writes, "'[a]lready motility, in its pure state, possesses the basic power of giving a meaning.'"[11] Body intentionality captures precisely the body in movement from the individual, immediate, and actual intentionality to the community, world, potential, and operative intentionality. The two movements form a unique relationship that demonstrates the intertwining of the self and the world.[12] The movement from the immediate to the surrounding world is a movement from the space of the concrete now to the space of the abstract future. The immediate vicinity that the body in action, the habitual body, establishes around itself provides the setting for body movement to extend toward possible and creative space. Merleau-Ponty describes the movement from the lived to the abstract space as a spiraling centrifugal movement.[13] The body in movement projects beyond itself.[14]

With the understanding that body movement connects act and operative intentionality from somewhere between a physical or mental force, what is the source for the beginning of body motility? Martin Dillon argues that body movements arise from habitual body movement, which possesses a nonending impetus of continual, ritualized movement.[15] Although this sounds persuasive, I do not find this explanation to sufficiently or fully explain body movement. Dillon explains habitual movement already in motion, but he does not explain what initiates habitual movement. All bodies do not develop exactly the same habitual body movements. Moreover, habitual body movements do not all continue forever. Habits and habitual movements begin, change, and end.[16] Body movement, and especially that which initiates and ends habitual movements, still requires explanation.

The Body Generates Space and Time

At this point, drawing from the understanding that body intentionality moves us from actual space to potential space, and to determine what initiates body movement, I turn to a lesser-known position from Merleau-Ponty that body movement generates space and time.[17] Let me begin by citing a few tan-talizing lines that initially led me to this conclusion. Merleau-Ponty writes, "[t]here must be as Kant conceded a 'motion which generates space' which is our intentional motion, distinct from 'motion in space,' which is that of things and of our passive body."[18] And alternatively, "[m]y body takes pos-session of time . . . it . . . creates time."[19] Additionally, he writes, "by consid-ering the body in movement, we can see better how it inhabits space (and, moreover, time) because movement is not limited to, submitted passively to space and time, it actively assumes them."[20] The possibility of body move-ment generating space and time is the inevitable, remarkable conclusion from Merleau-Ponty's works.

To elaborate how and exactly in what sense the body generates space and time, let me address each in turn. First, in turning to the possibility of generating space, Iris Marion Young's classic essay, "Throwing Like a Girl," demonstrates well Merleau-Ponty's notion of phenomenal space as distinct from objective space. Whereas in objective space all positions are external to each other and hence interchangeable, in phenomenal space positions are distinctly personal. Body motility establishes such subjective experience of space.[21] Upon describing girls' body movements when throwing a baseball, Young explains that girls' body movements characterize the specific space they occupy. Without going too much into the details of Young's well-known article, she describes three features of girls' body movements as demonstrat-ing "ambiguous transcendence," "inhibited intentionality," and "discontinu-ous unity."

Within Merleau-Ponty's phenomenology, all body movements ambigu-ously transcend to a certain extent because the subject is embodied. Exis-tentialism forwards that subjectivity demands transcendence; nevertheless, Young contends girls' body movements never quite transcend as much as boys' body movements. The lack of fluidity and confidence in girls' body movements while throwing a baseball illustrate ambiguous transcendence. Girls' body movements are overlaid with immanence.[22]

Consistent with act intentionality and body motility, Young explains that generally body intentionality represents a resolve, an "I can" to carry out one's aims.[23] Yet, Young argues that girls' body movements, not drawing from the entire body and full body strength, exhibit an overlay of a sense of fragil-ity conveying a broken intentionality, an inhibited intentionality.

Finally, recall that Merleau-Ponty understands the body as intrinsically reflexive between subjectivity and the world. As reflexive, the body pos-sesses an immediate intertwining with the world. Young writes about body movements that, "[b]y projecting an aim toward which it moves, the body brings unity to and unites itself with its surroundings."[24] Yet, again, girls' body movements exhibit, in their limited and nonfluid use of space, a discontinuous unity with their surroundings.

These body movements correlate—indeed create—a specific space that circumscribes the girls' bodies. Young distinguishes three ways the space around girls' bodies differs from that of boys. She argues that girls establish horizons that set the far reaches of one's sense of space circling closer to the body than do boys. Within this restricted or smaller horizon, girls utilize the space in more limited ways. Young explains that girls divide the space in ways that do not make full use of spatial depth. Finally, the yonder beyond the horizon influences girls' body movements less than boys' body movements. In other words, girls do not reach out to move into the space beyond the horizon, into the yonder.[25]

Young's essay is groundbreaking in its descriptions of the possible meanings of girls' body movements when throwing a baseball, but she has been criticized as essentializing girls' body movements—something she writes that she took pains to avoid. Rather, or in addition to reading Young's work as essentializing girls' body movements, a more generous reading suggests that her descriptions relay the historical sedimentation of bodily interactions, expectations, and scripts of girls and boys that have resulted in such body movements for at least until the 1980s and to some extent continues today. She is not saying such body movements are essential to girls, but that they are a result of a specific social historical horizon. Important to my present concern is not the accuracy of Young's depiction of girls' body movements and their associated space, but her illustration of Merleau-Ponty's insistence on an immediate *correlation* between body movements and space. Young writes, "[f]or Merleau-Ponty, the body is the original subject that constitutes space; there would be no space without the body . . . Because the body as lived is not an object, it cannot be said to exist in space as water is in the glass . . . Body is space."[26] Merleau-Ponty posits that body movements generate space; our body movements correlate to a size, type, and kind of space—a phenomenal space—which we create. Our body movements generate and establish a particular lived space.

Turning to the possibility that body movement generates time, I find it helpful to begin with some of Merleau-Ponty's disagreements with previous philosophical attempts to understand time. Concurring with Henri Bergson, Merleau-Ponty opposes the idea that time objectively and successively flows. He writes, "the space and time of culture is not surveyable from above . . .

[and] do[es] not hold under their gaze a serial space and time nor the pure idea of series."[27] Rather, time links distinctly to our body in movement. To illustrate this point, let us look at Bergson's insistence on the importance of the *speed* of time. Bergson's example of the flow of a film reel demonstrates that if time simply flows in infinitesimal, successive, and distinguishable moments, the speed at which a film strip plays would be inconsequential. At any speed, the film strip—discrete, serial pictures representing moments of time—is flowing. Yet we, human beings only appreciate the film within a small range of speeds; there is an *ideal* speed for the flow of the film. What exactly establishes this *ideal* speed? The speed of the film, the ideal pace of the flow of time depends on the subjects as embodied sitting and viewing the film.[28] The subject determines when time is flowing too fast or too slow. Both the constraints of the speed of thinking and the constraints of the speed of perceiving, because of the physicality of embodiment, sets the ideal speed of time. For this reason Bergson refers to time as intuition or as duration, for the speed of time's flow is intimately tied to subjectivity. Bergson posits the existence of an experiential, a phenomenal time.

In stressing time's intimacy with embodied subjectivity, however, Merleau-Ponty distinguishes his notion from Bergson's conception of time as internal to the subject. Merleau-Ponty's disagreement with Bergson is less well known than his agreement with Bergson on time's status as external to the subject. Although appreciative of Bergson's insight in establishing time's tie to the subject, Merleau-Ponty writes in a footnote that "[t]he lived-through which Bergson sets over against the thought-about is for him an experience, an immediate 'datum.' But this is to seek a solution in ambiguity. Space, motion and time cannot be elucidated by discovering an 'inner' layer of experience in which their multiplicity is erased and really abolished."[29] Merleau-Ponty opposes Bergson's solution of "intuition" or "duration" because these notions simply hide the problem by burying it deep within the subject. Bergson's solution of positing another layer of existence leaves time unintelligible.

If time is not objective and serialized, and time is not an intuitive duration, what does Merleau-Ponty offer? Consistent with other phenomenologists, Husserl and Heidegger, Merleau-Ponty's theory of time is a theory of the present. He writes, "[t]he true place of philosophy is not time, in the sense of discontinuous time, nor is it the eternal. It is rather the 'living present'— that is, the present in which the whole past, everything foreign, and the whole of the thinkable future are reanimated."[30] Time flows; the past flows toward the present and the present continues into the future. Because time flows, it

is impossible to divide the flow of time into distinct moments statically identified as the past, the present, and the future. Yet, although time flows, the
past does not predetermine the present,[31] and the future must remain unpredictable, for the present cannot decide the future. He describes the present
as possessing an internal horizon—since past events accumulate within the
present—and an external horizon—since the future lies beyond the present;
"[t]he lived present holds a past and a future within its thickness."[32]

The indeterminateness, the openness of time, even as it flows, eludes
or defies identification as objective/external or intuitive/internal. To capture this particular sense of the flow of time, Merleau-Ponty focuses on the
embodied subject's particular situation at the present moment, from which
one experiences time. He writes, "[c]hange presupposes a certain position
which I take up and from which I see things in procession before me: there
are no events without someone to whom they happen and whose finite perspective is the basis of their individuality."[33] From the subject's perspective,
one experiences the flow of time.

So if time flows, but in a sense in which the present does not determine
the future, in what sense does time flow? What are the meaning and the
significance of the subject's perspective in experiencing the flow of time?
Merleau-Ponty writes, "[t]ime is the one single movement appropriate to
itself in all its parts . . . It is nothing but a general flight out of the Itself, the
one law governing these centrifugal movements, or again, as Heidegger says,
an *ekstase.*"[34] Drawing from Heidegger's notion of *ekstase* in its intimate connection with freedom,[35] Merleau-Ponty speculates that time self-generates;
time self-produces. "Time is 'affecting of self by self,' what exerts the effect
is time as a thrust and a passing towards a future: what is affected is time as
an unfolded series of presents: the affecting agent and affected recipient are
one, because the thrust of time is nothing but the transition from one present
to another."[36] Only in this sense does the present flow into the future. The
present does not determine the future although the future must go through
the present.[37] Because time self-generates, time does not flow like a stream,
but rather like a fountain; time flows through a spout that constantly generates and renews itself at the present time. In place of a linear picture of time,
Merleau-Ponty offers, "a cycle defined by a central and dominant region and
with indecisive contours—a swelling or bulb of time."[38]

The present is primary, yet the present lies always beyond grasp. In *The
Visible and the Invisible*, Merleau-Ponty highlights the transcendence of the
present. One cannot live the present in its immediacy. A gap lies between
the moments of living the present and awareness or reflection of living in

the present. In a sense, the present always escapes us and lies just beyond our attention.[39] The present is inherently transcendent. In other words, "[w]e have to pass from the thing (spatial or temporal) as identity, to the thing (spatial or temporal) as difference, i.e., as transcendence, i.e., as always 'behind,' beyond, far-off."[40]

In positing the integral link between time and the body, Merleau-Ponty draws two conclusions. He presents an embodied subject whose body movement, much like the *ekstase* of time, self-generates and whose body movement *generates* time.[41] To stress this kinship between the body and time, Merleau-Ponty writes, "[i]f . . . the subject is identified with temporality, then self-positing ceases to be a contradiction, because it exactly expresses the essence of living time."[42] The *ekstase* of time and time's integral tie to the body explains body movement as self-generating. The *ekstase* of time and that the subject as embodied establishes the speed of time explains that body movement generates phenomenal time.

To accept that body movement self-generates requires a novel understanding of causality. Merleau-Ponty offers what he calls a *motivation* to explain the indeterminate self-generation in body movement. He draws the conclusion of a motivation from Sigmund Freud. Merleau-Ponty writes, "[i] nto the sexual history, conceived as the elaboration of a general form of life, all psychological constituents can enter, because there is no longer an interaction of two causalities and because the genital life is geared to the whole life of the subject."[43] Freud's work posits and explains how sexuality can function as a drive that does not immediately and directly lead to one inevitable expression or result, but rather leads toward a possible variety of ends. Motivations can come in the form of objects, events, or "nonthetic or not-explicitly-experienced motive[s]."[44]

This open-ended force or drive is a motivation distinct from the causality of formal logic, physics or the act intentionality of consciousness. The rigid causality of formal logic and physics—a causality defined within the parameters of repeatability and predictability—never escapes the facticity of the material world. The determinateness of consciousness does not recognize that fulfillment of one's intentions depends on the material conditions of my body and the circumstances of the world. As Mark Wrathall writes, motivations have an ambiguous presence because it speaks more to our bodies and less to reason and our minds.[45] Both causalities do not address that the body as subject is both matter and ideas. The causalities of physics and act intentionality do not explain the variety and the creativity of human projects, human endeavors, and human responses. Guy Widdershoven explains, "[t]he

notion of motivation offers an alternative to the concept of cause, engen-
dered by empiricism, and the notion of reason which is central to idealism.
A motive is not the cause of the resulting action, since its meaning cannot
be defined apart from the action; on the other hand, the action is not a
totally free response to the motive."[46] Because motivational relations depend
on the context and the agent—the embodied subject matters. Motivation
describes how sometimes, some individuals can perceive something different and beyond the familiar scope of everyday perceptions; how the body
can move in multiple expressive ways; and how one can create a broad range
of experiences and explanations. The notion of a motivation coheres with
the phenomenological existential tradition, which places much responsibility on the choices and actions of individual human beings.[47] For these self-
generated and nondeterminative body movements give birth to the human
subject. Through body movement, one shapes the quality of the space and
time and one moves from the given world to the sphere of the potential and
abstract world.

Through self-generated motivations, body movement generates phenomenological space and time. I should say something about the relationship
between the objective understanding of space and time and the phenomenological understanding of space and time. I suspect that Merleau-Ponty
intended for the phenomenological conception of space and time to replace
the objective conception of space and time. This is not to deny the very real
existence of space and time, but admits the epistemic limits of experiencing
pure space and time.

Responsibility for a Situation

Merleau-Ponty's embodied subject and his phenomenology as a whole insists
on the intimate ties between the subject and the world. He demonstrates
such intimate relations with the world without reducing the subject as the
result of causal forces from the material world or as the construct of nor-
malizing ideas. Merleau-Ponty maintains the existential dimension of the
subject exercising open-ended motivations for body movement. To appreciate the importance of body movements generating space and time within
our existential capabilities and responsibilities, I turn to ethics. In ethics and
whiteness studies, questions persist about responsibility not only for one's
immediate actions, but also for the situations, one finds oneself in, including
situations not of one's own intentional making.

Traditional liberal conceptions of agency and ethics too narrowly focus only on individual actions and ethical responsibilities. To illustrate this, let us look at Immanuel Kant's *Groundwork of the Metaphysic of Morals*, which is considered to be one of the most important—if not the most important—treatises on ethics and freedom. His work serves as a foundation for Western ethical theory. He argues for the importance of ethical life for human beings because human beings possess reason. How should reasoning human beings demonstrate their freedom, especially in situations defined by questions of morality? Kant's famous moral imperative states: "Act only on that maxim through which you can at the same time will that it should become a universal law."[48] One uses reason to exercise freedom when one follows one's own laws—laws one has made for oneself, because the "will is therefore not merely subject to the law, but is so subject that it must be considered as also making the law for itself."[49] Regarding these laws, Kant argues, one should imagine what would happen if all individuals act similarly in like circumstances. Only by acting with the belief that all individuals would behave similarly can one claim to act freely; Kant insists that only moral beings can claim freedom.

For Kant, autonomous individuals—subjects who can separate themselves from the world—exercise freedom. Within Kant's framework it is not clear whether his subjects are embodied, and so it seems unimportant. Kant's analysis presumes three criteria: first, his theory relies on the possibility and the imperative to separate the ethical decision-making moments from their context, to develop a universal criterion. Second, he insists on the essential commonality of all human beings facing and making decisions because of human beings' ability to reason. Kant believes that all reasoning individuals can and will ultimately reach the same conclusions. Finally, and most importantly, Kant's ethical system centers on autonomous individuals who are responsible for only their individual actions.

Merleau-Ponty's understanding of freedom and agency challenges all three of these tenets. Within the *Phenomenology*, he only explicitly addresses freedom in the last chapter; there he writes, "[t]here is free choice only if freedom comes into play in its decision, and posits the situation chosen as a situation of freedom."[50] In other words, choice only arises within a situation *and* one chooses a situation. Rather than reducing the ethical decision and action into isolated moments, Merleau-Ponty's freedom requires accounting for the history of one's past, which leads to the present situation with its available set of choices evolving to specific future options. Merleau-Ponty explains, "choice presupposes a prior commitment" and "the normal person *reckons* with the possible."[51] He concludes, "the real choice is that of whole character and our manner of being in the world. But either this total choice is never uttered . . . or else our choice of ourselves is truly a choice, a conversion involving our whole existence."[52] One does not exercise freedom in spurts of isolated moments but as a continuum, built into the minutia of choices. Based on one's past decisions, one faces different and fewer or greater opportunities in the present. As such, the ethical decision-making moment is not isolatable from its context. Rather, moments of ethical decision making, moments of exercising freedom, demand an acknowledgment of the importance of the circumstances within which human beings' started their lives and their history of choices. This position refutes Kant's first two criteria. The moments of ethical decision making cannot be isolated from their context. Contextually situated human beings do not essentially face the same ethical decisions. All human beings can reason, but, from a series of past decisions, they develop into subjects who utilize their reason in varying complex ways. Human beings face different decisions because they occupy different subjective contexts and situations.[53]

Finally, and most importantly for the present concerns, Merleau-Ponty's freedom requires assessments of normative demands for situations not of one's own making. Merleau-Ponty's conception of freedom suggests that individuals are responsible for more than personal decisions, but also for the situations in which they find themselves. Either human beings are not free because the circumstances of birth define and constrain human freedom, or human beings are truly free and accountable for the entirety of the situations in which they find themselves. In distinction from Kant, Merleau-Ponty broadens our ethical responsibilities to include one's situatedness. Merleau-Ponty stresses this conception of freedom and agency, well aware that human beings do not choose their situations of birth. His work demonstrates the extent of our existential possibilities, including challenging the formative influences of the world and the conditions of our situatedness that include the societies and communities we find ourselves.

Recall my earlier position that body movement generates space and time. Because of embodied subjectivity and because body movement generates the very space and time circumscribing the subject, Merleau-Ponty insists on the broadened responsibility for freedom, including responsibility for one's situation. Because body movements possess such power in their intimate relation with matter and ideas—because body movements generate two of the most fundamental features of being-in-the-world—one is responsible not only for one's immediate choices, but also for one's situations. "With great power comes great responsibility."[54]

The Benefits of Whiteness in a Situation

Merleau-Ponty's work illuminates the far reaches of both the broadened weight of embodied subjectivity and the extent of human existential possibilities in positing that our body movements generate space and time. Consistent with Merleau-Ponty's phenomenology holding human beings responsible for their situations, his phenomenology also attributes to body movements the ability to create the very feel of two of the most basic dimensions of being-in-the-world. For individual, minute, and small body movements build within a community to establish the phenomenal quality of a situation and a society. Maxine Sheets-Johnstone illustrates this especially poignantly in the case of dance movements that can be generalized here. She writes, "[t]he possibilities of the situation at any moment do not then stand out as so many recourses of action possible to take; they are adumbrated, mutely or tacitly given, in the immediacy of the evolving situation itself, a situation which moment by moment opens up a certain world and a certain way of being in the world."[55] To solidly illustrate this buildup of individual body movements generating space and time and responsibility for one's circumstances, let me end with one concrete example of the importance of claiming responsibility for one's situation.

    One of the most intriguing positions voiced in whiteness studies is the insistence that white people experience benefits simply from the location of whiteness in society. Because of this society's history, simply having a white body confers benefits. Theorists who write about whiteness aim to clarify this particular advantage that comes from merely possessing a body that looks white. Such clarification is necessary for understanding how to become responsible race traitors. In this specific context, race traitors are whites who endeavor to disavow their whiteness by repeatedly acting to defray their white privileges. Linda Martín Alcoff's caution to race traitors illustrates the informative role of body features; she writes, "in one important sense, whites cannot disavow whiteness. One's appearance of being white will still operate to confer privilege in numerous and significant ways, and to avow treason does not render whites ineligible for these privileges, even if they work hard to avoid them."[56] So, even race traitors, whose behavior does not passively absorb the social benefits of being white, who actively work to dispel these privileges, nevertheless profit from being white. For white people who want to conscientiously address the inequities of race, isolated actions do not suffice to dispel the personal benefits of whiteness. Isolated individual actions do not suffice because isolated individual actions cannot address the injustices inherent in a social structural situation. Rather, sometimes, individual acts of transgression of whitely scripts by whites are dangerous because unsuspecting black people are abruptly reprimanded in addition to or in place of whites.[57] Individual responsibility for one's own actions does not suffice to address the benefits inherent in social situations; Kant's moral imperatives center on autonomous individuals whose ethical behavior focuses only on individual actions. Kant's moral framework does not address the history of past injustices that now leads to the injustice's inherent in the present social situation with its structural benefits for whites.

To be a race traitor, Lisa Heldke writes, "involves taking responsibility for one's social location."[58] Heldke and Alison Bailey recognize that white people concerned with racial injustice, who recognize the benefits of simply possessing white bodies, must take responsibility for the social situations in which they live. This is quite an acknowledgment, for this requires taking responsibility for a history that one is not personally responsible for creating. Owning such responsibility remains one of the most radical and intriguing insights in whiteness studies. A general acceptance of this position could provide a thorough argument for affirmative action policies. For a much repeated argument against affirmative action policies is that present-day white people did not commit the atrocities of past white people. As Michael D. Barber explains, one of the arguments against affirmative action is "that white males who did not discriminate against blacks unfairly bear the brunt of the compensation burden."[59] This position that present-day whites should not be held accountable for the sins of their forebears is widely accepted today. But if we follow Heldke and Bailey's position and accept responsibility for a situation, including the historical moment of our birth, then present-day whites *can be held* accountable for the past injustices of their forebears that have resulted in today's social circumstances.

Here Merleau-Ponty's position that body movements generate space and time become pertinent. Bailey explains that history sediments into social meanings in the form of body comportments. The performance of whiteness has and requires white scripts that white and black bodies enact. Bailey writes, "[r]acial scripts are internalized at an early age to the point where they are embedded almost to invisibility in our language, bodily reactions, feelings, behaviors, and judgments."[60] The history of colonialism has not only sedimented into the social structural situation in terms of laws and institutions or conscious and unconscious beliefs and prejudices about different racialized body features, but into the very way one lives one's body, in one's body movements. In other words, how one stands, sits, walks, and greets another human being, how slowly, or quickly, one moves in a social situation are body movements that develop within a history and exhibit how comfortable one feels and is made to feel in any given context. Feminists have already argued that many public spaces in social institutions provide comfort for white men and intimidate women and minorities. Here I want to add that the architecture does not solely permit such levels of comfort and discomfort, but also the body comportment—the body movements of men and women, whites, blacks, or otherwise racialized people—in these spaces also establish the phenomenal feel of the space as welcoming or forbidding. Some obvious and well-known examples include the body comportment of resorting to smiling more frequently exercised by blacks and women; the use of handshakes for greeting, which is more frequent among white men, compared to greeting with more body contact, which is more frequent among certain people of color and women; or the notion of colored people time (CP time), referring to the likelihood of lateness by certain groups of people of color. Not only do specific racialized and sexualized subjects more frequently exercise each of these of body movements, but specific racially and sexually embodied subjects read each of these body comportments differently. Some read the tendency to smile as welcoming and endeavoring to put others at ease, while others read excessive smiling as obsequious and a sign of a lack of intelligence.[61] Some read handshakes as tasteful, while others read handshakes as cold. Some read greetings with more body contact such as kisses and hugs as more intimate and welcoming, while others read these greetings as unnecessarily invasive of personal space. I have noticed that I welcome hugs from women while feeling suspicious of hugs from men, especially men I do not know well. Some read CP time as demonstrating flexibility, patience, and the spirit that one should not take life so seriously, while others read CP time as demonstrating an inability to follow directions and disrespecting other people's time. Because the subject is embodied and in the world, not only does the existing architecture or institutional practices constitute space, but also body movements generate a phenomenal space and time around oneself.

Conclusion

The history of colonialism has sedimented into racialized body movement to generate phenomenal spaces and times that are also racially specific.[62] As a result, today, body comportment and movement are racially specific, and one understands the intentions and the significances of the body movement in racially specific ways. In this society, the sedimented scripts in the embodiment of white bodies and black bodies illustrate the depth of the racial benefits and disadvantages of the present social situations.

Whiteness studies' position that one is responsible for one's situation coheres well with Merleau-Ponty's claim that one is truly free only in accepting responsibility for the entirety of one's situation. Rising to the challenge of such freedom is an important consequence of understanding that our body movements generate space and time. Only in recognizing responsibility for one's situations, even if one was not personally complicit in creating such contexts, can one truly recognize the broad scope of one's existential power and ethical responsibility. To take responsibility for the history of racial injustice that has resulted in a social situation where simply possessing a white body confers benefits, following Bailey's account that such benefits are embedded in body scripts, requires changing the prevailing meanings of white and black bodies and our own body movements.

Phenomenology's account of freedom requires reconceptualizing our responsibilities as beings-in-the-world. Let me end with a hint here; recall Merleau-Ponty's understanding of the body as "a heavy signification." Ultimately, I suspect that he would attribute to body movement the generation of significations.[63] In other words, in addition to, or perhaps more than, addressing the linguistic signs about race, developing and accumulating different and new body movements can ultimately generate new meanings about white and black bodies.

Notes

1. Maurice Merleau-Ponty, *The Visible and the Invisible*, trans. Alphonso Lingis (Evanston, Ill.: Northwestern University Press, 1968), 114, 248–249.
2. Maurice Merleau-Ponty, *Phenomenology of Perception*, trans. Colin Smith (Evanston, Ill.: Northwestern University Press, 1962), 164, 166, 181. I follow this translation, although I understand that this translation confuses body image and body schema. See footnote 5 below.
3. Merleau-Ponty, *Visible*, 136, 249.

4. Helen Fielding, "Depth of Embodiment: Spatial and Temporal Bodies in Foucault and Merleau-Ponty," *Philosophy Today* 43, no. 1 (Spring 1999): 78.

5. Shaun Gallagher clarifies that there has been quite a bit of confusion over the uses of the terms *body image* and *body schema* across various disciplines, including among Merleau-Ponty scholars. Nevertheless, Gallagher believes Merleau-Ponty was consistent in his reference to the body schema, "to signify a dynamic functioning of the body in its environment. The schema operates as a system of dynamic motor equivalents that belong to the realm of habit rather than conscious choices" (*How the Body Shapes the Mind* [Oxford: Oxford University Press, 2005], 20). Gallagher points out, "however, the term 'schema corporel' was rendered 'body image' in the English translation of his work in the *Phenomenology of Perception* (1962)." Gallagher offers the following definition of a body image and body schema. Body image "consists of a system of perceptions, attitudes, and beliefs pertaining to one's own body. In contrast, a body schema is a system of sensory-motor capacities that function without awareness or the necessity of perceptual monitoring" (24). Gallagher continues, "[t]his conceptual distinction between body image and body schema is related respectively to the difference between having a perception of (or belief about) something and having a capacity to move (or an ability to do something)." I do not follow Gallagher here, mainly because I worry about the possible loss of reflexivity between perception and action.

6. Merleau-Ponty, *Phenomenology*, 110.

7. Merleau-Ponty, *Phenomenology*, 387.

8. Merleau-Ponty, *Phenomenology*, xviii.

9. Merleau-Ponty, *Phenomenology*, 136.

10. See Galen A. Johnson, "Inside and Outside: Ontological Considerations," *Merleau-Ponty, Interiority and Exteriority, Psychic Life and the World*, ed. Dorothea Olkowski and James Morley (Albany: State University of New York Press, 1999).

11. Merleau-Ponty, *Phenomenology*, 142.

12. Merleau-Ponty, *Phenomenology*, 110.

13. Merleau-Ponty, *Phenomenology*, 111.

14. Lawrence Hass, "Sense and Alterity: Rereading Merleau-Ponty's Reversibility Thesis," *Merleau-Ponty, Interiority and Exteriority, Psychic Life and the World*, ed. Dorothea Olkowski and James Morley (Albany: State University of New York Press, 1999), 94.

15. Martin Dillon, *Merleau-Ponty's Ontology* (Evanston, Ill.: Northwestern University Press, 1997), 124.

16. See Richard Shusterman, "The Silent Limping Body of Philosophy," *The Cambridge Companion to Merleau-Ponty*, ed. Taylor Carman and Mark B. N. Hansen (New York: Cambridge University Press, 2005), 151–180.

17. Although Merleau-Ponty uses the word *generate*, I do not believe that he uses the word in the sense referred to in Anthony Steinbock, "Generativity and Generative Phenomenology," *Husserl Studies* 12 (1995): 55–79. Steinbock talks about generating to refer to becoming over the generations (57). Unfortunately the same word is used here, but even Steinbock admits that Husserl never fully developed a generative philosophy (75).

18. Merleau-Ponty, *Phenomenology*, 387.

19. Merleau-Ponty, *Phenomenology*, 240. Although later he clarifies that he does not mean create, exactly, but generate.

   Martin Heidegger suggests a similar relation: "Spaces, and with them space as such—'space'—are always provided for already within the stay of mortals. Spaces open up by the fact that they are let into the dwelling of man. To say that mortals *are* is to say that in *dwelling* they persist through spaces by virtue of their stay among things and locales" ("Building Dwelling Thinking," *Basic Writings*, ed. David Farrell Krell [San Francisco: Harper San Francisco, 1993], 359).

20. Merleau-Ponty, *Phenomenology*, 102; see also 142, 148.

21. Iris Marion Young, "Throwing Like a Girl," *The Thinking Muse: Feminism and Modern French Philosophy*, ed. Jeffner Allen and Iris Marion Young (Bloomington: Indiana University Press, 1989), 62.

22. Young, "Throwing Like a Girl," 59.

23. Young, 59.

24. Young, 60.

25. Young, 63.

26. Young, 63.

27. Merleau-Ponty, *Visible* 115. See Henri Bergson, *The Creative Mind*, trans. Mabelle L. Andison (New York: Citadel Press, 1946), 18.

28. Bergson, 1946, 55.

29. Merleau-Ponty, *Phenomenology*, 276. Or see 420 for another reason why Merleau-Ponty disagrees with Bergson's analysis. Merleau-Ponty writes, "Bergson was wrong in *explaining* the unity of time in terms of its continuity, since that amounts to confusing past, present, and future on the excuse that we pass from one or the other by imperceptible transitions; in short it amounts to denying time altogether."

30. Maurice Merleau-Ponty, "Phenomenology and the Sciences of Man," *The Primacy of Perception*, ed. James M. Edie, trans. John Wild (Evanston, Ill.: Northwestern University Press. 1964), 90.

I understand that Jacques Derrida criticizes phenomenology for being "presentists," but this critique does not suffice to completely dismiss phenomenological theories on time.

31. Merleau-Ponty, *Visible*, 114.

32. Merleau-Ponty, *Phenomenology*, 275.

33. Merleau-Ponty, *Phenomenology*, 411; see also 331, and 1968, 114, 184.

34. Merleau-Ponty, *Phenomenology*, 419.

35. Martin Heidegger, "On the Essence of Truth," *Basic Writings*, ed. David Farrell Krell (San Francisco: Harper Collins Publishers, 1993), 126.

36. Merleau-Ponty, *Phenomenology* 425–426. He continues to write, "[t]he primary flow, says Husserl, does not confine itself to being; it must necessarily provide itself with a 'manifestation of itself' without our needing to place behind it a second flow which is conscious of it. It 'constitutes itself as a phenomenon within itself'" (1962, 426). He cites Heidegger, *Kant und das Problem der Metaphysik*, 180.

37. Merleau-Ponty, *Phenomenology*, 85.

38. Merleau-Ponty, *Phenomenology*, 184.

39. Merleau-Ponty writes, "the present is us; it awaits our consent or our refusal. . . . The proximity of the present, which is what makes us responsible for it, nevertheless does not give us access to the thing itself" (1964b, 194).

40. Merleau-Ponty, *Visible*, 195.

41. Merleau-Ponty, *Phenomenology*, 426. He cites Husserl, *Zeitbewusstein*, 436.

42. Merleau-Ponty, *Phenomenology*, 425, 423–424

43. Merleau-Ponty, *Phenomenology*, 158.

44. Mark A. Wrathall, "Motives, Reasons, and Causes," *The Cambridge Companion to Merleau-Ponty*, ed. Taylor Carman and Mark B. N. Hansen (Cambridge, UK: Cambridge University Press, 2005), 117.

45. Wrathall, "Motives, Reasons, and Causes," 115.

46. Guy A. M. Widdershoven, "Truth and Meaning in Art: Merleau-Ponty's Ambiguity," *Journal of the British Society for Phenomenology* 30, no. 2, (1999): 231. Merleau-Ponty also writes, "Plato and Kant, to mention only them, accepted the contradiction of which Zeno and Hume wanted no part . . . There is the sterile non-contradiction of formal logic and the justified contradictions of transcendental logic" ("The Primacy of Perception and Its Philosophical Consequences," *The Primacy of Perception*, ed. James

M. Edie, trans. William Cobb [Evanston,Ill.: Northwestern University Press, 1964], 19).

In other words, motivational relationships "lack extensionality. Causal relationships, by contrast, are extensional, in the sense that the relationship holds up between the relata regardless of the mode by which the relata are presented to us" (Wrathall, 116).

47. See Wrathall, 118.
48. Immanuel Kant, *Groundwork of the Metaphysic of Morals*, trans. H. J. Paton (New York: Harper Torch Books, 1964), 88. This categorical imperative can also be stated as: "Act in such a way that you always treat humanity whether in your own person or in the person of any other, never simply as a means, but always at the same time as an end" (96).
49. Kant, 98–99.
50. Merleau-Ponty, *Phenomenology*, 437; see also 164.
51. Merleau-Ponty, *Phenomenology*, 439 and 109, respectively.
52. Merleau-Ponty, *Phenomenology*, 438–439
53. Merleau-Ponty's position dissolves the strict distinction between ethical and practical decisions.
54. I am facetiously quoting *Spiderman* (2002, directed by Sam Raimi, written by Stan Lee and Steve Ditko, screenplay David Koepp). This individual responsibility for the situations of one's birth, of one's history suggests responsibility by the "winners" of history for all the possibly atrocious acts committed to be able to portray themselves as the winners of history *and* the "losers" of history for all their failures and calamitous endeavors. In this chapter, I only explore responsibility for the history by the so-called winners of past atrocious acts. It would be interesting to think of responsibility for a history of loss. But I leave this exploration for another occasion.
55. Maxine Sheets-Johnstone, "Thinking in Movement," *The Journal of Aesthetics and Art Criticism* 39, no. 4 (Summer, 1981): 405.
56. Linda Martín Alcoff, "What Should White People Do?" *Decentering the Center: Philosophy for a Multicultural, Postcolonial, and Feminist World*, ed. Uma Narayan and Sandra Harding (Bloomington: Indiana University Press, 2000): 273.
57. See Alcoff, "What Should White People Do?" 215.
58. Lisa Heldke, "On Being a Responsible Traitor: A Primer," *Daring to Be Good: Essays in Feminist Ethico-Politics* eds. Bat-Ami Bar On and Ann Ferguson (New York: Routledge, 1998), 96.

59. Michael D. Barber, *Equality and Diversity: Phenomenological Investigations of Prejudice and Discrimination* (Amherst, NY: Humanity Books, 2001), 223.

60. Alison Bailey, "Locating Traitorous Identities: Toward a View of Privilege-Cognizant White Character," *Decentering the Center: Philosophy for a Multicultural, Postcolonial, and Feminist World*, ed. Uma Narayan and Sandra Harding (Bloomington: Indiana University Press, 2000): 290.

61. See Martha Nussbaum, "'Don't Smile So Much': Philosophy and Women in the 1970s," *Singing in the Fire: Tales of Women in Philosophy*, ed. Linda Martin Alcoff (New York: Rowman and Littlefield Publishers, 2003), 81–92. See also Toni Morrison's description of Clarence Thomas's laugh in, "Introduction: Friday on the Potomac," *Race-ing Justice, En-Gendering Power: Essays on Anita Hill, Clarence Thomas, and the Construction of Social Reality*, ed. Toni Morriosn (New York: Pantheon, 1992), xii.

62. I am not claiming absolutely all body movement conforms to their racialized scripts, but that the tendency is distinguishable.

63. This position coheres with Gallagher's analysis of gesture. Carving a middle space between theories that gesture develops either from linguistic or from motor capabilities of the body, Gallagher argues for an integrative understanding of gesture. He describes gesture to be "first, embodied (constrained and enabled by motoric possibilities); second, communicative (pragmatically intersubjective); and third, cognitive (contributing to the accomplishment of thought, shaping the mind)" (123).

ELEVEN

THE FUTURE OF WHITENESS

Linda Martín Alcoff

The most trenchant observers of the scene in the South, those who are embattled there, feel that the southern mobs are not an expression of the southern majority will. Their impression is that these mobs fill, so to speak, a moral vacuum and that the people who form these mobs would be very happy to be released from their pain, and their ignorance, if someone arrived to show them the way. I would be inclined to agree with this, simply from what we know of human nature. It is not my impression that people wish to become worse; they really wish to become better but very often do not know how.

—James Baldwin

As Nell Painter observes in her recent, masterful study, *The History of White People*, "being white these days is not what it used to be."[1] The present-day character and experience of whiteness as a lived, embodied identity in the context of the contemporary United States is undergoing as significant a transformation, as it did during the period over a century ago when southern Europeans and the Irish became accepted members of the club. This provides a highly opportune moment to observe the fluidity of racial categories in action, as meanings mutate and practices shift, but it also provides an opportunity for strategic intervention and normative analysis. This paper will thus approach the question of the future of whiteness not simply as a project of prediction but as a normative project with a plan for positive change, as Baldwin, on one of his optimistic days, evokes for us in the passage above.

The emerging whiteness studies, as full of wonderful work as it is, can leave one with a sense of doom and confusion. Whiteness is often portrayed as essentially racist, despite the antiessentialist leanings of most of the theorists. If white identity is doomed by its history, there is literally nowhere to go but to a kind of self-erasure. But if we attempt to eliminate the category, the question is what can replace it, given the diminished importance for most white families of their distant European lineages, and the bankruptcy of generic deraced individualism? Social categories of identity are indices of historical experience, and history doesn't go away, even if it can be radically reinterpreted. This chapter is an attempt to think aloud about this dilemma, the dilemma of a whiteness few want to see in the future.

I. Demographic Realities

White, European Americans living in the United States, will soon share the unprecedented experience of slipping below 50 percent of the population. Some say this will happen by 2050, some say 2042. For the first time in its history, the United States will be a majority nonwhite nation. The mind reels. Will this make a difference to its foreign policy, or its domestic policy? Will the nonwhite majority revise and correct the prettified ideological image of the history of the United States and its role in the world, bringing slavery, genocide, colonialism, and imperialism out from the footnotes? And how will whites respond?

Let's look first at the numbers. The predictions are based on facts such as the following: between 2000 and 2010, the U.S. population increased by nearly 10 percent to 308 million souls. Latino and Asian numbers increased the most, with each group increasing its numbers by 43 percent, but African Americans went up as well, by 12 percent. Even the category of "American Indian and Alaska Native" jumped 18 percent. The white population lagged markedly behind, increasing only by 1 percent, losing five points of its market share in the overall population. Whites dropped from 69 percent of the whole down to 64 percent during this single decade, but even this number is misleading since the category of white includes Arabs and north Africans.[2] But the important point is that the confluence of factors leading to the loss of a white majority cannot be "corrected" by changing immigration rates, since the majority of new Latinos are born in the United States. The writing on the wall for whiteness in America is unmistakable, and irreversible, and it may not be written in English.

It is important to note that whites will remain the largest plurality even after 2050. More importantly, the economic advantages in home equity and other forms of inherited capital—cultural and otherwise—wrought over hundreds of years are likely to persist for generations. The distribution of economic resources will not change as quickly as the demographics because, as many studies reveal, the main way that race affects a household's economic condition is not measured in wages but in real estate. When the measure of wealth rather than wage income is used, it turns out that white families have 44.5 times more wealth than African Americans families.[3] The recent mortgage crises hit the newest and poorest homeowners the hardest, disproportionately people of color. United for a Fair Economy estimates that the subprime mortgage bubble caused losses between 146 billion dollars to 190 billion dollars for African Americans and Latinos. These facts together with our liberal inheritance laws mean that there will be a cross-generational payoff of white privilege for some time.

Yet, given the clear signs of hysteria we can witness across the country, the likely recalcitrance of material advantage is not enough to offset the psychic turmoil that has resulted from an impending loss of majority status. I argue that this is not merely a media orchestration, producing hysteria where there is no basis. It is clear to whites that things will not continue to operate in the future in quite the same way as they have operated in the past. Unlike the manufactured German hysteria about an imagined Jewish world domination, the fear of losing white dominance is not merely a projection of pure paranoia or a manipulation by elites.[4] Millions of urban whites in the United States have been experiencing minority status for decades. New York, Miami, Denver, Los Angeles, San Francisco, Houston, Atlanta, Washington DC, Detroit, Tampa, Baltimore, and Philadelphia are all major cities with a white minority, and there are now four states with minority white populations. The absolute cultural and political hegemony of whiteness has already been lost: even the Tea Party must drag its nonwhite participants up to the front of every major public event.

Whites are split over the Tea Party: according to a *Newsweek* poll in 2010, 45 percent of *white southerners* disapprove of its negative politics. Fearful, racist, and violent responses by whites to their impending minority status are clearly not the only sort out there. Opinion polls continue to reveal significant divergences between whites and nonwhites on race-related matters, but we may be overlooking the important data from such surveys. For example, according to recent Gallup Polls, 56 percent of whites disapprove of the treatment of immigrants in the United States, fully half believe racism is widespread, and 44 percent believe racism is a factor in blacks' rates of incarceration.[5] In the post–civil rights era, white attitudes have changed significantly about issues such as neighborhood integration, interracial dating, and racism. While the disparity between whites and nonwhites on racial issues remain significant, we shouldn't overlook the fact that nearly half of white Americans agree with the overwhelming majority of people of color on many political questions concerned with race. Does this mean they are divided and will soon be conquered?

II. The Experience of Whiteness

Younger whites are no doubt the main game changers here. They have grown up in more diverse environments in their schools, neighborhoods, and worksites, with interactions that are often egalitarian, not simply interacting with servants. Many young whites gravitate toward strongly assertive forms of African American expressive cultural productions, from musicians to comedians. The support among white youth for Obama was well known, but white youth also populates the ranks of more progressive social movements outside the electoral arena.

Living among diversity, even when this occurs in fairly egalitarian conditions, is not sufficient to explain a lessening of racist attitudes, as Gordon Allport's study on racism showed many years ago.[6] The contact zone has to be of a certain sort. Take the comparison once again with Germany, in which Jews experienced much more social integration than in other countries in Eastern Europe and Russia, where pogroms made everyday living such a nightmare that whole families sent away their precious young people knowing they would never return. In contrast to these countries, German Jews attended university, entered many of the professions, owned property, and achieved a measure of cultural and economic success. But there was a general nonconfrontational and pro-assimilation attitude among German Jews since the nineteenth century, when Karl Marx's family, for example, converted so that his father could practice law. Gentile Germans in those historical periods were not confronted by the angry assertiveness of aggrieved Jewish sensibilities expressed in popular music or street demonstrations, nor did they experience the moral challenge of a civil rights movement that showcased the harrowing effects of social inequality and segregation. They could live their lives in relative ignorance of Jewish perspectives about anti-Semitism in German society.[7]

Thus, merely living alongside others, even in relations of relative equanimity, is insufficient to change dominant consciousness. There must also be an awareness of the others' subjective point of view, including their assessments of the dominant group and dominant culture, that is, the shared social world. Without an awareness of the subjectivity of the other, people truly become Ellison's invisible man, someone with the object-like status that Fanon describes as a corporeal malediction, or what Lewis Gordon calls simply "a form of absence."[8] Without knowing the subject-self of the other, the other is "a body without a perspective."[9]

The importance, and the effects, of intersubjective relations, are apparent in Simone de Beauvoir's memoir of visiting the United States for the first time in 1947. Beauvoir spent four months lecturing and touring across the country, and, though many parts of the culture animated her interest, the differences between and relations among whites, blacks, Latinos, and Native Americans was a central chord in the subsequent observations she published. Some of these observations clearly stereotype racial differences: for example, when she describes "puritan" whites and "sensual" blacks. But she also astutely described the intensity of racism in Jim Crow America, the hypocrisies of urban sophisticated white liberals, and the effects of living in a racist society on white subjective life. These experiences, especially her visits to Harlem and New Mexico, instigated Beauvoir's own self-examination. As she recounts experiences of shame or deep-seated discomfort, she was not simply commenting on the racism of others, but awakening to the deep and complicated nature of her own white subjectivity. Socializing with Richard Wright in the Jim Crow New York of the 1940s, Beauvoir notes the hostile glances and feels herself "stiffen with a bad conscience."[10] She observes:

> Harlem weighs on the conscience of whites like original sin on a Christian. Among men of his own race, the American embraces a dream of good humor, benevolence and friendship. He even puts his virtues into practice. But they die on the borders of Harlem. . . . And all whites who do not have the courage to desire brotherhood try to deny this rupture in the heart of their own city; they try to deny Harlem, to forget it. It's not a threat to the future; it's a wound in the present, a cursed city, the city where they are cursed . . . And because I'm white, whatever I think and say or do, this curse weighs on me as well. I dare not smile at the children in the squares; I don't feel I have the right to stroll in the streets where the color of my eyes signifies injustice, arrogance, and hatred.[11]

Individual antiracist intentions count for naught in a social realm overdetermined by histories of slavery, lynching, and sanctioned racism. A smiling white face would signify condescension, or hypocrisy, in a society where shared water fountains constituted the threat of pollution. Beauvoir rightly notes that whites knew, even then, that there were double standards for civility, justice, and benevolence. Many recognized that the platitudes of national moral superiority were so hollow as to be cruel. As a result, she opines, the white person who enters a space like Harlem "feels hated; he knows he is hateful." His or her true reason for avoiding the area is not crime, but the psychic discomfort of guilt.

Such accounts must problematize the claim many theorists have made that whiteness has been, until recently, an invisible identity. Under Jim Crow, whiteness was quite visible, even though it did not require the practices of marking or announcing used with nonwhites (as lampooned by the title "national black correspondent" on Jon Stewart's *Daily Show*) because whiteness was the *normative* identity—normative for "Americans," for professionals, for leaders in all fields. Whiteness went unnamed because white presence required no explanation or justification, not because it was invisible. Whiteness was always a critical element of social situations, determining the possibilities for action and modes of interaction. The commonly used phrase, "That's mighty white of you," that one can find in movies as soon as talkies began, as well as in novels like Sinclair Lewis's *Babbitt*, reveals that whites were aware of white identity and its perks.[12] When Katherine Hepburn declares in the 1938 film *Bringing Up Baby*, "I am free, white, and over 21," she is saying she has three positive goods that enable her to do what she wants.[13] One cannot navigate a segregated or hierarchical social landscape without becoming schooled in the specific practices accorded to one's identity, wherever one stands with respect to the divide.

Of course, there have been more recent cultural shifts in the visibility of whiteness, without a doubt, prompted by the (relative) success and visibility of the civil rights struggle. Beauvoir's "bad conscience" appears to be more openly acknowledged in recent times. The most significant difference between today and the period of Jim Crow is the increasing visibility of the subjective experiences of nonwhites in our society, as expressed mainly in artistic and cultural forms but also in opinion polling and voting. Even high art, so called, is no longer a white-only space, and though much of the culture industry is distorted by the effects of (white) capital, there is still the strong presence of nonwhite sensibilities, reactions, interpretations, and values on our shared daily events. Niche media marketing is not strong enough to completely block the nonwhite point of view.

The meanings of identity are always relational, as Judy Rohrer argues in her instructional study of *Haoles in Hawai'i*, a group of whites who have been minoritized for longer than those on the mainland.[14] Rohrer traces the shifts in the meaning of *haole*, or white, identity in relation to the shifting populations on the islands, as well as shifts in the colonial political economy and labor market. Whiteness cannot remain still while its social context is radically rearranged, however much it may try. For some time now some *haoles* in Hawai'i have been claiming that whiteness is victimized, a far cry from the idea of happily being "free, white, and over 21."

The very idea of white supremacy is, of course, a relational claim, and it seems clear that the increasing disaffection of whites from such ideas is a result of their changed relational position, as people who can no longer pretend to be unaware of the point of view of nonwhites. If whites felt uncomfortably self-conscious entering Harlem in 1947, they are likely to feel self-conscious today in a great deal more public spaces, including many public schools and universities. In Charles Gallagher's study, young white students evince a palpably painful, and confused, sense of "feeling white": "I mean now I really have to think about it. Like now I feel white. I feel white," one student laments.[15] The denial and avoidance Beauvoir reports on are more difficult to maintain in less segregated social landscapes where whites are a minority or near-minority, or at least not the overwhelming majority. The main catalyst of this developing self-awareness among whites that they are racialized subjects whose point of view on the world is only partial and limited comes, thus, not from whites themselves, but from the increasingly visible sensibilities of nonwhites, who have for a long time seen the limitations of white points of view.

Whiteness is in transition, then, not because it is becoming visible for the first time, but because it's meaning is changing in ways that call white cultural dominance to account. Whiteness was visible before, as necessarily so in any segregated society, but its dominance was naturalized to such an extent that it required no justification, no commentary, no analysis. By contrast, Gordon argues that the very presence of blackness had to be justified in many public spaces, such as university classrooms, while the presence of whiteness enjoyed an a priori justification. That is what is being lost, such that some whites may in fact feel today that *their* presence requires some justification, in certain neighborhoods, for example, or at certain concerts. What is becoming more widely visible, then, is not whiteness but white domination, that is, the hegemony of whiteness in the public domain. This is what is fueling the

ferment of white identity: its lost sense of unquestioned legitimacy, and its
sense of uncertainty about where this transitional national moment is leading.

It remains the case, however, that the phenomenological experience of
white embodiment—that first-person sense of self—will provide a limited
source for understanding what whiteness is today in any fully adequate sense.
Many whites continue to operate in the world with ideological blinders about
the reality of their history, their economic position relative to other groups,
and the whole range of their unconscious habits of privilege.[16] Gallagher's
subjects, for example, mistakenly place slavery in the far distant past, believing it to be four generations older than it in fact is.

Self-delusion is a common theme in whiteness studies. Delusion applies
not only to white beliefs about the past and the present, but also the future.
Some whites even seem to believe that the D-Day date of 2050 can be avoided
if we quickly stop immigration and make the life of the undocumented such
a living hell that they will return to their home countries or just die on the
job or in prison.[17] The fact that Mexican laborers in the United States already
die in on-the-job accidents at a rate four times higher than other workers,
and the harassment daily heaped on immigrants, both legal and illegal, makes
this plan more than a rhetorical flourish. However, and despite the ample
evidence of whites' delusions, it is a mistake to assume, as some critical race
theorists do, that the first-person lived experience of whiteness should be
approached *only* as something that needs to be deconstructed and critiqued.
The phenomenal experience of whiteness is sometimes presented as a they-
self or chatter, in Heidegger's sense, as if it emanates from an alienated consciousness that lacks all self-awareness and exhibits only ignorance. Certainly
there is ample evidence of ignorance, denial, confusion, and problematic
habits of perception, but is that all there is to whiteness? Are there any useful
first-person insights that might provide a re-visioning of possibilities toward
a changed national landscape that would include whites *as whites?*

Whiteness, without a doubt, poses unique challenges to the formation of
a culturally pluralist, egalitarian society in which group identities can be present in the public sphere without rancor, enforced assimilation, or reductive
essentializing. There are always conflicts between various groups, but when
conflicts arise among people of color it is possible to invoke shared histories
of identity-based oppression as a common experience. Negotiating and managing the conflicts between oppressed racial/ethnic groups and whites pose
different challenges.

The idea of whites operating in the public domain *as* whites, as a group
that defines its own group related interests and grievances, raises the specter

of white landowners fighting Native American treaty recognition, or whites filing legal suits against affirmative action. Such examples return us, understandably, to pessimism. Might there be other ways in which it is possible to operate in the public domain as white, without either delusion or self-erasure? This hinges on the larger question: Can whites change?

III. A Relational Substance

Pessimism may be in order, but determinism is not, neither is an essentialist take on the meanings of white identity. One can say that the doctrine of National Socialism was irretrievably racist, but historically developing races and ethnicities are not bound in the same way to any set of originary doxastic commitments. Social groups have no specifiable origin, or even a textual basis, that inhibits their flexibility. The genesis of black identity in concepts of natural slavery did not keep African peoples of the new world from transforming the accepted meanings of blackness from natural slavishness to more positive connotations, such as community solidarity, emotional strength, cultural brilliance, and sophisticated coolness. The connotations and meanings of blackness have shifted as a result of changing group conditions and practices, and someday the concept may wither away or be entirely replaced. Nuyorican identity has undergone a similar transformation from its genesis in forced economic migration under colonial conditions. Long derided by both island Puerto Ricans and non-Latinos in the United States, Nuyorican identity has become a positive and powerful self-ascription signifying survival, political resistance, and cultural and linguistic dexterity. The genealogy of whiteness—even though it has an origin in domination rather than oppression—is not necessarily any more determinative of all the future meanings whiteness might develop. Outside the United States, there are a number of similarly challenged transformations, from the mestizo identities in Latin America that include the conquistadors alongside the conquered, to German national identity, British identity, Tutsi identity, Japanese identity, each wrestling with histories of evil.[18] These forms of identity share with whiteness a past attachment to supremacist narratives that have now lost their power of persuasion. They are in a process of similar turmoil with varied strategies of redemption. Whiteness is not alone in its quest.

Moreover, it is far from clear that whiteness *can* be successfully eliminated. The phenomenology of white identity retains its effects over the micromodes of interaction and understanding, and the imaginary collectivity

of whiteness continues to affect and infect subjective ways of being. Whiteness certainly affects the political discourses and debates about entitlements,
reparations, and both foreign and domestic policy. But even those whites
who come to participate in the coalition for social change, whether in the
Occupy Wall Street movement or their local labor unions, come *as whites*, not
just as women, gays and lesbians, working-class people, the disabled, or any
one of another group-related identity that might offset potential conflicts
and jumpstart an easy talk of commonality.

White identity has substantive features beyond being embroiled in the
history of racism, just as oppressed identities are not reducible to their
oppression. It has its own material reality in the social and economic context
of the West, its own set of broad historical experiences, and its own modes
of subject formation including the development of modes of comportment, perception, and intersubjective interaction, sometimes grounded in a
pan-European ethnicity, sometimes in white supremacy, sometimes in white
inflected versions of missionary Christianity. We need the analytic category
of whiteness to be able to mark and name these specifics, whether or not the
persons so named self-ascribe as whites. As Michael Monahan's new study
shows, the laborers who came to Barbados from Ireland as indentured servants in the eighteenth century had rough lives that led them sometimes to
make common cause with the forced laborers from Africa. But to understand
their particular position in the organization of labor in the Caribbean and the
Americas, we need the category of whiteness. Despite their racialization as a
distinct race from the British, the skin color of the Irish differentiated them
from the Africans in their specific opportunities, challenges, and experiences,
and in their future transformed interpellations.[19] The category of whiteness
in this case does not depend for its analytical utility on self-ascription. We
must let go of the idea, once and for all, that workers have ever entered
the modern colonial world system as generic workers, as if their class identity and class interests and class-related opportunities can be separated from
other elements of their identity.

White workers come to their union bargaining committees with a set
of experiences and interests to be taken into account in determining overall
priorities, some of which are legitimate. They are also likely to come with
some baggage of chauvinism and racism, like all other groups, but with one
important difference: whites are likely to be influenced by the ideology of
white vanguardism, the idea that white people—generally meaning Anglo-
Saxons or those from Western Europe—are the moral, political, scientific,
and technological vanguard of the human race. White vanguardism is a

powerful cross-class phenomenon, conferring a sense of dignity and entitle-ment on men of modest means. It has been such a powerful aspect of white subject-formation that it becomes difficult to imagine what whiteness would be without it.

Thus, many academic theorists today are fatalistic about the possibility of transforming whiteness in positive ways. From eliminativists like Garvey and Ignatiev, to cosmopolitanists, to the critics of identity politics that would have us cease and desist bringing identities into the political realm (except for a "generic" class), there are a number of theorists who hold that whiteness is constituted through and through by racism, that racism is its founding moment, and will be its dying gasp. Whiteness, they argue, needs to disappear.

IV. A Realistic Realism

I have three arguments against the eliminativists.

First, the idea that social identities are unchangeable is as wrong as the idea that we can just volitionally change our self-ascriptions. Eliminativists have a wrong account of social identity in general. To fully justify such a claim would require a different paper, but consider the following four ele-ments of social identity.

1. Social identities are not created entirely from the top down, as whiteness is often imagined to have been. Michael Omi and Howard Winant's theory of racial formation provides a realistic account of historical processes wherein multiple actors influence events from varied social locations.[20] Racial concepts are products of both resistance movements and oppressive forces. Whiteness cannot be blamed exclusively on state and corporate actors. This means, however, that future alterations in white subjectivity and practice can alter what it means to be white.

2. Social identities are rough indices of relations between individuals and macrohistorical events, such as slavery, genocide, land annex-ation, famines, religious persecution, and imperial wars. These indices have explanatory value for both individual lives and his-torical events. Groups are positioned differently in regard to such histories, as subject to violence or as benefiting from the spoils of war. Such collective differences can partially determine affective responses for generations, such as empathy for the veterans of

selected wars, or rage at orchestrated famines, or fear of renewed persecution. A category like whiteness can name a broad and diverse collective experience with the capacity to explain phenomena today, from wealth differentials, to political dispositions and voting patterns, to selective empathy.

3. Social identities are also correlated to unconscious practices, modes of comportment, and habits of perception, as a wealth of social psychology has revealed in recent studies.[21] But really, these empirical studies simply confirm a general idea that we already accept: that different people interact, think, and perceive differently, in sometimes group-related ways. Sonia Sotomayor's controversial claim that a "wise Latina" would judge differently simply names the commonly held belief that identities can sometimes affect our judgments and interpretations, and the fact that we sometimes weigh an interlocutor's claims in light of that person's identity. There is no perfect coincidence here, in such a way that every individual's dispositions can be predicted, and yet patterns persist across groups. It would make no sense, for example, to conduct a survey about public attitudes toward the police that includes only whites. The greater tendency of whites to trust the police affects their judgment, modes of comportment, and habits of perception.

4. Finally, social identities need to be understood as aspects of our shared, material world in the sense that they are (generally) visible features that produce a kind of visual registry directing us toward specific forms of interaction. Identities are not merely a discursive overlay on top of materially instantiated differences, in which case it might indeed seem that we could simply, and volitionally, change the discourse and thus change the society. Rather than being simply "in our heads," identities are part of our phenomenologically accessible material world. Changing the meanings and significance of social identities will require changing the materiality of our social worlds.

These four elements show social identities to be real material aspects of social worlds, rather than mythic overlays that can be discursively corrected.

My second argument against eliminativism is that the history of those people marked as white indicates a specific experience as well as some level of consciousness about their different social situation and options. In other words, whiteness meets the criteria listed above. The new and excellent race-conscious labor and social histories beginning to emerge reveal the ways in which whiteness has been manifest in historical and subjective experience, and not just as an ideological formulation. See, for example, Peter Linebaugh and Marcus Rediker's work about the multiracial mariner working-class, *Many Headed Hydra: The Hidden History of the Revolutionary Atlantic.*[22] This book has been heralded for its retrieval of a history of cross-racial collaborations, a history that is remarkable precisely because of the material reality of racial formations. It also exemplifies a new form of historical work that reads whiteness back into history, showcasing the ways in which white workers were precisely *white* workers, whether self-ascribed or not.

To speak meaningfully of whites requires further specifications of the domain, because "white experience" or "white history" is just too broad and internally diverse to have any content. But a suitably contextualized or hyphenated whiteness is an aspect of people's experiences coming to the new world as Irish economic refugees, or French farmers, or German shopkeepers. The integration of whites across national and ethnic distinctions, and their treatment *as whites*, led to the formation of expressive cultures, such as clogging and what we today call country music. The fact that none of these forms emerged without being profoundly influenced by the cultures of other groups simply means that white cultures share the same hybrid, multiple genealogy as all other cultures; the only difference was that white racists claimed that whiteness was the "uncaused cause," a pure self-invention that never in fact obtained. However, while "white history" is a myth, the fact is that there is a historical experience of diverse groups of whites for whom the fact of their interpellation as whites played a role in the practices and customs they developed.

Monica McDermott's excellent ethnography, *Working-Class White*, and Dana Ste. Clair's history of the folklore of Florida Crackers, titled simply *Cracker*, provide further good examples of contextualized studies.[23] McDermott illustrates the experiences and subjectivity of contemporary working-class whites while Ste. Clair describes early-twentieth-century rural white Floridians. These works give a content to white identities beyond either the myths of supremacists or the manipulations of elite institutions, which included of course, until recently, most academic research.

Yet eliminativism may be intended more as prescription for the future than as description of either the present or the past. My third argument addresses this prescriptive project. The quest, or desire, to eliminate whiteness in the future may in fact be motivated by a desire for escape from uncomfortable histories that bear on present-day material distributions, or the simple desire to transcend historical guilt. Let's consider this idea, for a moment, in the context of the award-winning film *Avatar*.[24] *Avatar*, as has often been stated, is a version of *Dances with Wolves* set in space, the latter of which is a movie that won the Academy Award for Best Picture of 1991.[25] The two movies have a strikingly similar plot, but important political differences. In *Dances with Wolves*, Lieutenant John Dunbar of the Union Army discovers anti-indigenous racism, has a conversion experience, and then learns the high price of treason to the white power structure. But by the end of the movie, Dunbar nevertheless commits to return to white society and spread the word of what he has learned. He considers assimilation to the Lakota people who have befriended him, but realizes this would not be the most responsible action. Thus, he rides off into the sunset to a difficult and uncertain future, with a white woman at his side who did assimilate but who now joins him in his effort to change their own white countrymen.

Now let's jump ahead nearly twenty years to *Avatar*, a movie whose magnum profits indicate that it's narrative resonates with broad numbers of the white public. It's not just the visuals that drew viewers, but also the *Star Wars*–like story, which pits a plucky group of underdog anti-imperialists in space against a death star of corporate bad guys.

The main protagonist is again a white guy who has a conversion experience, eventually becoming a traitor to his people. This time it is set in the future and not the past (though both movies take us comfortably out of the present to reimagine white possibilities). Jake Sully is a disabled Marine veteran who is recruited to a new mission at an outpost where an indigenous people, the N'avi, are standing in the way of an aggressive quest for resources. The evil community is this time no longer purely white but multiracial, since an all-white representation would not make the movie a realistic representation of the future. And while it is no longer completely male dominated, there is no indication that this is a society that has achieved real racial or gender equality; the principle leaders are white and male, and they act with impunity despite opposition from white women and people of color.

Sully is able to achieve a kind of literal double-consciousness through a science fiction device of avatar existence, in which he can escape the limits of his paraplegic body and experience life fully as an able-bodied N'avi, or at least as himself in N'avi form. As he moves back and forth between his white and his new blue identity, Sully seems at first to retain a white subjectivity with only a change of bodily form, but by the end it has become clear that Sully wants to shed his white identity entirely, and to become "one of them."

The interstellar imperialists from Earth that Sully works for are referred to as Sky People by the N'avi. As an avatar, Sully must learn to navigate between two sets of names and titles and terms, as well as two ways of interacting with others and of inhabiting a planet. Watching Sully navigate his bipolar world must resonate with whites sitting in the audience, I would suggest, who are beginning to realize that theirs is *not* the only language, philosophy, morality, or aesthetics around, and further, that theirs may not be the best in all respects, even if it has the superficial superiority of instrumental domination over an environment.

Importantly, the white male protagonist in *Avatar*, just as in *Dances With Wolves*, must accept the position of novice student to the nonwhite culture, requiring him to put up with being the class dunce for awhile. Sully is teased and called both a baby and a moron while he is trying to learn N'avi ways. But he not only has to learn everything from scratch; he also has to unlearn everything he already knows. There is a telling moment when the elder female leader of the N'avi expresses some skepticism about changing the Sky People's thinking, asking, "How can we fill a thing that is already filled up?" In other words, how can we teach the Sky People about ourselves or about our world when they think they already know all there is to be known? Indeed, the movie plays out a constant epistemic contestation between knowledge systems as well as ways of knowing or modes of justification, between the N'avi's spiritual metaphysics of nature and the Sky People's instrumental rationality and environmental atheism.[26] Here, then, is presented in dramatic form the obstacle to conversion and transformation: How can whiteness revise itself when this requires not merely learning new things but a fundamental *unlearning* that will change all it believes about *itself*?

Sully is representative of the white everyman as a nonelite. He's been forced into his current position in the lower ranks of a colonizing power by a lack of access to health care, since it was his disability that propelled him to take the position as an avatar for a chance of a transplant. Interestingly, this is a similar element from *Dances with Wolves*, since it was Dunbar's impending disability—his fear that he would lose his injured leg at the overtaxed army hospitals of the civil war—that propelled him to the suicidal ride that classified him (mistakenly) as a hero and, thus able to escape to the western frontier. The filmmakers seem to be assuming that audiences will identify with protagonists motivated by the desire to escape disability even at the risk of death. But this narrative device also means that the white hero is, in both cases, someone with enough of a relationship to disability that he begins to dis-identify with the idea of white male invincibility, as well as the idea that white or white-dominant society can always be relied on to take care of their own. Dunbar knows that the indifferent, overworked army medics will simply cut off his leg, and Sully knows that the indifferent military corporation could easily fund his cure but will only do so, like any good Mafia Don, after he performs an important and unsavory service. White dominant social institutions have let them down.

Despite their similarities, *Avatar* ends in a significantly different way than *Dances with Wolves*. Unlike Dunbar, Sully loses his whiteness in the close of the movie and becomes fully assimilated to the N'avi, both physically and culturally, refusing to return to his own people. The imperialist culture of the Sky People is portrayed as so monolithically evil that, although there are other critical voices besides Sully's, the idea of a revolution is hopeless. It is notable that in fewer than twenty years, we might read the collective white unconscious as becoming more rather than less pessimistic about the possibility of changing white culture. However, in *Avatar*, although the white culture apparently cannot be changed, it can be beaten, at least in a specific battle-site. In a burst of implausible physical prowess and military leadership, Sully beats back the imperial army to become the greatest warrior the N'avi have ever known. This too marks a significant difference from *Dances with Wolves*, where Dunbar's capacity as a warrior is never presented as superior to the Lakota. The difference in ending is significant. I would suggest that in *Avatar*, even though Sully ostensibly assimilates and literally turns blue, he maintains a dominant positions over the nonwhites—as the smartest and the bravest and the recognized military leader. The white audience has the reassuring experience of seeing the white man move from dunce to leader in the time it takes to watch a movie. And he also wins the love of the chief's beautiful daughter, despite her prior betrothal to another N'avi.

If we read *Avatar*, then, as an expression of at least one important trend within collective white consciousness, we can see that it is still within the same broad historical moment as *Dances with Wolves*, a moment characterized by the disaffection with white vanguard narratives. But we can also read in *Avatar* a regressive development from *Dances with Wolves*. Sully does not take the difficult path of returning to the white world to enact social change from within. Instead, we see him at the end enjoying the benefits of the nonwhite communal culture. He loses his whiteness not only in the sense of physical form but also in the sense of losing a specific and substantive cultural way of life, yet this loss is portrayed, interestingly, as holding nothing of value. "Avatar" provides white audiences who are uncomfortably conscious of the false claims of white vanguardism with a way out of this discomfort that requires no sacrifice. The movie titles themselves signal this regression, from a title that conveys the indigenous point of view—the Lakota name for Dunbar—to a title that signifies a mobile transformer, the very activity of which is associated not with the heavily tradition-bound nonwhite ethnic cultures but with the mercurial capacity of Western capital, and Western man, to go anywhere and become anything.

Such a contradictory outcome—losing one's whiteness, but retaining white dominance—is clearly not what the race traitor, white abolitionists, or even the cosmopolitans have in mind. And yet, Sully's repudiation of white-dominant culture and his rejection of his own white identity is as dramatic and complete as any eliminativist could want. Thus, I want to suggest here a concordance between the eliminativist's quest to escape whiteness and the avatar's beatific assimilation as both symptomatic of the current turmoil of whiteness.[27] Having a white identity has become a heavy burden to bear, with its indelible connection to a disquieting past, troubling present, and correlate responsibilities. The regressive quest then becomes how to maintain a pride in one's identity and one's forebears without sacrificing, à la the Tea Party, one's rational faculties.

V. White Double Consciousness

Contemporary white anxiety is manifestly in a quest for a coherent resolution to its troubled double consciousness, but this takes both regressive and a progressive forms. The regressive versions aim for an easy, comforting escape hatch, while the progressive version seeks a morally responsible and politically plausible route to acknowledge the horrific history of white vanguardism without foreclosing the possibility of playing a role in future positive change. Avatar symbolizes the regressive version with near perfection.

Although I have placed this quest in a contemporary frame of reference, connecting it to post-Vietnam U.S. culture and current anxieties about the impending demographic shifts, there were many earlier manifestations. The best-selling novelist Graham Greene began linking U.S. imperialism to racism in the 1950s in a series of novels with a wide American readership. The organized left began to grapple seriously with issues of race in the 1930s, and sectarian differences between parties often centered precisely on issues of nationalism and degrees of support for anticolonial movements. The Beat's famously attempted to escape from whiteness through a self-presentation of sensibilities that they identified as nonwhite. They presented themselves as having nonwhite modes of comportment—modes of being—and not simply as adopting nonwhite styles of cultural expression, music, or writing. Jack Kerouac, in particular, expressed a poignant alienation from his white identity and the general normative whiteness of heterosexual suburbia, and he emphatically identified with the more intense existential registers of nonwhite affect that he took to be common among African Americans and Mexicans.[28]

Although Kerouac was humorously blind to the racist way he characterizes African Americans and Mexicans, I would suggest that we should take his alienated consciousness seriously as a phenomenological datum from which to understand the transformations of whiteness. That is, we should take seriously his experience of alienation from the normative cultural and political meanings that a white appearance would convey in the 1950s, and thus we should take seriously his discomfort with his embodied identity. It's useful to consider Kerouac's alienated consciousness in relation to Du Bois's notion of double consciousness, which invokes the idea that one sees oneself both by how one knows one is seen in the dominant mainstream, and also by how one is seen by one's own community. When there are contradictions between these two points of reference, as there are for minoritized communities, the result is a troubled, split consciousness that is hyperaware. The contradictions Kerouac experienced had a different source yet similar effects. Kerouac knew how middle-class whites viewed the world; he also knew how limited and partial this view was and he had an inkling (though just an inkling) of another possibility. Thus, he experienced a kind of split self, unable to immerse fully into his normative white identity, yet still powerfully haunted by its expectations.

Du Bois's concept of double consciousness is interestingly resonant with the incoherence of white subjective experience, although there are important differences with the experience of African Americans. The way in which oppressed groups are seen by the dominant mainstream is almost wholly false, but this is also true for whites who are taken as the vanguard of the human race. Yet the main source for white enlightenment often comes from outside their racially organized communities. Like Beauvoir, whites may come to realize the social meanings of whiteness, its unearned privileges and moral collusion, from their intuited sense of how they are viewed by nonwhite others. This is a critical difference. Whites who experience a split consciousness between the way they see themselves and they way they are seen by nonwhite others are not thereby oppressed by a racist gaze. Rather, they are living out the effects—the necessary effects—of white vanguardist ideologies. The double consciousness that can result, for whites who begin to sense an incoherence in the way whiteness is viewed, serves as a potential source for a new understanding of social conditions.

For both whites and nonwhites, double consciousness signifies a kind of impossible incoherence between incommensurable paradigms of representation. Coming to an awareness of this incoherence means coming to an awareness of the social obstacles in the way of creating a morally livable white identity, one that is both white and morally defensible. This is an obstacle that can be approached in a number of different ways, from denial to political activism.[29]

I want to suggest that the current subjectivity of many whites today does not correspond to the dominant narrative of whiteness that holds itself ahead of and better than every other culture. In some cases, their own experience of their lives may cohere little with supremacist claims. So beyond Kerouac's cultural alienation from the aesthetic norms and values of his upper-middle-class family, there can also be an alienation felt by poor whites, rural whites, or less educated whites, whites who work as waitresses and as sanitation workers and as schoolroom cafeteria workers, or whites who come as new immigrants from Eastern Europe to fill low-wage jobs. For these whites the notion of privilege and the promised entitlements to the vanguard feel pretty meaningless. There are also those whites whose multiracial families, neighborhoods, and workplaces are changing their affective lives as well as their perceptual practices and habits of action, perhaps making them not quite as white as they used to be. This is not just (or necessarily) a doxastic repudiation of the tenets of white supremacy, or a change at the level of belief, but, more importantly, an alteration of lived context and resultant consciousness and modes of behavior.

In some cases the turmoil in white subjectivity and embodied existence, and the incoherence of an alienated consciousness, produces a genuine disaffection from white supremacy, even if occurring in confused, inchoate form. But there is without a doubt a growing awareness about how whites are viewed by others as well as a significant decrease in white cultural domination and segregated social life. In saying that "being white these days is not what it used to be," Nell Painter points to the following four trend-lines as important markers of contemporary change. I would note here that these are trends and not, alas, consolidated achievements with universal scope, but they are significant nonetheless.

1. *Whiteness is neither as normative nor as positive an identity as it used to be.* It is no longer so easy to see whites simply as the singular norm or default position.[30] Critical race and whiteness studies have helped bring this about in the academy, but ethnographic research shows young whites beyond the campuses acutely self-conscious about their whiteness and decidedly uncomfortable with its associated meanings.[31] Although they express a disinclination to think about their whiteness, avoidance of nonwhite perspectives and cultural expressions takes a great deal of effort. Whites, thus, find themselves the object of a new gaze that foregrounds their whiteness in ways that are not always flattering.

2. *The degree to which white identity alone confers privilege is mediated more so than in the past by the significance of other variables—class, gender, region, age, able-bodiedness, sexuality, and so on.* According to economist Richard Wolff, the real wages of white workers rose steadily over a century until the 1970s, from which time there has been a steady drop.[32] The increasing gap between rich and poor has thrown millions of whites into economic instability, and the new feudal relations of production have shown evidence of a clear-cut disregard for the well-being of white workers in industrialized nations. The attack on the wages and benefits of millions of unionized public sector workers has mobilized white workers from Wisconsin to Maine. And the loss of well-paid manufacturing jobs—from steel to auto to textile—and the forced march to the service sector has notably hit white male workers, who made up the bulk of that sector of the workforce. A recent study by Michael Zweig, Michael Porter, and Yuxiang Huang shows that the number of U.S. casualties in Afghanistan are disproportionately white, very different from the deaths in Vietnam, which were disproportionately black and Latino.[33]

    Thus, Painter may be right that the terms of the old racial contract have shifted. This is not about white victimization: whites are not targeted as white in the way nonwhite racial and ethnic groups are targeted, but their whiteness provides little defense against the contractions of Western standards of living.

3. *White expectations of being able to have a white-dominant or white-only home or personal space is decreasing.* White-dominant neighborhoods and schools are becoming less white, and the media that constantly invades our homes is less white as well. In 1990 one-seventh of whites were closely related to someone of another race. Whites remain less likely than any other racial group in the U.S. to marry outside their race, and yet the numbers of white exogamous unions are steadily rising so that, by 2050, it is projected that 10 percent of whites will marry people from other races. This phenomena can coexist with racism, as Obama's family, Bush's family, and my own can attest, and yet the *younger* generations that grow up in such families may be less "filled up" with the old ideas of their parents and grandparents, ideas that seem to survive for the older generation despite experiential changes wrought by having mixed-race families. Even if the older generation remains less changed, however, the children who grow up in such mixed families may indeed learn new ways of being in the world by seeing their society and world through multiple lenses.

4. *The promulgation of new racial categories may confuse the meaning of the concept of race and lessen its power.* There are certainly many confused and confusing new categories of race: in the 2010 census, the ability to check more than one box means that a full sixty-three racial types are now recognized. The singular significance of race, Painter suggests, loses its punch when it gets diluted to this degree.[34] We cannot forget that the promulgation of mixed race categories can easily coexist with white dominance and antiblack and/or anti-indigenous, racisms, as it does in Latin America. Nonetheless, Painter is hopeful that the current trend is less an expansion of types than a muddying of distinctions that will render racism's directive more obscure. What will eventually develop in the United States will undoubtedly have its own dynamic given the particular history, mix of groups, and forms of resistance *here*, rather than being determined merely to repeat and replay dynamics elsewhere.

These trends represent the objective foundation for the turmoil in white subjectivity. The experiences of whites are changing, not because the society they live in is multiracial, since this has always been the case, but because their society is more racially integrated in cultural and political practice, a trend that will expand as the demographic picture changes. And the meaning of both whiteness and of white privilege is changing as race categories are multiplied and increasingly diversified within. Charting these trends against the real turmoil in white consciousness should help us, I would hope, to avoid being deterministic about the future.

Part of the turmoil of whiteness today is, however, as we all know, pure reaction. Within two years after the election of Barack Obama in 2008, the number of hate groups nationwide increased to over 900. Antigovernment, or so-called patriot, groups tripled to 1,200. And nativist extremist groups of the kind that harass immigrants—engaging in what they call "beaner hunting"—saw the largest increase, 80 percent, to a total of 1,600. Don't assume you know where all of these groups are: while there are 32 hate groups in Alabama, there are 31 in New York state, 44 in New Jersey, and 60 in California. And don't assume these groups are harmless. The month that Obama was elected, in November 2008, gun sales reached a record high of 1.5 million.[35]

We might easily, and plausibly, blame Fox News for spreading disinformation and directing the action just as effectively as I remember Cuban-owned radio stations in Miami in the 1970s and 1980s directing guys to show up with bats whenever we organized an anti-imperialist march in the area. But the message of Fox News is working today because it connects to an already felt turmoil. And the white movement that has emerged in the form of the Tea Party is not made up of the rich or the educated but, according to recent Harris and Quinnipiac polls, decidedly nonelites. Rational, economic-based motivations are simply insufficient to explain the psychic attachment many whites feel to white vanguardism.

Yet the current turmoil in white subjectivity provides a new opportunity to revise the narrative of whiteness. Such a revision must address the motivational question—the question of what motivates whites as whites—and in a larger way than reducing this to material gain. If eliminativism is a pipe dream, we must explore the basis on which whites might join a coalition for social change on their own grounds, for their own reasons.

What might those reasons be? Antiracism is, at least on the face of it, a negative agenda directed at repudiating and overcoming racism and its long legacy. But we also need a positive agenda that addresses the white motivations for changing society. Imagining the motivations whites may have for reassessing the meaning of whiteness is not, in fact, rocket science. I would argue it consists of three strong elements.

1. Whites have a motivation to face the full-on truth of history, to avoid being duped any longer or blindsided by the feel-good education of (white) nationalist narratives. (And this means that academics need to find a way to talk about historical truth without feeling like they are being merely strategic.) The best resistance to Tea Party ideology is to displace the narratives of vanguardism, with its mythical entitlements for all whites, with new narratives that get the actual histories of the United States and Europe in clearer focus, including both the atrocities of colonialism and the actual variety of white experience under white racist regimes. Such narratives would make sense of the present economic difficulties and cultural contestations in a way that vanguardist narratives cannot, and will suggest new ways to make alliance and coalition. History is a weapon.[36]

2. Social progress by any measure cannot be advanced or achieved by a white majority, given its decreasing numbers and increasing disunity. Whiteness is no longer a sufficient, stand-alone predictor of job prospects or likelihood of death in war. Nor is it determinative of majority attitudes about race and racism, since white responses to such questions are increasingly divided. Whites who support even the milquetoast social reforms offered by the Democratic Party must find allies. Progressive unions have realized this for some time and have initiated a number of new policies to better represent the multiracial working class, from establishing quotas for representation at conventions to ending the jingoist "buy American" campaigns. But coalitions are now a necessity for whites of nearly all political persuasions, just as has long been true for other groups. Whiteness remains a salient aspect of some of this coalitional work, requiring its own specific intersectional analysis and policies. (This also means that academic leftists need to become more adept at intersectional theorizing and leave class reductionism behind.)

3. Whites have a motivation to live in communities where they can hold up their heads, and smile unself-consciously at the neighbor's children. Vanguardism worked in part because it offered a moral account of the role of whites in the world. Whites could view themselves as having a positive role, as providing charity rather than benefiting from the conditions that produced the need for

charity, as on the side of civility in a barbarous world rather than exacerbating barbarism. The rise of the Christian right is due in part to the power of moral motivations and the desire to live a moral life. The left needs to learn this lesson.

What would it mean for whites to become more positively embodied as white within a multipolar social landscape? Perhaps the critical element will involve coming to understand whiteness as a particular among other particulars, rather than the universal that stands as the exemplar of civilization. The Mexican philosopher Leopoldo Zea explained that, while every culture tends to see itself at the center of the world, it was the West that uniquely created a worldview in which it regarded itself "as universal," in which its own history is "world history."[37] What whites do advances the species; what others do reflects only on themselves. Against such a worldview, living whiteness mindfully as a particular would have a deflationary effect, and produce an opening to the possibility of learning from others rather than always leading them. It would also place whiteness within a complex history involving multiple relations with others, some of which were constitutive of whiteness itself.

A recent documentary, titled aptly *The Inheritance*, charts the effects of Nazism on German, non-Jewish children.[38] Documentarian James Moll focused on Monika Hertwig, the real-life daughter of the brutal concentration camp commander Amon Goeth, memorably portrayed by Ralph Fiennes in *Schindler's List* as the sort of sadist who enjoyed shooting prisoners while lounging on his back terrace.[39] With quiet and simple integrity, Hertwig shares her story of slowly uncovering the facts about her parents as a child and then actively pursuing more information as an adult. She eventually reaches out to one of the victims, Helen Jonas, who worked as a servant in the Goeth household and knew her father personally. With some trepidation, Hertwig asks to meet with Jonas. She is indeed overcome with sadness at the further facts that she discovers about her father from the meeting, yet her relationship to a grandchild seems to clarify her position. We cannot change the past, as she explains, we can only, possibly, change the future.

Notes

1. Nell Painter, *The History of White People* (New York: W. W. Norton, 2010), 389.
2. Go to http://www.workingimmigrants.com/2011/03/portrait_of_middle_eastern_and.html) and http://www.census.gov/prod/cen2010/briefs/c2010br-02.pdf.

3. The Economic Policy Institute is a nonprofit, nonpartisan think tank, with regular analysis of these and related facts that appears at http://www.epi.org/publication/trends-median-wealth-race/. Accessed on June 27, 2013. Another useful resource is United for a Fair Economy, found at http://www.faireconomy.org/. See Andrew Hacker, *Two Nations: Black and White, Separate, Hostile, Unequal* (New York: Scribner, 2003).

4. Paranoia clearly marked earlier anti-immigrant movements in the United States, such as the Know Nothings anti-immigrant party of the 1850s, and the anti-German and anti-Japanese hysteria during the two world wars of the twentieth century.

5. http://www.gallup.com/poll/109258/majority-americans-say-racism-against-blacks-widespread.aspx.

6. Gordon Allport, *The Nature of Prejudice*. Reading (Mass.: Addison- Wesley, 1979).

7. G. J. Pulzer, *Jews and the German State: The Political History of a Minority, 1848-1933* (New York: Blackwell, 1992).

8. Lewis Gordon, *Bad Faith and Antiblack Racism* (Atlantic Highlands, N.J.: Humanities Press. Gordon 1995), 99.

9. Ibid., 100.

10. Simone de Beauvoir, *America Day by Day,* translated by Carol Cosman (Berkeley: University of California Press, 2000), 37.

11. Ibid., 36.

12. Lewis, of course, was making use of the phrase for social criticism. See Sinclair Lewis, *Babbitt* (New York: Harcourt, Brace, and Company, 1922).

13. Dudley Nichols and Hagar Wilde, *Bringing Up Baby*, directed by Howard Hawks, Los Angeles, California, RKO-Radio Pictures, 1938.

14. Judy Rohrer, *Haoles in Hawai'i* (Honolulu: University of Hawai'i Press, 2010).

15. Charles Gallagher, "White Reconstruction in the University," *Socialist Review* 94, nos. 1 and 2, (1994): 165.

16. Shannon Sullivan, *Revealing Whiteness: The Unconscious Habits of White Privilege* (Bloomington: Indiana University Press, 2005).

17. Groups such as the Pioneer Fund and the Federation for American Immigrant Reform (FAIR) express this sort of "optimism."

18. One might be tempted to think that most of these are national, not racial or ethnic identities. Yet the idea of being "Japanese" or "British" has clear associations with ways of being in the world we associate with ethnicities, with specific cultural histories and practices. The way the concept of "nationality" is understood colloquially, I'd argue, is not entirely

distinct from ethnic or ethno-racial concepts. This is why we have trouble imagining Latinos and Asians, in particular, as capable of serving as paradigms of "American" identity.

19. See Michael J. Monahan, *The Creolizing Subject: Race, Reason and the Politics of Purity* (New York: Fordham University Press, 2011).
20. Michael Omi and Howard Winant, *Racial Formations in the United States: From the 1960s to the 1980s* (New York: Routledge, 1986).
21. See, for example, Claude Steele, *Whistling Vivaldi.* (New York: W. W. Norton, 2010).
22. Peter Linebaugh and Marcus Rediker, *Many Headed Hydra: The Hidden History of the Revolutionary Atlantic* (Boston: Beacon Press, 2000).
23. Monica McDermott, *Working-Class White: The Making and Unmaking of Race Relations.* (Berkeley: University of California Press, 2006); and Dana Ste. Clair, *Cracker: The Cracker Culture in Florida History* (Gainesville, Fla: University Press of Florida, 2006).
24. James Cameron, *Avatar*, directed by James Cameron, Twentieth Century Fox, Los Angeles California, 2009.
25. Michael Blake, *Dances with Wolves*, Tig Productions, Burbank, California, 1990.
26. In another similarity with *Dances with Wolves*, *Avatar* stereotypes both dominant and oppressed cultures, portraying the former as irredeemably violent as well as willfully and dogmatically ignorant, and the latter as naturally peaceful and communal. There is a little more complexity in *Dances with Wolves*, although this is achieved by portraying native peoples as coming in two simplistic archetypes: civilized and peaceful, like the Lakota, and bloodthirsty and uncivilized, like the Pawnee. Yet despite the stereotyped character of the white dominant culture, which lends itself to a certain essentialism, both movies convey the message that sharp political differences exist among whites. Unlike Dunbar, who was a lone voice among whites in the imagined past, Sully has some strong allies among the Sky People. Though these allies come from less dominant subgroups—female or nonwhite—it is still clear that the future world imagined by *Avatar* has more white traitors.
27. And anecdotally, the avid left wing (white) fans of *Avatar* in the blogosphere would confirm this concordance.
28. I discuss Kerouac's identity issues at greater length in *Visible Identities* (New York: Oxford University Press, 2006), chapter 11.
29. A further form of reaction might be the development of a specific identity in a different form, such as the Guido identity that became public

with the television show *Jersey Shore*. Guido identity is within the rubric of whiteness, but it provides a substantive ethno-cultural identity that one might place in a multicultural mix as deserving of recognition and acceptance alongside nonwhites. Whiteness itself is too general and broad to provide much of the specificity we associate with ethnic identities, and its cultural association is increasingly coming to be negative and the butt of jokes (as in the website, "Stuff White People Like"). Guido identity provides a substantive, noneliminativist alternative.

30. Painter, 388
31. See, for example,. Gallagher 1994, op. cit.; Danielle Allen, Danielle S., *Talking to Strangers: Anxieties of Citizenship since Brown v. Board of Education* (Chicago: University of Chicago Press, 2004); J. A. Richeson, and S. Trawalter, "The threat of appearing prejudiced and race-based attentional biases," *Psychological Science* 19, (2008): 98-102.
32. Richard Wolff, *Capitalism Hits the Fan: The Global Economic Meltdown and What to Do About It* (Ithaca, N.Y.: Olive Branch Press, 2009).
33. See Michael Zweig, Michael Porter, and Yuxiang Huang, "American Military Deaths in Afghanistan, and the Communities from Which These Soldiers, Sailors, Airmen, and Marines Came," http://www.stonybrook.edu/workingclass/publications/afghan_casualties.shtml, 2011.
34. Painter, 385.
35. These and other related facts can be found at the Southern Poverty Law Center website: http://www.splcenter.org. The gun sales statistics are from the FBI.
36. See historyisaweapon.com.
37. Leopoldo Zea, *The Role of the Americas in History*, edited by Amy A. Oliver, translated by Sonja Karsen (Savage, M.D.: Rowman and Littlefield, 1992) 75-76.
38. James Moll, Director, *Inheritance*, Allentown Productions, Los Angeles, California, PBS POV, 2008.
39. Steven Zaillian (based on a book by Thomas Keneally), *Schindler's List*, directed by Steven Spielberg, Universal Pictures, Los Angeles, California, 1993.

CONTRIBUTORS

Linda Martín Alcoff is professor of philosophy at Hunter College and the Graduate Center of the City University of New York. Her writings have focused on social identity and race, epistemology and politics, sexual violence, Foucault, and Latino issues in philosophy. She has written two books, *Visible Identities: Race, Gender and the Self* (Oxford University Press, 2006), and *Real Knowing: New Versions of the Coherence Theory* (Cornell University Press, 1996); and she has edited ten books. *Visible Identities* won the Frantz Fanon Award in 2009. She was named the Distinguished Woman in Philosophy for 2005 by the Society for Women in Philosophy. She is currently at work on two new books, a book on sexual violence, and an account of the future of white identity. She is a coeditor of *Hypatia: A Journal of Feminist Philosophy*. She was president of the American Philosophical Association, Eastern Division.

Alia Al-Saji is associate professor of philosophy at McGill University. Her work brings together and critically engages twentieth-century phenomenology and French philosophy, on the one hand, and critical race and feminist theories, on the other hand. Running through her works is an abiding concern with time and embodiment. She has recently published articles on the racialization of veiled Muslim women's bodies, the uses of Husserlian phenomenology for feminist theory, and the temporality that constitutes philosophical thinking. Her work has appeared in venues such as *Continental Philosophy Review, Philosophy and Social Criticism, Research in Phenomenology*, and *Southern Journal of Philosophy*, among others. She is a coeditor of the *Symposia on Gender, Race and Philosophy* and the editor for the "Feminist Philosophy" section of *Philosophy Compass*.

Edward S. Casey is distinguished professor of philosophy at State University of New York, Stony Brook, where he has taught since 1978. A recent president of the American Philosophical Association, Eastern Division, he has published a series of books on place (including *The Fate of Place* and *Getting Back into Place*), as well as books on imagination and memory. *The World at a Glance* appeared in 2007, and he is currently completing a companion volume called *The World on Edge*. With Mary Watkins, he is bringing out *Up Against the Wall: Re-imagining the U.S.-Mexico Border*.

Namita Goswami is associate professor of philosophy at Indiana State University. Her work combines Continental philosophy, postcolonial, critical race, and feminist theory. She has published in a wide range of journals such as *SIGNS*, *Angelaki*, *Critical Philosophy of Race*, *Contemporary Aesthetics*, and *South Asian Review*, and in edited volumes such as *Rethinking Facticity* (edited by Eric Nelson and François Raffoul) and *Constructing the Nation: A Race and Nationalism Reader* (edited by Mariana Ortega and Linda Martín Alcoff). She is currently finishing revisions on her book manuscript on philosophy, feminism, and postcolonial theory (State University of New York Press).

David Haekwon Kim is associate professor of philosophy at the University of San Francisco. His research interests include political philosophy, philosophical psychology, phenomenology, Asian and comparative philosophy, philosophy of race, and postcolonialism. His current work focuses on embodiment, the politics of emotion, xenophobia, critiques of U.S. imperialism, and the extension of various forms of Asian thought to concepts of modernity, like rights, race, civilization, and hegemony.

Emily S. Lee is associate professor of philosophy at California State University, Fullerton. Her research interests include feminist philosophy, philosophy of race, and phenomenology, especially the works of Maurice Merleau-Ponty. She has published articles on phenomenology and epistemology in regard to the embodiment and subjectivity of women of color in journals, including *Hypatia: A Journal of Feminist Philosophy*, *Southern Journal of Philosophy*, and *Philosophy Today*. She is currently finishing a book concerning the phenomenology of race.

Donna-Dale L. Marcano is associate professor of philosophy at Trinity College in Hartford, Connecticut. She has written several articles on race and philosophy, including essays on Julia Kristeva, Jean-Paul Sartre, bell hooks, and Black feminist philosophy. She is coeditor of the volume *Convergences: Black Feminism and Continental Philosophy* (2010).

Charles W. Mills is John Evans Professor of Moral and Intellectual Philosophy at Northwestern University. He works in the general area of oppositional political theory, with a particular focus on race. He is the author of five books: *The Racial Contract* (Cornell University Press, 1997); *Blackness Visible: Essays on Philosophy and Race* (Cornell University Press, 1998); *From Class to Race: Essays in White Marxism and Black Radicalism* (Rowman & Littlefield, 2003); *Contract and Domination* (with Carole Pateman) (Polity, 2007); and *Radical Theory, Caribbean Reality: Race, Class and Social Domination* (University of the West Indies Press, 2010).

Mariana Ortega is professor of philosophy at John Carroll University, University Heights, Ohio. She received her PhD from the University of California, San Diego. She is interested in Latina feminism, race theory, twentieth-century Continental philosophy, specifically Heideggerian phenomenology, and aesthetics. Her research focuses on questions of self and sociality, visual representations of race, and identity. She has published articles in journals such as *Hypatia: A Journal of Feminist Philosophy*, *International Journal of Philosophical Studies*, *International Philosophical Quarterly*, and *Radical Philosophy Review*. She is coeditor with Linda Martín Alcoff of the anthology *Constructing the Nation: A Race and Nationalism Reader* (State University of New York Press, 2009). She is currently working on a monograph that elaborates a notion of multiplicitous selfhood in light of Latina feminisms and existential phenomenological views.

Gail Weiss is Chair of the Department of Philosophy and professor of philosophy and Human Sciences at the George Washington University (Washington, DC). She is the author of *Refiguring the Ordinary* (Indiana University Press, 2008) and *Body Images: Embodiment as Intercorporeality* (Routledge, 1999); the editor of *Intertwinings: Interdisciplinary Encounters with Merleau-Ponty* (State University of New York Press, 2008); and coeditor (with Debra Bergoffen) of the Summer 2011 Special Issue of *Hypatia: A Journal of Feminist Philosophy* on "The Ethics of Embodiment" (vol. 26, no. 3). She is also the coeditor of three anthologies: *Feminist Interpretations of Maurice Merleau-Ponty* (Penn State University Press 2006), *Thinking the Limits of the Body* (State University of New

York Press, 2003) and *Perspectives on Embodiment: The Intersections of Nature and Culture* (Routledge, 1999). Her publications include journal articles and book chapters on philosophical and feminist issues related to human embodiment.

George Yancy is professor of philosophy at Duquesne University and coordinator of the Critical Race Theory Speaker Series. He is the author of *Black Bodies, White Gazes: The Continuing Significance of Race* (Rowman & Littlefield, 2008), which received an Honorable Mention from the Gustavus Myers Center for the Study of Bigotry and Human Rights. He is also the author of *Look, a White! Philosophical Essays on Whiteness* (Temple University Press, 2012). He has authored numerous articles in scholarly journals. In addition, he has edited fourteen influential books, three of which have received *Choice* Awards.

INDEX